LIBRARY AND INFORMATION SCIENCE

LIBRARY
AND
INFORMATION SCIENCE

By

Bhagwatiben Govindbhai Prajapati

M.A., B.Lib., M.Lib., B.Ed.

Librarian

Special Education College

Palanpur

(India)

DPH

DISCOVERY PUBLISHING HOUSE PVT. LTD.

NEW DELHI-110 002

Published by:
Tilak Wasan

DISCOVERY PUBLISHING HOUSE PVT. LTD.
4383/4B, Ansari Road, Darya Ganj
New Delhi-110 002 (India)
Phone : +91-11-23279245, 43596064-65
Fax : +91-11-23253475
E-mail : discoverypublishinghouse@gmail.com
sales@discoverypublishinggroup.com
parul.wasan@gmail.com
web : www.discoverypublishinggroup.com

***First Edition:* 2013**

ISBN: 978-93-5056-386-1

Library and Information Science

Printed at:
Dynamic Printers
Delhi

Contents

Preface

Libraries played a very effective role in exchanging views on social issues and in giving direction to the social and political movement. However, things have changed today. The modern public and academic libraries are starved for want of proper funds. This has caused a deterioration of the services in libraries. It is time that a proper infrastructure is drawn up for the public, college, university and school libraries.

Library and Information Science is a merging of the two fields: library science and information science. The phrase "*library and Information Science*" is associated with schools of library and information science, which generally developed from professional training programs to university institutions during the second half of the twentieth century. This book aims to serve the students of *Library and Information Science* and professionals who propose to site for UGC examination.

—Author

1

Information

INFORMATION SCIENCE

What is information science? The question, while seemingly simple, begs another, more complex one: *How is information science, or for that matter any field, to be defined?* This is a complex problem dealt with at length in philosophy and in other fields. Lexical definitions are necessary for providing a broad description and boundaries of the subjects covered by a field, but they cannot provide for a deeper understanding. Webster does not a field define. This is not to reject clear lexical definitions—not at all—just to establish their limitations.

In approaching the discussion of information science, I am taking the problem point of view as elaborated by Popper who argued that:

* [S]ubject matter or kind of things do not, I hold, constitute a basis for distinguishing disciplines. . . .*We are not students of some subject matter, but students of problems.* Any problem may cut right across the border of any subject matter or discipline.

Our emphasis is on problems addressed by information science. Although we provide definitions of information science and other fields in interdisciplinary relations with information science later in the chapter, we are doing this solely to advance the understanding of problems addressed by different fields and their relation to information science problems. Debates over the "proper" definition of information science, as of any field, are fruitless, and in expectations naive.

Information science, as a science and as a profession, is defined by the problems it has addressed and the methods it has used for their solutions over time.

Any advances in information science depend on whether the field is indeed progressing in relation to problems addressed and methods used. Any "fixing," if in order, will have to be approached by redefining or refocusing either the problems addressed, or the methods for their solutions, or both. Information science has three general characteristics that are the leitmotif of its evolution and existence. These are shared with many modern fields.

They can also be viewed as problem areas with which infor-mation science has to deal on a general level:

* First, information science is interdisciplinary in nature; however, the relations with various disciplines are changing. The interdisciplinary evolution is far from over.
* Second, information science is inexorably connected to information technology. A technological imperative is compelling and constraining the evolution of information science, as is the evolution of a number of other fields, and moreover, of the information society as a whole.
* Third, information science is, with many other fields, an active participant in the evolution of the information society. Information science has a strong social and human dimension, above and beyond technology.

A number of works that I freely consulted dealt with various historical aspects of information science.

Among those works are:

* Shera and Cleveland,
* Bourne,
* Herner,
* Salton,
* Cleverdon,
* Swanson,
* Lilley and Trice,

* Farkas-Conn,
* Buckland and Liu, and
* Rayward.

Still, a comprehensive history of information science is a project for a future historian of science. As yet only historical pieces and different perspectives of pieces exist. A history of any field is a history of a few powerful ideas. I suggest that information science has three such powerful ideas, so far. These ideas deal with processing of information in a radically different way than was done previously or elsewhere. The first and the original idea, emerging in 1950s, is *information retrieval,* providing for processing of information based on formal logic. The second, emerging shortly thereafter, is *relevance,* directly orienting and associating the process with human information needs and assessments.

The third, derived from elsewhere some two decades later, is *interaction,* enabling direct exchanges and feedback between systems and people engaged in IR processes. So far, no powerful ideas have emerged about *information,* as the underlying phenomenon, or *"literature"*, as the object of processing.

However, one can argue that the idea of mapping of "literature," that started with exploitation of citation indexes in 1960s, may also qualify as a powerful idea. In a non-historical sense this stage deals with these powerful ideas and with leitmotifs. They form a framework for understanding the past, present, and future of information science.

ORIGIN AND SOCIAL CONTEXT

Information science is a field that emerged in the after-math of the Second World War (WW II), along with a number of new fields, with computer science being but one example. The rapid pace of scientific and technical advances that were accumu-lating since the start of the 20th century, produced by mid-century a scientific and technical revolution. A most visible manifestation of this revolution was the phenomenon of "information explosion," referring to the exponential and unabated growth of scientific and technical publications and information records of all kinds, so masterfully synthesized and illuminated by de Solla Price.

In a remarkable turn of events, the impetus for the development of information science, and even for its very origin and agenda, a respected MIT scientist and, even more importantly, the head of the U.S. scientific effort during WW II.

Bush did two things:

* He succinctly defined a critical and strategic problem that was on the minds of many, and
* Proposed a solution that was a "technological fix", and thus in tune with the spirit of the times.

Both had wide appeal and Bush was listened to because of his stature. He defined the problem in almost poetic terms as "the massive task of making more accessible a bewildering store of knowledge". In other words, Bush addressed the problem of information explosion. The problem is still with us. His solution was to use the emerging computing and other information technology to combat the problem. But he went even further. He proposed a machine named Memex, incorporating a capability for "association of ideas," and duplication of "mental processes artificially." A prescient anticipation of information science and artificial intelligence is evident.

Memex, needless to say, was never built, but to this day is an ideal, a wish list, an agenda, and, some think, a utopia. We are still challenged by the ever-worsening problem of the information explosion, now universal and in a variety of digital formats. We are still trying to fix things technologically. We are still aspiring to incorporate Memex's basic ideas in our solutions. A number of scientists and professionals in many fields around the globe listened and took up Bush's challenge.

Governments listened as well and provided funding. The reasoning went something like this: Because science and technology are strategically important for society, efforts that help them, information activities in particular, are also important and need support. In the U.S., the *National Science Foundation* (NSF) Act of 1950 established NSF and provided a number of mandates, among them "to foster the interchange of scientific information among scientists in the U.S. and foreign countries" and "to further the full dissemination of information of scientific value consistent with the national interest".

The 1958 National Defence Education Act enlarged the mandate:

> "The National Science Foundation shall..undertake programme to develop new or improved methods, including mechanized systems, for making scientific information available".

By those mandates, an NSF division, which after a number of name and direction changes is now called the Division of *Information and Intelligent Systems* (IIS), has supported research in these areas since the 1950s. Importantly, the field-defining studies that NSF supported included, among others, Cranfield IR evaluation studies in the 1950s and 1960s, large chunks of SMART studies from the 1960s to 1990s, and now the Digital Libraries Initiatives.

In the U.S., information science developed and began flourishing on its own in a large part due to government support by a host of agencies, as did many other fields. Historically, the support was a success—it was instrumental in creation of the whole enterprise of information science and even of the information online industry based on IR. But to the credit of information science it kept growing on its own even after government support slackened substantially. This cannot be said of a number of other fields or areas that floundered after government stopped being their main source and resource.

Social Context

It is a truism to state that information was always important for any society in any historical period. But the role of information and its degree of importance differed. With the evolution of the social order to a "post-industrial" society, or "post-capitalist" society or what we now commonly also call "information society," knowledge and information is assuming an increasing central role in every aspect of life. The classic study by Machlup, followed by a number of similar studies, documented the startling structural changes in the economy and society as driven by the growth of information and knowledge production and processing.

Popularly, they were summarized by Drucker:

> The change in the meaning of knowledge that began two hundred fifty years ago has transformed society and economy. Formal knowledge is seen as both the key personal and the key economic resource. . . [K]nowledge proves itself in action. What we now mean by knowledge is information effective in action, information focused on results.... The actual products of the pharmaceutical industry is knowledge; pill and prescription ointment are no more than packaging for knowledge.

Addressing the problem of information explosion, information science found a niche within the broader context in the evolution of the information society. In its various manifestations and attempted solutions, the niche is getting broader and bigger. But by no means does information science hold a monopoly in that niche. As the importance of information is increasing in society, more and more resources and expenditures are channeled into various information-related activities. More and more research funds, projects, and initiatives are devoted to information in various disguises. It is not surprising then that more and more fields, researchers, professionals, and businesses are turning to information, and even "discovering" information. There is gold in information. Information science has many competitors—it may be even swamped by them.

WHAT IS "INFORMATION" IN INFORMATION SCIENCE

In a scientific sense, the answer to the question is "We don't know." Yes, we can and do provide various lexical definitions of information, and we have an intuitive understanding of its meaning that we apply daily and widely. Thus, we do understand the message-sense in which we deal with information in information science. But that does not provide for a deeper and more formal understanding and explanation. Information is a basic phenomenon. For all basic phenomena—energy or gravity in physics, life in biology, justice in jurisprudence—the same "we-don'tknow" answer applies.

However, the investigation of the basic phenomena is proceeding—that is the basic point of all these fields. It is proceeding by investigating the *manifestations, behaviour,* and *effects* of phenomena under question. While we do not know what information is, or what some of its derivative notions, such as relevance, may be, over the years we have learned a lot about their various manifestations, behaviours, and effects. And we are continuing to learn about them through scientific investigations. "Information" has a variety of connotations in different fields. For instance, from the standpoint of physics and biology, a number of highly ambitious attempts have undertaken to explore information as a basic property of the universe.

In psychology, information is used, at times, as a variable dealing with sensory perception, comprehension, or other psychological processes. These senses of information are very different than the one in information science. In some fields, information science included, the notion of information is broadly associated with messages. For this sense, a number of interpretations exist, which are assumed in different theoretical and pragmatic treatments of information. We can present them as related, but differing manifestations of information in an ordered sequence or a continuum of increasing complexity.

Narrow Sense

Information is considered in terms of *signals or messages for decisions* involving little or no cognitive processing, or such processing that can be expressed in algorithms and probabilities. Information is treated as the property of a message, which can be estimated by some probability. Examples are information in terms of uncertainty in information theory, "perfect information" in game theory, or information as related to decision-making and market equilibrium in the theory of uncertainty and information in economics of information.

The latter has been surveyed by Hirshleifer and Riley, who provide this illustrative explanation: In the economics of uncertainty, an individual is assumed to act on the basis of current *fixed beliefs, e.g.*, deciding whether to carry an umbrella based on one's present estimate of the chance of rain, while in the economics of information a person typically is trying to arrive at *improved beliefs, e.g.*, by studying a weather report before deciding to take an umbrella.

Information may be considered as causing a difference between fixed and improved beliefs. The value of information is calculated as the difference between the decision maker's expected utility of the decision made without the information, and the expected utility of the best possible choice in decision made after receiving and analysing the information. The huge, and sometimes insurmountable, problem, of course, is estimating appropriate probabilities. A number of pragmatic applications follow this interpretation, such as computerized trading.

Broader Sense

Information is treated as directly involving *cognitive processing and understanding*. It results from interaction of two cognitive structures, a "mind" and a "text." Information is that which affects or changes the state of a mind. In cases of information services, information is most often conveyed through the medium of a text, document, or record, *e.g.*, what a reader may understands from a text or document.

The interpretation by Tague-Sutcliff fits:

* Information is an intangible that depends on the conceptualization and the understanding of a human being. Records contain words or pictures absolutely, but they contain information relative only to a user... Information is associated with a transaction between text and reader, between a record and user.

Broadest Sense

Information is treated in a context. That is, information involves not only messages that are cognitively processed but also *a context*—situation, task, problem-at-hand, and the like.

Using information that has been cognitively processed for a given task is an example. In addition to other senses, it involves motivation or intentionality, and therefore it is connected to the expansive social context or horizon, such as culture, work, or problemat-hand.

In information science, we must consider the third and broadest sense of information, because information is used in a context and in relation to some reasons. The point was implicitly understood from the beginning of information science, particularly as reflected in the practice of information retrieval. This interpretation of "information" in information science is not new. Such a broad interpretation of information that explicitly incorporates cognition and context was, among others, elaborated by Wersig and Neveling and Belkin and Robertson. It is also implicit in the social role of information science.

THE BIG PICTURE: STRUCTURE OF INFORMATION SCIENCE

Any field is structured along some distinct, larger areas or subdisciplines of enquiry or practice. Think of a number of areas of medicine, computer science, librarianship, and so forth. Information science is not an exception. It has a distinct, two-partite structure. A number of authors observed that the work in information science falls in two large areas or subdisciplines, each, of course, with further subareas or specialties.

White and McCain conducted a monumental bibliometric study of the domain of information science by providing extensive analysis of co-citation patterns for 120 authors over a period of 23 years. Borrowing from White and McCain, visualize a map of information science as an ellipse with authors inside, distributed or clustered according to their connections. There are two large clusters at each end of the ellipse, with only a few authors spanning both. In other words, there are two major areas or subdisciplines.

I liked their metaphor:

> *As Things Turn Out, Information Science Looks Rather like Australia*: Heavily coastal in its development, with a sparsely settled interior.

In one of the coastal sections, fall authors that worked on analytical study of literatures; their structures; studies of texts as content-bearing objects; communication in various populations, particularly scientific communication; social context of information; information uses; information seeking and behaviour; various theories of information and related topics. As yet, there is no good label for that cluster. Some call it "information analysis." For simplicity, lets call this the *domain cluster*, as did White and McCain, although "basic" may be a good label. In the other coastal section are authors who concentrated on IR theory and retrieval algorithms; practical IR processes and systems; human-computer interaction; user studies; library systems; OPACs; and related topics.

Let's call this cluster the *retrieval cluster,* although "applied" may also be a good label. Basically, most of the areas in the domain cluster are about study of fundamental manifestations and behaviour of phenomena and objects that information science is all about. They are centered on the phenomenon of information and its manifestations in literature. The retrieval cluster deals, by and large, with a variety of implementations, on both practical and theoretical levels. It is about implementation, behaviour, and effects of the interface between literatures and people, including, of course, all kinds of retrieval aspects. Unfortunately, these two main clusters are largely unconnected.

Only a very small number of authors spanned the two clusters. In other words, there are very few integrating works. The last text that undertook an integrative approach encompassing both clusters. A rare example of such an effort in research is the last work by Tague-Sutcliffe, where she related the notion of informative-ness with evaluation of IR systems.

Several modern texts are specifically aimed at IR but none on information science as a whole. I dare to venture a prediction: fame awaits the researcher who devise a formal theoretical work, bolstered by experimental evidence, that connects the two largely separated clusters, *i.e.*, connecting basic phenomena with their realization in the retrieval world. And a bestseller is awaiting an author that produces an integrative text in information science. Information science will become a full-fledged discipline when the two ends are connected successfully. The two clusters are not equally populated. The retrieval cluster has significantly more authors, not to mention total number of works. As in many other fields, more effort is expanded on the applied side than on the basic side.

In part, this is due to availability of funds for given topics—not surprisingly, research goes after moneyed topics. By and large, over the last decade or so, major granting agencies funded only applied research in information science. For instance, I have been unable to identify a single grant addressing any of the topics in the domain or basic cluster from NSF Division of Information and Intelligent Systems since its preceding Division of Information Science and Technology was reorganized and included in the Directorate for *Computer and Information Science and Engineering* (CISE) in 1985. In de Solla Price's concepts and words, the domain cluster is "little science", while the retrieval cluster is "big science," and the connection between the two has presently no science.

PROBLEMS ADDRESSED

General

Webster routinely defines information science as "the science dealing with the efficient collection, storage, and retrieval of information." It is a general definition of problems addressed by information science. The definition follows pretty much an early and popular one given by Borko as a part of a wide discussion and controversy about the nature of the field in the 1960s. More specifically, information science is a field of professional practice and scientific enquiry addressing the problem of effective communication of knowledge records—"literature"—among humans in the context of social, organizational, and individual need for and use of information. The key orientation here is the problem of need for and use of information, as involving knowledge records.

To provide for that need, information science deals with specifically, oriented information techniques, procedures, and systems. To elaborate, the specific concentration of information science is on human knowledge records as *content-bearing objects,* in all forms, shapes, and media. The primary emphasis is on content of these objects, in terms of their potential for conveying information. "Literature" may be used as a generic term for these knowledge records, but "literature" has many other connotations, thus requiring a careful restriction in its use in information science. Because of these connotations, "literature" will not become popular in information science.

Realizing this, I am using the term here only as a shorthand, as did White and McCain, when they elegantly stated:

> "The proper study of information science is the interface between people and literature . . . modeling the world of publications with a practical goal of being able to deliver their content to enquirers on demand . . . While many scientists seek to understand communication between persons, information scientists seek to understand communication between persons and certain valued surrogates for persons that literature comprises.

In all of this there is a technological imperative, reflected in efforts to take advantage of modern information technology. While information science is not about technology, the problem of providing effective computer applications pervades the field. Following is a word on the extent and borders of information science.

Focusing information science on the content-bearing properties of literature, and on associated techniques and systems dealing with providing effective access to and use of literature, provides a restriction for information science.

Thus, the field does *not* deal with great many other information systems, such as payroll, inventory, decision support systems, data processing, airline schedules, and a zillion others, nor does it deal with direct communication among and between persons. Information science is about a specific manifestation or type of information that defines its scope and its systems. Information science, as many other fields, also involves a professional component. Starting in 1950s, the profession of information science grew from research and applications in IR, to become a powerful component of the field, and in many ways a leading one in respect to innovation.

As in many other fields, there is an uneasy relation between the scientific or research-oriented component and the professional or practice-oriented one. The profession is responding in its own way to needs of its users and organizations, and chartering its own technological applications, many times independently of research advances, and even in different directions. At present, the connection and feedback between profession and research in information science is not as well established as it is in older fields, such as engineering or medicine. This is a serious inhibitor for progress of both.

More Specific

A number of authors suggested a breakdown of specific areas of information science, beyond the structural analysis offered above. The breakdown among different authors is in significant agreement, although the labels differ somewhat. I will take the breakdown and labels provided by White and McCain. They provided a factor analysis of co-cited authors and extracted 12 factors as specialties.

In descending order of how authors loaded, they labelled the specialties as:

* Experimental *information retrieval* (IR);
* Citation analysis;
* Practical retrieval;
* Bibliometrics;
* General library systems theory;
* Science communication;
* User studies and theory;
* OPACs;
* General imported ideas—other disciplines;
* Indexing theory;
* Citation theory; and
* Communication theory.

While one may quibble with some of the classes and labels, these specialties provide a fairly accurate picture of problem areas in which information scientists worked over the past quarter of a century.

Over time, there were shifts in emphasis and there were movements between specialties. Nothing is permanent. But these are the specialties of information science. New areas are clearly on the horizon. For the 1990s, I would suggest that the major new areas include interaction studies; searching of the Internet; multimedia IR; multilanguage IR; and digital libraries.

These are prime examples of the new significant areas of concentration, not yet evident in the historical record. At the same time, the old area of experimental retrieval is blossoming like never before, courtesy of the *Text Retrieval Conference* (TREC), a government-sponsored mechanism for comparative evaluation of a variety of IR techniques and approaches that involves large test beds. IR was, and still is, the major and most populated area of information science. Thus, a separate discussion of IR follows.

INFORMATION RETRIEVAL

In the early and mid-1950s, a critical mass of scientists, engineers, librarians, and entrepreneurs started working enthusiastically on the problem and solution defined by Bush. By 1960s this became a large and relatively well-funded effort and organized activity. Often, there were heated arguments and controversies about the "best" solution, technique, or system.

These arguments brought on the tradition of evaluation, a major staple of IR research and development. What is now TREC started with Cranfield evaluations in the late 1950s and early 1960s. Remarkably, the basic evaluation principles developed then are still the underpinning of TREC today. Calvin Mooers, an active and highly visible pioneer of information science, coined the term *information retrieval* in 1951. The term took hold, and today is a part of the English language.

At that time, Mooers not only coined the term, but also defined the problems to be addressed:

> "Information retrieval embraces the intellectual aspects of the description of information and its specification for search, and also whatever systems, techniques or machines that are employed to carry out the operation.

Today, we would add that IR also and particularly involves interaction in all of these, with all the contextual-cognitive, affective, situational—aspects that interaction embraces. An expanded Mooers' conception is still valid. As it advanced, IR produced a number of theoretical, empirical, and pragmatic concepts and constructs. Numerous IR systems were developed and successfully deployed.

A great many historical examples can be given to illustrate the remarkable evolution of IR systems and techniques, adapting the ever-evolving information technology, from punch cards in the midcentury to the Internet at its close. Based on IR, an online information industry emerged in the 1970s, and grew through its own version of information explosion, as chronicled by Hahn. IR is one of the most widely spread applications of any information system worldwide. It has a proud history. Surely, information science is more than IR, but many of the problems raised by IR or derived from objects and phenomena involved in IR, are at its core.

Approaches and Paradigm Split

The approach taken by Mooers was to concentrate on the building of systems. This systems emphasis which was formulated early in the 1950s, was the sole approach to IR for some decades. It still predominates in a good part of IR research to this day.

Consequently, most of the IR research and practice concentrated on retrieval systems and processes. However, starting in the late 1970s and gaining steam in the 1980s, a different line of reasoning and research evolved-one that concentrates on the cognitive, interactive, and contextual end of the process. It addressed users, use, situations, context, and interaction with systems, rather than IR systems alone as a primary focus.

The retrieval cluster started splitting into subclusters, as noted by White and McCain, and before by others such as Saracevic and Harter. We now have two distinct communities and approaches to research in the retrieval cluster. They became commonly known as *systems-centred* and *user-centred.* Both address retrieval, but from very different ends and perspectives. The split is not only conceptual, looking very differently at the same process, but also organizational. The systemscentered side is now mostly concentrated in the *Special Interest Group on Information Retrieval* (SIGIR) of the *Association for Computing Machinery* (ACM), while the user-centered cluster congregates around the *American Society for Information Science* (ASIS).

Each has its own communication outlets-journals, proceedings, and conferences. There is less and less overlap of authors and works between the two outlets. We have two camps, two islands, with, unfortunately, relatively little traffic in-between. The systems-centered approach is exemplified by work on algorithms and evaluation based on the traditional IR model, a model that does not consider the users or interaction. The massive research that evaluates a variety of IR algorithms and approaches within TREC is a culmination of this approach.

In contrast, cognitive, situational, and interactive studies and models, involving the use of retrieval systems exemplify the human-centered approach. Following that approach, interactive models, differing significantly from the traditional IR model, started to emerge. Even in TREC, a group of researchers started an interaction track, but so far have a hard time conceptually and methodologically, thus demonstrating the difficulty in merging the traditional and interactive models and approaches. Let me characterize, in a simplified way, the relationship between the two approaches or subclusters addressing different sides of retrieval.

On the one hand, the human-centred side was often highly critical of the systems side for ignoring users and use, and tried valiantly to establish humans as the proper center of IR work.

The mantra of human-centred research is that the results have implications for systems design and practice. Unfortunately, in most human-centred research, beyond suggestions, concrete design solutions were not delivered. On the other hand, the systems side, by and large, ignores the human side and user studies, and is even often completely ignorant of them. As to design, the stance is "tell us what to do and as suggested, do it." But nobody is really telling, or if telling, nobody is listening.

As a rule, in systems-oriented projects, people and users are absent. Thus, there are not many interactions between the two camps. Let me provide some examples. A rough analysis of the 1997 SIGIR proceedings found only 3 papers of some 34 that dealt in some way with people and users; in the ACM's Digital Libraries 1997 conference proceedings, of 25 papers only 3 mentioned people and users. If one reads authors such as Dervin and Nilan, and many of their successors, who champion the human centered approach, one gets the impression that there is a real conflict between the two sides and approaches, and that there is an alternative way to the "dreadful" systems approach.

In a way, this stance is a backlash caused by the excesses, failures, and blind spots of systems-centered approaches not only in IR, but also in great many other technological applications. Unfortunately, sometimes the backlash is justified. All of us who work on the humancentered side are not that dismissive of the systems side. But the issue is not whether we should have systems-*or* humancentered approaches. The issue is even less of human*versus* systems-centered. *The issue is how to make human*and *systems-centered approaches work together.* In this sense, a number of works have addressed integrating usercentered and systems-centered approaches in IR, but this has been discussed mostly by researchers from the usercentered side.

Examples are works by:

* Bates,
* Belkin,
* Cool,
* Stein,

* Thiel,
* Fidel
* Efthimidiadis,
* Robertson and
* Beaulieu.

To reiterate, it is not one camp against the other but how can we incorporate the best features of both approaches and make them work jointly. The issue is how to deliver and incorporate the desired design features that will improve systems orientations towards users, integrate them with systems features, and use advantages provided by both, humans and technology. In other words, the issue is *putting the human in the loop* to build better algorithms and to exploit computational advantages. Real progress in information science, and by extension in IR, will come when we achieve this. Lately, the NSF has championed human-centered design involving an interdisciplinary approach to information systems. Hopefully, this will go beyond rhetoric. It is not easy to do. But, that is what research is for—to address difficult, not only easy problems.

Proprietary IR

By the 1980s, the commercial information industry based on IR became successful and profitable. Out of academe, grants, and government, IR became a money-making proposition. This, of course, is another and important sign of success. Not surprisingly, a number of former IR researchers, practitioners, and graduates of IR programmes ventured out to become IR entrepreneurs.

Sure enough, throughout information science history there were many entrepreneurs, and they were highly significant in development of the field. But this generation of entrepre-neurs was different. They ventured to develop and market a variety of IR procedures based on algorithms, applicable and scalable to large files, multiple applications, and/or various advanced technologies. It was knowledge industry at its purest. But, as in all commercial knowledge industries, the product was proprietary. While it was not that hard to guess the base of these various proprietary algorithms and how they worked—after all they were derived from publicly available knowledge and experiences, such as those that came from SMART experiments—they remain unpublished and "secret."

A new kind of IR evolved, separate from the rest, not communicating as to intellectual advances with the rest. None of these ventures became a high commercial success, as measured by Silicon Valley standards. But the World Wide Web, emerging in the first half of the 1990s, changed all this. The acceleration of the growth of the Web is an information explosion of the like never before seen in history. Not surprisingly then, the Web is a mess. No wonder that everybody is interested in some form of IR as a solution to fix it.

A number of academic-based efforts were initiated to develop mechanisms, search engines, "intelligent" agents, crawlers, and so forth, to help control the Web. Some of these were IR scaled, and adapted to the problem; others were a variety of extensions of IR. Many had few, if any original, developments, besides new packaging or labeling; and a good number were just the usual hype. The wheel was reinvented a number of times. But out of this, and fast, came commercial ventures, such as the pioneering Yahoo!, whose basic objective is to provide search mechanisms for finding something of relevance for users on demand.

And to make a lot of money. These enterprises pride themselves on having proprietary methods by which they are accomplishing the retrieval tasks. The connection to the information science community is tenuous, and almost nonexistent. The flow of knowledge, if any, is onesided, from IR research results into proprietary engines. The reverse contribution to public knowledge is zero. A number of evaluations of these search engines have been undertaken simply by comparing some results between them or comparing of their retrieval against some benchmarks.

Some evaluations were done within, others outside of information science. Results were not complimentary. The Web-based proprietary IR is expanding and flourishing outside of the field. It is addressing a vexing problem, the like we have not seen before. But as yet, the success is elusive and questionable.

RELEVANCE

As information science pioneers developed IR processes and systems in the 1950s, they defined as the main objective retrieval of *relevant* information. Effectiveness was expressed in terms of relevance. From then to now, IR is explicitly geared not towards any old kind of information, but towards *relevant information*. Various IR approaches, algorithms, and practices were, and still are, evaluated in relation to relevance. Thus, relevance became a key notion in information science. It is also a complex phenomenon with a long and turbulent history in information science transcending IR, going back to early 1950s. Of course, there was a choice.

Relevance did not have to emerge as the key notion. Uncertainty was one choice suggested by a number of theorists to be the base of IR, and thus to reflect effectiveness. But it did not take. In contrast, uncertainty is the basic notion underlying expert systems. If the pioneers had not embraced relevance, but instead, let's say, uncertainty, as the base for IR, we would have today a very different IR, and probably not that successful. In general, relevance, according to *Webster*, means having significant bearing on matter at hand. As with many other concepts, relevance assumes related but more specific meaning in more specific contexts and applications.

In the context of information science, relevance is the attribute or criterion reflecting the effectiveness of exchange of information between people and IR systems in communication contacts based on valuation by people. With relevance as the criterion, and human judgments of relevance of retrieved objects as the measuring instrument, the measures of precision and recall are widely used in evaluation of IR systems. The strength of these measures is that they involve people—users—as judges of effectiveness of performance. The weakness is the same: it involves judgment by people, with all the perils of subjectivity and variability. Relevance indicates a relation. For relevance, many relations have been investigated.

An consensus has emerged in information science that we can distinguish between several differing relations that account for different manifestations or types of relevance:

* *System or Algorithmic Relevance:* Relation between a query and information objects in the file of a system as retrieved, or as failed to be retrieved, by a given procedure or algorithm. Comparative effectiveness in inferring relevance is the criterion for system relevance.
* *Topical or Subject Relevance:* Relation between the subject or topic expressed in a query and topic or subject covered by retrieved texts, or, more broadly, by texts in the system file, or even in existence. Aboutness is the criterion by which topicality is inferred.
* *Cognitive Relevance or Pertinence:* Relation between the state of knowledge and cognitive information need of a user and texts retrieved, or in the file of a system, or even in existence. Cognitive correspondence, informativeness, novelty, information quality, and the like are criteria by which cognitive relevance is inferred.
* *Situational Relevance or Utility:* Relation between the situation, task or problem at hand and texts retrieved by a system, or in the file of a system, or even in existence. Usefulness in decision making, appropriateness of information in resolution of a problem, reduction of uncertainty, and the like are criteria by which situational relevance is inferred.
* *Motivational or Affective Relevance:* Relation between the intents, goals, and motivations of a user and texts retrieved by a system, or in the file of a system, or even in existence. Satisfaction, success, accomplishment, and the like are the criteria for inferring motivational relevance.

Practically, IR systems assess systems relevance only-that is, they respond to queries-hoping that the objects retrieved may also be of cognitive relevance, and even more so of utility. However, a user may judge an object by any or all types of relevance-for a user they may interact dynamically. Difficulties arise when an object is of system relevance but not of cognitive relevance or utility, or conversely.

If items are of cognitive relevance or utility, but were not reflected in the query, they are not and cannot be retrieved. At the bottom of IR research is a quest to align systems with other types of relevance. People all over have a strong intuitive understanding of relevance, thus, they intuitively understand, without manuals, what IR is all about. This makes IR systems generally understandable and acceptable-a critical attribute in their widespread application.

DISCIPLINARY RELATIONS

Two things introduced interdisciplinarity in information science. First and foremost, the problems addressed cannot be resolved with approaches and constructs from any single discipline-thus, intedisciplinarity is predetermined, as it is in many modern fields. Second, interdisciplinarity in information science was introduced and is being perpetuated to the present by the very differences in backgrounds of people addressing the described problems. Differences in background are many; they make for richness of the field and difficulties in communication and education. Clearly not every discipline in the background of people working on the problem made an equally relevant contribution, but the assortment was responsible for sustaining a strong interdisciplinary characteristic of information science. I will concentrate on interdisciplinary relations with two fields: librarianship and computer science. Obviously, other fields, most notably cognitive science and communication, have also interdisciplinary relations, but these are the most significant and developed ones.

Librarianship

Librarianship has a long and proud history devoted to organization, preservation, and use of graphic records and records in other media. This is done through libraries not only as a particular organization or type of information system, but even more so as an indispensable social, cultural, and educational institution whose value has been proven manifold throughout human history, and across all geographic and cultural boundaries.

Researcher defines the library as:

* . . .Contributing to the total communication system in society. . . Though the library is an instrumentality created to maximize the utility of graphic records for the benefits of society, it achieves that goal by working with the individual and through the individual it reaches society.

The common ground between library science and information science, which is a strong one, is in sharing of their social role and in their general concern with effective utilization of graphic and other records, particularly by individuals.

But there are also very significant differences in several critical respects, among them:

* *Selection of Problems Addressed and the Way they were Defined*: A majority of the problems were not and are not addressed in library science;
* *Theoretical Questions Asked and Frameworks Established*: The theories and conceptual frameworks in librarian-ship have no counterpart in information science, and *vice versa*;
* *The Nature and Degree of Experimentation and Empirical Development and the Resulting Practical Knowledge and Competencies Dderived*: There is very little overlap in experimentation and development between the two, and professional requirements differ as well to a significant degree;
* *Tools and Approaches Used:* A most telling example is the very different approach undertaken in relation to utilization of technology in IR and in library automation; and
* *The Nature and Strength of Interdisciplinary Relations Established and the Dependence of Progress on Inter-disciplinary Approaches*: Librarianship is much more selfcontained.

All of these differences warrant a conclusion that librarian-ship and information science are two different fields in strong interdisciplinary relations, rather than one and the same field, or one being a special case of the other. This is not a matter of turf battles, or of one being better or worse than the other. Such arguments, while common between many fields, matter little to progress of either field. But differences in selection and/or definition of problems addressed, agenda, paradigms, theoretical base, and practical solutions *do* matter. Thus the conclusion that librarianship and information science, while related, are different fields. The differences are most pronounced in the research agenda and directions.

Interestingly, research on OPACs, now that they are incorporating more and more IR features, is bringing the two fields in closer relation. Probably, so will the research in digital libraries, but at this time, it is too early to tell. The conclusion is not without heated controversy.

Among other authors, Vakkari contends on information science and librarianship being one and the same field, with the now commonly used name of "library and information science." Does it matter? Administratively yes, very much so, particularly in universities and professional societies. Otherwise, no. The issue is, and always will be, in the problems addressed and solutions undertaken. I contend that they differ significantly.

Computer Science

The basis of relation between information science and computer science lies in the application of computers and computing in IR, and the associated products, services, and networks. In the last few years, this relation also involves research on the evolving digital libraries, with their strong technological base.

To illustrate the connection, we use a definition by Denning:

> "The discipline of computing is the systematic study of algorithmic processes that describe and transfer information: their theory, analysis, design, efficiency, implementation, and application. The fundamental question underlying all of the computing is: "What can be automated?"

Computer science is about algorithms related to information interpreted in the first, whereas information science is about the very nature of information and its use by humans, interpreted in the third or broadest sense. Computer science is about symbol manipulation, whereas information science is about content manipulation, where symbol manipulation is the indispensable infrastructure. The two concerns are not in competition, they are complementary—they lead to different basic and applied agendas. Computer science is also many times larger than information science.

A number of computer scientists have been involved in research and development on information and its many spin-offs, to the point of being recognized leaders in information science. Gerard Salton is a prime example. In addition, there are several streams of research and development in computer science that had no connection with the early evolution of information science, but have addressed information problems similar to those in information science. Among others, these include works on expert systems, knowledge bases, hypertext, and human-computer interaction.

More recently, this involves research and development on digital libraries, a "hot", financially heavily supported area by a host of government agencies in the U.S. and many other countries. Bolstered by heavy support, interest in digital library research exploded on the scene in 1990s, attracting the attention of computer scientists from a wide variety of streams, as well as people from many other disciplines. These areas have a significant informational component that is associated with information representation, its intellectual organization, and linkages; meta-information, information seeking, searching, retrieving, and filtering; use, quality, value, and impact of information; evaluation of information systems from user and use perspective; and the like-all traditionally addressed in information science.

Conversely, these streams of computer science research and development provide a different outlook, framework, and approach, and even a different paradigm, not only for information science research and development, but also for its academic and continuing education. Again, as with librarianship, the issue is not about turf. It is about paradigms, theoretical foundations, and pragmatic solutions; and ultimately, it is about their appropriateness to human information problems.

EDUCATION

That education is critical for any field is a truism that hardly needs to be stated. In particular, research lives by education, it cannot be better than the education that researchers receive and then extend and plow back into education. Unfortunately, education in information science has not received the attention that it deserves. This may explain the many difficulties in the field that I have discussed. Educational models that evolved differed to a degree or even substantially from country to country. I am concentrating here on the U.S. models only.

In the United States, two educational models evolved over time. I call them the Shera and Salton models, after those that pioneered them. Both have strengths and weaknesses. Jesse H. Shera was a legendary library school dean from the 1950s until the 1970s at Western Reserve University. Among others, he was instrumental in starting the Center for Documentation and Communication Research in 1955. Shortly thereafter, the library school curriculum started to include courses such as "Machine Literature Searching" and several other more advanced courses and laboratories on the topics of research in the Centre.

The basic approach was to append those courses, mostly as electives, to the existing library school curriculum, without modifications of the curriculum as a whole, and particularly not the required core courses. Information science became one of the specialty areas of library science. The base or core courses that students were taking rested in the traditional library curriculum. Information science education was an appendage to library science. A few attempts to spin off information science as an independent degree and curriculum were not followed widely. But Shera's model was. Library schools in the U.S. and in many other countries imitated Shera's model.

They used the same approach and started incorporating information science courses in their existing curriculum as a specialty. Out of this was borne the current designation "library and information science." Shera's model is still the prevalent approach in schools of library and information science. The strength of the Shera model is that it posits education within a service framework, connects the education to professional practice and to a broader and user-oriented frame of a number of other information services, and relates it to a great diversity of information resources.

The weakness is a lack of a broader theoretical framework and a total lack of teaching of any formalism related to systems, such as development and understanding of algorithms. The majority of researchers in the human-centered side, as I described earlier, came from or are associated with this educa-tional environment. Gerard Salton was first and foremost a scientist, a computer scientist, and the father of modern IR.

As such, he pioneered the incorporation into IR research a whole array of formal and experimental methods from science, as modified for algorithmic and other approaches used so successfully in computer science. His primary orientation was research. For education, he took the time-honoured approach of a close involvement with research. Salton's model was a laboratory and research approach to education.

As Shera's model resulted in information science education being an appendage to library science education, Salton's model of IR education resulted in it being a specialty of and an appendage to computer science education. Computer science students that were already well-grounded in the discipline, got involved in SMART and other projects directed by Salton, worked and did research in the laboratory, completed their theses in areas related to IR, and participated in the legendary IR seminars.

They also published widely with Salton and with each other, and participated with high visibility in national and international conferences. From Harvard and Cornell, his students went to a number of computer science departments where they replicated Salton's model. Many other computer science departments in the U.S. and abroad took the same approach.

The strength of Salton's model is that it:

"Starts from a base of a firm grounding in formal mathematical and other methods, and in algorithms, and

* Relates directly to research.

The weakness is in that it:

* Ignores the broader aspects of information science, as well as any other disciplines and approaches dealing with the human aspects that have great relevance to both the outcomes of IR research and the research itself, and
* Does not incorporate professional practice where these systems are realised and used. It loses users.

Consequently, this is a successful, but narrowly concentrated education in IR as a specialty of computer science, rather then in information science. Not surprisingly, the researchers in the systems-centred approach came out of this tradition. The two educational approaches are completely independent of each other. Neither is connected to the other. Neither reflects fully what is going on in the field. While in each model there is an increase in cognizance of the other, there is no educational integration of the systems-and usercentered approaches.

The evident strengths that are provided by Shera and Salton model are not put together. Their weaknesses are perpetuated. It is high time for communities from each model to try to integrate education for information science. It is an open question whether the human-and systems-centered approaches can fruitfully work together as urged in all those calls for human-centered design until an educational integration occurs.

While library education receives formal attention from the *American Library Association* (ALA), and education for computer science from ACM, no such formal attention is paid by any professional/scientific society to education for information science, or for IR in particular. Neither ASIS nor SIGIR, as primary homes for information science, have been involved to any great extent in educational matters, such as setting of standards or devising model curricula. Clearly, there is a need and an opportunity for more substantive involvement by both organizations in educational issues.

INFORMATION SOCIETY

First, the general development of the information society is pushing to re-evaluation of all the institutions which work with information, data, and knowledge-indirectly also with culture. In this connection the roles of education and media have been discussed already quite largely also in the European Union. But libraries — as well as other memory institutions like archives and museums-have not been considered. Still, there is a clear need in the information society to maintain an institution which is concentrating in collecting and organizing information and offering general access to it.

Until now, this work has been underestimated, but I argue the situation will change! Libraries are especially important now when the whole idea of education is stressing more and more independent learning and acting. All citizens must be able to find and use information. It is the key raw material-but it is a zero resource, if there are no access points to it and if documents are in chaotic order.

Here we can see libraries enter the stage:

* The unique function of libraries is to acquire, organize, offer for use and preserve publicly available material irrespective of the form in which it is packaged in such a way that, when it is needed, it can be found and put to use. No other institution carries out this long-term, systematic work.

Culture must be nominated especially: it has an important and unique role in mobilizing resources of human beings. It has been described: *T*o some extent, culture makes its influence felt more indirectly than knowledge, but it is impossible to imagine how people's creative powers could be fully activated without the impact of culture, which extends into the depths of the mind. The challenge to modern societies is that the basic resource, knowledge, is developing from information in very individual, capricious and unpredictable process. It cannot be commanded.

Still, societies can support this development, *e.g.* by offering acces to cultural and knowledge treasures. This can even be translated into economic language: to get out the best from the human resources in Europe, this resource must be feeded up with rich and various cultural and information contents! I would like to stress especially the idea of organising information by libraries. It is often shadowed by the second important side of library work: offering access. But in the life-long learning and new technology context just all forms of organising documents are getting more to the focus. This is clear to anybody who has tried to find something from not-so-often-used Internet websites.

NEW LINES IN THE EU AND IN THE UNITED STATES

In accordance with these phenomenons, there are new political lines in the European Union (EU): The Maastricht Treaty in 1992 launched the cultural aspects. This was only after a long discussion, which made it clear that we have to remember to separate the national view and the European view. The Amsterdam Treaty in 1997 declared citizenship as an impor-tant theme. A significant part of this are a.o. granting infor-mation skills and access to information to every European.

In addition to this, the European future strategies need to meet the democratic aspects of the information society development. One of the crucial points is again general access to information. Libraries, especially public libraries, are a good tool in all of these new areas. But the European union does not support whichever cultural or citizen concentrated projects in Europe. In the interests of the European Union there is always to find the European element.

So, what can be done in library policy on the European level, taking in account that libraries are primarily a part of national education and cultural policies?:

> "The own-initiative report "The role of libraries in modern societies", adopted by the European Parliament in October 1998, is the first effort to answer these questions.

The same topics have been dicussed in the United States. They have reached the point where especially the problems of those lacking access to digital resources have been studied. The report Falling Through the Net: Defining the Digital Divide by the U.S. Department of Commerce was released earlier in July 1999. The report finds that minorities, low-income persons, the less educated, and children of single parent households, particularly when they reside in rural areas or central cities, are risk groups.

The report calls for public policies and private initiatives to expand affordable access to critical information resources. But it also shows,, for the first time as far as I know, that libraries and community centres really can diminish the information gap between haves and not-haves. The 1998 data from the U.S. demonstrates very clearly that community access centers, primarily public libraries, are particularly well used by those groups who lack access at home or at work: *e.g.* unemployed groups used Internet in libraries three times as often as an average citizen.

EARLIER ACTIONS IN EU

In the European Union, there have been some efforts to mobilize "the treasures of the European libraries" since the mid-80'ies. These discussions and resolutions led to two special library programmes under the 3rd and 4th Framework programmes of research and development. The later programme has been known as "Telematics for Libraries".

They have been strongly concentrated in IT, because it has been seen as a good tool to produce better access to the existing, underused library resources. These programmes have had a clear impact in the European library co-operation and development.

Benefits of this work come to public libraries indirectly: common standards and working methods help in the end all kind of libraries. But a fact is, that nearly all the libraries active in these EU projects are national libraries or big research and university libraries. Two main exeptions are PubliCA, a network of European public libraries, and ECUP, which was a copyright awareness raising project, and reached public libraries as well. A new beginning was the so called Morgan report in 1997.

In this report libraries were for the first time put clearly onto the place where they belong in the information society. As one result of the Morgan report, the European Commission informed that it will produce a Green Paper about the role of libraries in the information society.

For one or another reason, this was made quite ready but was never published. In this situation the Committee on Culture, Youth, Education and the Media in the European Parliament decided to produce an own-initiative report about libraries.

The main reason was that they wanted to influence the big issues under work in the EU, first of all the copyright directive and the 5th framework programme, which will have a direct impact to libraries.

DECISIONS OF THE EP CONCERNING LIBRARY POLICY

In short, when adopting the own-initiative report, the EP (European Parliament) was calling the Commission and/or the member states to following actions:

* Libraries must be taken in account in national and EU information society strategies and in the respective budgets.
* Libraries need more resources for acquiring expensive books.
* The Green Paper on libraries by the Commission must be completed.
* The users position must be taken in account in the copyright directive process, the balance must be maintained-this was politically the most important decision in short run.
* Support to libraries was demanded from the 5th

Framework programme of research and development, *e.g.* for networking, drafting standards, preserving, and transferring information; there is no more named library programme under the 5th framework programme.

* A clearing-house to solve problems of long-term conservation should be founded.
* Studies concerning permanent paper should be done on European level.
* The member states should take care of digitizing their cultural heritage for future.
* There should be studies and concrete support to libraries in licensing matters, which are–will be the next big issue in library work.
* The EU cultural and information budget should be opened to libraries as well, libraries and their co-operation should be taken in account in planning new programmes.
* Problems of legal deposit in international and multinational materials, especially in electronic materials should be solved.
* The member states should provide all types of libraries with modern equipment, particularly with Internet connections.
* Free of charge use of public libraries, in the spirit of the UNESCO Public Library Manifest, was demanded.
* Free and easy access via libraries to material produced with the aid of tax revenues was demanded.
* The members states should organize for their library professionals up-dating education and training.
* A European Union focal point for libraries should be set up.
* The member states should found European information points at libraries in countries where they do not yet exist.
* Library statistics should be better and more comparable both on national and European level.
* The national Parliament libraries should be opened

to the MEP's in countries where this is not yet the practice.

In addition to these, the report strongly stresses that the library financing must be re-thougt in the information society. Without new resources libraries are unable to do everything they are expected to do! After the EP adoption of this report, the European Commission informed that it will next prepare a communication about actions to do. It was stated that the report had already served as a discussion paper, and so the need for the Green Paper had disappeared. The communication is in summer 1999 still under work in the Commission DGXIII/2.

TRADITIONS AND NEW FORMS OF WORK IN THE SAME HOUSE

The European Commission R&D framework programmes have concentrated in IT matters. The three cultural programmes, Caledoskope, Ariane and Raphael, have not been very useful for libraries, because their scope has been quite narrow, *e.g.* the books and reading programme Ariane has concentrated in translations. In the coming framework programme Culture 2000 libraries will have more possibilities to get support also for their cultural actions. What then will be the fate of the traditional tasks of libraries in general? Will the information society wipe out book loaning and poems? These elements will survive, but will get completed by new media forms.

It was stated earlier that culture has a special role in building up the modern society and in mobilizing the capacity of its members The significance of reading is only growing in future. Demands to enlargen and deepen literacy skills get greater and greater. Literacy has a special role in guaranteeing the basic citizen competence to everybody. It is in general interests of the society to offer possibilities to all people for maintaining and developing their literacy. In library work new technologies offer new possibilities to raise service level, too. Good examples can already now be found all over the world, mainly of course in those countries where Internet is used largely.

Some models: Library catalogues are available via Internet, the patron can check her/his loaning data from Internet, and even renew the loans a country/areawide information service via Internet and e-mail; there are versions for link libraries or virtual libraries, where libraries collect and describe high-level link-ups discussion lists of librarians, whre they can share their professional skills and knowledge, even take part in developing the library policy of the country/area.

There is one special comment concerning Internet which we have heard both from small libraries with rejected printed collections in Finland and from African libraries: In case you got reach in Internet, the resources your library can offer to the patrons are suddenly multiplied. All of once we have exactly the same resource as British Library or the Library of Congess.

It is amazing, it is revolutionary, and we can use it! In the complicated modern society libraries have many kinds of answers to many demands of the society, as well as those of the citizens.

They have potential means to serve both the information society development and their traditional human-istic tasks. Maybe information technology will even make it easier to combine these elements in future than in the past!

ROLE OF INFORMATION IN PLANNING

WHAT IS PLANNING

Planning is a simple process used every day. In the process, one decides where he is, where he wants to be, and how he gets there. Getting to work every day, grocery shopping, preparing for a vacation or trip, and saving for retirement are examples of events that require planning. More formally, planning is an organizational process of envisioning a desired future and developing the necessary infrastructure to achieve it.

WHY PLAN

Overall, the purpose of planning is to achieve excellence in public library service.

Some specific benefits:

* Planning provides information to use in decision-making.
* Planning provides a blueprint for future library development.
* Planning guides decision-makers in setting necessary priorities about who receives what service with what efficiency.
* Planning provides information to use in the allocation of resources, particularly when they are scarce.
* Planning leads to structured positive change resulting in improved library service.
* Planning makes crises less critical.
* Planning encourages staff creativity and cooperation.
* Planning encourages accountability.
* Planning provides a basis for evaluating the library's performance.
* Planning can improve communication and give everyone who works with the library a sense of common purpose.
* Planning pays off—organizations that plan out-perform those that do not.

WHAT ARE THE STEPS IN THE PROCESS

There are many approaches to planning. Significantly, the Public Library Association published a new approach to public library planning; *Planning and Role Setting for Public Libraries: A Manual of Options and Procedures* is designed to meet the special needs of this community. The following is a summary of the eight major steps recommended.

PLANNING TO PLAN

* Organizes the planning process,
* Shapes the planning process to the library's needs and resources,
* Coordinates planning with other management activities,
* Defines the responsibilities of major planning participants, and

* Organizes and trains the Planning Committee.

LOOKING-AROUND

* Identifies information needed for planning,
* Collects information about the library and the community it serves, and
* Analyses information gathered for planning decisions.

DEVELOPING ROLES AND MISSION

* Describes eight distinct roles, or service profiles, that public libraries may emphasize in providing services to their comm-unities;
* Describes a method of determining which roles are to receive a major commitment in the library and which are to be supported only minimally;
* Guides planners in writing a mission statement as a concise expression of the roles chosen for emphasis;
* Helps the library communicate its service focus to the public, elected officials, and staff.

WRITING GOALS AND OBJECTIVES

* Translates the library's role choices and mission into statements of desired ends or targets,
* Defines goals as long-range and representing a vision of excellence in library service,
* Defines objectives as specific, time limited, and measurable or verifiable, and
* Provides a framework for implementation and evaluation.

TAKING ACTION

* Produces tangible evidence of the library's planning,
* Identifies possible activities to implement the goals and objectives,
* Selects activities best suited to the library's circumstances and resources, and
* Leads to cycle of annual objective setting and updating of five-year plan.

WRITING THE PLANNING DOCUMENT

* Describes creation of a formal report of the library's planning activities, and
* Provides an opportunity for communication with the public, the library staff, and governing officials.

REVIEWING RESULTS

* Reviews the plan and its implementation activities after a period of time,
* Reviews extent to which objectives were accomplished, and
* Starts the planning cycle again.

"LEVELS OF EFFORT" AS A PLANNING TOOL

Planning and Role Setting for Public Libraries introduces the concept of "levels of effort," an approach that allows library planners to adapt the process to a particular library's needs, purposes, and resources. There are three levels of effort — basic, moderate, and extensive. Any of these will result in acceptable plans. Each library's level-of-effort choice reflects the interplay of several different factors.

* *Participants:* The more individuals and groups represented, the higher the library's level of effort for planning will be.
* *Resources:* Higher levels of effort call for a proportionally greater commitment of the library staff's time and larger expenditures from the library's budget.
* *Library Context:* Libraries serving a community with rapid growth or change, a complex and diverse population, shifting economic conditions, or libraries facing a major change in funding may need to plan at a higher level of effort.
* *Planning Purposes:* What the library expects the planning process to accomplish may affect the level of effort chosen for some planning phases.
* *Planning Structure:* Libraries planning at a basic level of effort may approach many planning activities

informally; but as library complexity increases, the planning structure becomes more formal, thus increasing the level of effort.

* *Planning Schedule:* Some libraries may complete their first objectives cycle over a very short time period; higher levels of effort may require twelve to eighteen months to complete.

ROLE SETTING AS A PLANNING TOOL

Another unique feature of the planning process developed by the Public Library Association and introduced in *Planning and Role Setting for Public Libraries* is the concept of public library roles.

Public library roles are library service profiles that describe a combination of factors in planning and include:

* What the library is trying to do?
* Whom the library is trying to serve? and
* What resources the library needs to achieve these ends?

2

Communication

This chapter explains the nature of interpersonal communication in organizations, and should also help the reader become a more effective communicator. The chapter is based on the premise that understanding communication as well as good communication skills is required for success in managerial work. Presented first is a basic version of the communication process, followed by a description of nonverbal communication. Next is a description of formal and informal communication channels.

Extensive attention is paid to a description of major communication barriers, including cross-cultural differences and how they can be overcome. The chapter concludes with a brief description of organizational politics. The subject of politics would fit many places in the text, and is included here because organizational politics affects interpersonal communication. Poor communication is the number one problem in virtually all organizations and the cause of most problems. Communication problems can be expensive, and good communication skills can enhance sales.

THE COMMUNICATION PROCESS

Communication is the process of exchanging information by the use of words, letters, symbols, or nonverbal behaviour. Sending and receiving messages accurately is complex and difficult.

STEPS IN THE COMMUNICATION PROCESS

Two-way communication involves four major steps, and each step is subject to interference or noise:

* *Encoding the Message:* Encoding organizes ideas into

a series of symbols, such as words and gestures, designed to communicate with the receiver.

* *Communication Media:* The message is sent over a communication medium such as voice, e-mail, instant message, Web log, or telephone.
* *Decoding the Message:* In decoding, the receiver interprets the message and translates it into meaningful information. Communication barriers are most likely to surface at the decoding step.
* *Feedback:* Without feedback, it is difficult to know whether a message has been received and understood. If the receiver takes action as intended by the sender, the message has been received satisfactorily.

Many missteps can occur between encoding and decoding a message. Noise, or unwanted interference, can distort or block the message

NONVERBAL COMMUNICATION IN ORGANIZATIONS

A substantial amount of communication occurs through nonverbal communication, the transmission of messages by means other than words. Nonverbal communication supplements verbal communication; its purpose is to express the feeling behind a message.

Six categories of nonverbal communication are as follows:

* *Hand and Body Gestures:* Included here are frequent movements to express approval and palms spread outward to indicate perplexity. Gesturing should not be eliminated because it is a natural part of speech and thinking, and off loads some of the mental effort.
* *Facial Expressions and Movement:* A facial look and movements may show approval, disapproval, or disbelief.
* *Posture:* Posture can reveal attitude, such as leaning towards a person to shows a favourable attitude towards the message. Tilting your head and leaning in indicates you are concerned and engaged in the message.

* *Body Placement:* The placement of one's body in relation to someone else is widely used to transmit messages, such as moving close to indicate acceptance. A speaking coach says that to effectively relate to an audience, you need a *kinesthetic connection*. This would include other forms of nonverbal communication as well as moving around effectively.
* *Voice Quality:* The way something is said can be more meaningful than what is said. Another aspect of voice quality is a person's accent. Regional accents can sometimes
* *Clothing, Dress, and Appearance:* Dress can communicate how willing an employee is to conform to organizational standards.

Another application of nonverbal communication is to assist in screening airline passengers who could be a security threat. Unusual behaviour and odd gestures might signal potential problems. Screening possible security threats by nonverbal communication rather than cultural stereotypes is much more acceptable to defenders of civil liberties. Many nonverbal signals are ambiguous, such as a smile indicating warmth or nervousness.

ORGANIZATIONAL CHANNELS AND DIRECTIONS OF COMMUNICATION

Messages travel over different channels and follow different directions.

FORMAL COMMUNICATION CHANNELS

Formal communication channels are the official pathways for sending information inside and outside the organization, usually revealed by the organization chart. With e-mail it has become easier for lower-ranking people to communicate with top management. Other formal channels include newsletters, meetings, and memos. Management by walking around could be classified as formal or informal.

INFORMAL COMMUNICATION CHANNELS

Informal communication channels are the unofficial networks used to supplement the formal channels, and usually rise out of work necessity:

* *Networks Created by Leaders:* Leaders make extensive use of informal networks to accomplish goals. *Operational networking* is aimed at doing one's assigned task more effectively. Some of this networking is part of the formal channel. *Personal networking* engages people from outside the organization in a person's effort to develop personally and advance. *Strategic networking* focuses networking on attaining business goals directly.
* *Chance Encounters:* Unscheduled and informal contact between managers and employees can be an efficient and effective informal communication channel. Spontaneous communication events may occur at many places on the work premises.
* *The Grapevine and Rumor Control:* The grapevine is the informal means by which information s transmitted in the organization. Rumors and gossip are the two major components of the grapevine. Rumors are typically about something people wish to happen, or dread. Gossip is part of the human condition, and is fueled by the need for affiliation. Information travels rapidly over the grapevine, and three-fourths of its information is true.

Rumors can also create productivity and morale problems. Good employees may leave in response to rumors about layoffs. Severe negative rumors, especially about product defects or poisonings, must be neutralized to prevent permanent damage. Rumors about the financial health of a company are also damaging. Rumors can be combated by enhancing formal communication because employees seek more information during times of intense rumors. For example, explain why you cannot comment or give full information.

COMMUNICATION DIRECTIONS

Messages in organizations travel in four directions: downward, upward, horizontally, and diagonally. A communication network is a pattern or flow of messages that traces the communication from start to finish. *Downward communication* is the flow of messages from one level to a lower one. *Upward communication* is the transmission of messages from lower to higher levels.

Companies have developed mechanisms to facilitate upward communication, including:

* The open-door policy,
* Town hall meetings,
* Complaint programmes and hotlines, and
* Web logs.

Horizontal communication is the sending of messages among people at the same organizational level. *Diagonal communication* is the transmission of messages to higher or lower organizational levels in different departments.

ORGANIZATIONAL LEARNING AS PART OF COMMUNICATION IN ORGANIZATIONS

An important output of communication channels is to transmit information to other workers so as to advance knowledge and learning throughout the organization. A learning organization is skilled at creating, acquiring, and transferring knowledge. It also modifies its behaviour to reflect new knowledge and new insights. Managing knowledge and sharing information are also important. Knowledge management is the ways and means by which a company leverages its knowledge resources to generate business value. In addition to the specialized work of the *chief knowledge officer* in a learning organization, managers must also manage knowledge. A problem is that many workers jealously guard their best ideas.

BARRIERS TO COMMUNICATION

Barriers exist at every stage in the communication process, and they are considered to be noise or interference. Barriers are the *throughput* in the communication process.

Messages the most likely to be distorted are those that are complex, emotional, or clash with the receiver's mental set:

* *Low Motivation and Interest:* The most basic fact about communication is that the message must appeal to a need of the receiver.
* *Inappropriate Language:* Language can be inappropriate and can therefore create barriers for many reasons. Two factors of particular significance in a work setting are *semantics* and *difficulty level.* Contrary to popular sentiment, there are times when a low difficulty level is inappropriate. Jargon works well with insiders, and typically not well with outsiders.
* *Defensive Communication:* A general communication barrier is defensive communication—the tendency to receive messages in such a way that our self-esteem is protected. *Denial* of contrary information is part of defensive communication.
* *Insufficient Nonverbal Communication:* If verbal communication is not supplemented by nonverbal communication, messages may not be convincing.
* *Information Overload:* Information overload occurs when an individual receives so much information that he or she becomes overwhelmed. A message must have high impact to get around the overload problem. E-mail is exacerbating the problem of information overload. Many managers receive about 150 messages each day. Yet many workers at all levels are learning to manage e-mail better.
* *Poor Communication Skills:* Many messages fail to register because the sender lacks effective communication skills. The plain language movement instructs workers in government, the sciences, business, and the legal profession. Many messages left on voice mail systems are articulated so poorly that the receiver lacks enough information to act, including understanding the return phone number or electronic address. Poor listening is another communication problem.

* *Electronic Communication Problems:* Information technology has created several new communication barriers, as exemplified by the impersonality of e-mail. Most managers use e-mail as a substitute for face-to-face interaction with group members. The nuances of human interaction are usually lost in e-mail exchanges. Computer graphic presentations can create communication barriers. It is important to maintain eye contact and not overwhelm the audience with a large number of detailed slides.

OVERCOMING BARRIERS TO COMMUNICATION

Most communication barriers are surmountable.

The general strategy is to be aware that such barriers exist, and to develop a specific tactic to deal with each one:

* *Understand the Receiver:* Understanding the receiver can help overcome every communication barrier. *Empathy* is needed to understand the receiver, and also helps build rapport.
* *Communicate Assertively and Directly:* If the sender explains explicitly and directly what he or she wants—and conveys feelings—the message is more likely to be received. An application of assertive communication is the informative confrontation, a technique of enquiring about discrepancies, conflicts, and mixed messages. It is helpful to repeat your message and use multiple channels. A *spin measure* is another form of indirect communication that might be converted into direct communication.
* *Use Two-Way Communication and Ask for Clarification:* Two-way communication reduces barriers because a dialogue helps reduce misunderstanding by communicating feelings as well as facts. Also, two-way communication allows for questions and answers. Two-way communication also helps build connections with people and is useful in obtaining clarification on what the other person means by a particular phrase. The telephone is making a comeback because it enhances two-way communication.

* *Elicit Verbal and Nonverbal Feedback:* The effective communicator asks for verbal feedback, and looks for nonverbal indicators of acceptance and understanding.
* *Enhance Listening Skills:* Listening is a basic part of communication. A helpful technique is active listening, which means listening for full meaning without making premature judgments or interpretations. Active listening includes listening for total meaning, and reflecting the message back to the sender. An advanced skill for active listening is to ask questions instead of making statements. The receiver does not blurt out questions as soon as the other person is finished speaking.
* *Unite with a Common Vocabulary:* A management writer recommends that managers should first identify the core work of a business, and then describe it in a shared business vocabulary. In this way, the various functions would speak a common language. Business jargon can contribute to a common vocabulary but must be used cautiously to avoid misunderstanding.
* *Be Sensitive to Cultural Differences:* In order to overcome culturally based communication barriers:
  - Be sensitive to their presence,
  - Show respect for all workers,
  - Use straightforward language,
  - Be alert to cultural differences in customs and behaviour,
  - Be sensitive to nonverbal differences,
  - Do not be diverted by accent, grammar, or personal appearance, and
  - Be attentive to individual differences in appearance.
* *Engage in Metacommunications:* Many people make no particular effort to overcome communication barriers. Another possibility is to metacommunicate, or communicate about your communication to help overcome barriers or resolve a problem. In other

words, talk about how well, or not well, the communication is going.

HOW TO CONDUCT AN EFFECTIVE MEETING

Poorly conducted meetings are a productivity drain. Group meetings can also be improved by such means as:

* Meeting only for valid reasons,
* Starting and stopping on time and offering refreshments,
* Keeping comments brief and to the point,
* Avoiding electronic distractions,
* Capitalize on technology when appropriate,
* Encouraging critical feedback and commentary,
* Striving for wide participation,
* Solving small issues ahead of time with e-mail, and
* Considering "huddling" when quick action is needed.

ORGANIZATIONAL POLITICS AND INTERPERSONAL COMMUNICATION

Politics is related to communication because so much interpersonal communication in organizations is politically motivated. Organizational politics refers to informal approaches to gaining power or other advantages through means other than merit or luck. In recent years, as managers have to rely more on personal influence and less on hierarchy, the meaning of organizational politics has become more favourable.

RELATIVELY ETHICAL POLITICAL TACTICS

A political tactic might be considered relatively ethical when it is used to gain advantage or power that serves a constructive organizational purpose.

Useful and relatively ethical political tactics are:

* Develop power contacts,
* Be courteous, pleasant, and positive,
* Create a positive image,
* Ask satisfied customers to contact your boss,
* Be politically correct, and
* Send thank-you notes to large numbers of people.

RELATIVELY UNETHICAL POLITICAL TACTICS

In reality, not all organizations are ideal and many people use negative political tactics to fight for political advantage.

Four widely practiced unethical political tactics are:

* *Back Stabbing:* You pretend to be nice, but all the while plan someone's demise. E-mail is widely used for back stabbing.
* *Setting up Another Person to Fail:* Give another person an assignment with the hopes that he or she will fail and therefore be discredited.
* *Playing Territorial Games:* Also referred to as *turf wars,* territorial games involve protecting and hoarding resources that give one power, such as information and authority.
* *Be Unpredictable:* Some particularly devious executives behave unpredictably by design to keep people off guard.

EXERCISING CONTROL OF NEGATIVE ORGANIZATIONAL POLITICS

Carried to excess, organizational politics can damage productivity and morale, including hurting the careers of innocent people. *Being aware of the presence of organizational politics* leads to control. *Open communication* can also constrain the impact of political behaviour. *Avoiding favouritism* is a big help. Also, *managers should find a way to talk about territorial games.*

3

Intellectual Property Rights

INTRODUCTION

Computers and the concomitant capability they have provided for making copyrighted works available in digital form in networked environments have created many new kinds of expressive opportunities. Computer technology together with communications technology has enabled authors to create digital libraries and hypertext publishing systems. Active development of such systems is now underway. While some difficult technical problems must be solved to build these systems, technical obstacles are thought to be surmountable. Less clear, however, is what kind of intellectual property scheme can be used to make digital library or hypertext publishing systems commercially viable.

An intellectual property system works well when it embodies a reasonably accurate model of how people are likely to behave. Copyright law is based on a relatively simple and straightforward model of author and reader behaviour. Authors are motivated to produce interesting and valuable texts and to make these works available to others by copyright's reassurance that authors can control the sale of copies of their works. Readers are motivated to purchase the texts, or to urge institutions such as libraries to purchase the texts, so that they can have access to the work.

Authors have generally had little control over what uses readers make of the copies after the first sale of the work to the public. Commentators on U.S. copyright law have sometimes regarded this lack of control over uses as a virtue. But while it can be said that the absence of copyright control over uses has promoted the dissemination of knowledge, the truth is that in the print world it is infeasible to maintain meaningful control over uses anyway. Copyright should be accounted a great success at modeling author and reader behaviour, for the basic framework of this law has lasted nearly three hundred years.

During this period, copyright industries have flourished and copyright law has broadened to include a wide variety of intellectual products besides those manufactured by printing presses. While the copyright model is being utilized for all manner of texts in digital form, the behaviour of authors and readers is being changed by the new digital technologies. It is becoming increasingly likely that some adjustments will have to be made in the copyright model to make digital libraries and hypertext publishing environments as commercially viable as the print industries have been. But few new models have yet been constructed, and work in this direction has only just begun, After a brief discussion of some characteristics of informational works in digital form that challenge existing intellectual property systems.

It will then try to foresee how such rights might be handled if digital libraries become, as some in the technical community foresee they will, hypertext publishing systems (that is, systems in which users can become authors by linking portions of the digital library's contents-with or without any additional content contributed by them-whose link-based work can be published within the digital library). The most innovative and well-developed model for how intellectual property rights might be dealt with in a hypertext publishing system is that proposed by Ted Nelson (a hypertext developer and visionary—indeed the person who coined the term hypertext for which a whole field of endeavor is now known) in his book Literary Machines.

This book describes the Xanadu hypertext publishing system designed by Nelson, which was to have been commercialized by Autodesk, a software publishing firm.

Although the object ultimately concludes that the Xanadu intellectual property rights model is flawed because it does not accurately reflect how authors and users would likely behave, it praises a number of aspects of Nelson's model and the innovative concepts it embodies. The authors hope this critique of the Nelson model will aid in the formulation of a new conception about how intellectual property rights can be dealt with so that digital libraries and hypertext publishing systems can become commercially viable.

DIGITAL MEDIA AND INTELLECTUAL PROPERTY LAW

Six characteristics of works in digital form seem likely to change significantly the contours of intellectual property law, especially copyright. The ease with which such works can be replicated and the ease with which they can be transmitted and accessed by multiple users are the first and second of these characteristics. These characteristics would seem to create strong incentives for copyright industries to move away from their traditional focus on the sale of copies, and towards greater control over uses of protected works. That it is now feasible to control uses through controlling access to computer systems containing works in digital form will also affect this trend.

A third characteristic of digital works is the ease with which they can be manipulated and modified. While this plasticity offers users some important advantages over the print medium (printed works are sometimes too fixed to be maximally usable), copyright law is more geared towards dealing with works that are permanently fixed. The law may need to be adjusted to cope with the new benefits and new problems that this plasticity will entail, such as providing guidelines for circumstances in which plastic uses of digital information are permissible.

A fourth characteristic is the breakdown of copyright distinctions among different kinds of works when they are in digital form. The copyright statute identifies seven categories of protected works, each of which has somewhat varying degrees of protection, Is a hypertext version of Mozart's Magic

Flute that contains the music, the libretto, textual commentary, pictures of Mozart, and other media a "literary work," a "musical work," a "sound recording," a "pictorial work," or an "audiovisual work'? The answer to this question under copyright law cannot be all of the above—even if it really is.

Copyright's classification scheme, oriented as it is towards the appearance of works and the medium in which they are embodied, seems in need of adjustment if the statutory differences are absent from the digital representation. Because so many of the exclusive fights and special privilege provisions in the copyright statute depend on the category of the work, they will need some refinement to deal with digital multimedia works. A fifth characteristic is that digital works are virtually invisible to users/readers. Works in digital form are stored as a sequence of high and low voltage signals in computer memory. They cannot be perceived or read by humans except with the aid of a user interface.

One cannot tell from viewing one portion of such a work on a computer screen how large the work is, nor can one navigate through the text unless navigation aids have been specially constructed in software to permit this. Fortunately, the sixth and final characteristic of digital media is that they allow new kinds of search and linking activities to be achieved. This characteristic has given rise to new classes of protected intellectual property products, including hypertexts.

Intellectual property protection for innovative aspects of new kinds of digital works, such as software user interfaces and hypertext navigation aids, has been a subject of significant controversy, both on copyright and patent fronts, and seems likely to remain so for the foreseeable future. Despite repeated Supreme Court rulings that algorithms are unpatentable and evidence that practitioners believe strong protection by copyright and patent will have a negative effect on the software industry, the U.S. Patent Office has been issuing many software patents in recent years, some of which are for functions and user interface features for hypertext systems.

Some court decisions have taken such an expansive view of the scope of copyright protection that reuse of almost anything but very high level abstractions in software would seem dangerous, although other decisions have taken a far narrower view, seeming to confine "expression" to that which would readily be viewed as expressive in traditional categories of works. Some decisions have recognized that computer software is difficult to fit in the traditional copyright mold.

MODELS OF AUTHOR AND READER BEHAVIOUR IN RECENT ELECTRONIC INFORMATION SYSTEMS

Some clues about how authors and readers might behave in digital libraries and hypertext publishing systems can be perceived by looking at how people currently use computer bulletin boards, computer data bases, and other information services and electronic mail systems. Instead of viewing these systems as technical precedents, it is instructive to consider them as experiments in developing appropriate models for intellectual property and reader/user/author behaviour that might be adapted for more ambitious applications such as Xanadu.

PRODIGY AND CompuServe

Prodigy and CompuServe are commercial services that provide a variety of bulletin boards, electronic mail, information services, and entertainment. They embody significantly different models of user behaviour, and their pricing strategies are markedly different. Prodigy targets the consumer and home markets, and treats its users as relatively passive information consumers who do not interact much with each other. Prodigy offers users access to many different kinds of information, as well as bulletin boards, electronic mail, and some entertainment. Its services are made available for a fixed monthly fee.

Usage-insensitive pricing is made possible by the paid advertising that Prodigy presents along with nearly every screen of information displayed to users. When Prodigy imposed a usage-pricing scheme for sending electronic mail, many users felt that their contract with Prodigy, as well as their "free speech fights," had been violated. In contrast,

CompuServe has been oriented towards business and professional users and always had usage-based pricing based on connect time.

CompuServe information services are specifically focused, organized into a complex hierarchy of bulletin boards and data bases, many of which are moderated by an expert, who in some circumstances is compensated by CompuServe. This finer-grained categorization enables CompuServe to impose surcharges for supposedly more timely or valuable information, but its user population is presumably used to paying for information according to its value. Users engage in heated electronic dialogues with one another on bulletin boards, commenting on and criticizing one another's postings. Both Prodigy and CompuServe place some limits on user downloading.

Some materials, such as shareware or public domain software from both sources, can be downloaded without restriction, but other materials are restricted. The two systems differ, however, in the locus of restrictions. Prodigy is a centralized service which means it sets and enforces the downloading policy. CompuServe, by contrast, has a more decentralized policy because it is essentially an umbrella organization for a number of information services, and these services often have their own downloading policies. Quite recently, however, both Prodigy and CompuServe have expanded user opportunities to download materials, although this adds to the cost of the service.

THE INTERNET

The Internet is a vast network of networks that interconnect thousands of computing sites in government, industry, and academia. The Intermit has evolved from primarily providing electronic mail services to become the infrastructure for significantly broader services of information exchange and collaborative work. Like CompuServe, the heart of the Internet is a vast collection of newsgroups in which participants from around the world post and comment on messages. Some people take on the role of newsgroup moderators, but the overwhelming majority of newsgroups are unmediated.

Author and reader behaviour on the Internet are largely governed by norms or "netiquette" that have evolved over time and that are enforced both by system administrators and by the informal but effective sanctions of "flames" (critical messages) directed at violators. Included in these norms are rules about selecting newsgroups in which to post messages, sensitivity to authors of posted messages when citing or responding to them, and other matters that affect both authors and readers. Users of the Internet vary greatly in their perception of intellectual property laws as they apply to this new kind of publishing system. Some users, especially new users who are college students, act as if the Internet services and the information that can be had by exploring the Internet are completely free.

In fact, each host machine that serves as an Internet site has to pay a fee for the privilege. Institutions recoup these fees as well as other costs associated with use of host machines by passing them on, even if the costs are not immediately evident because they may be borne by a particular unit of the institution, rather than directly by those who use the machine for Internet services. Those who post information not authored by them on Intermit bulletin boards or in electronic newsletters delivered by Internet sometimes do so with a conspicuous notice that it is being posted without copyright permission, thereby asserting the poster's view of an appropriate scope of fair use.

But some who post materials on the Internet explicitly assert copyrights on the messages that they post. And it has become increasingly common for electronic journals distributed on the Internet to contain a notice that those who contribute items to the journals are responsible for obtaining whatever copyright permissions might be needed. Although "net" users generally regard it as fair to download items from the bulletin board for one's personal use, and even to send a copy to a friend who might otherwise not see the item, it is considered bad manners (or worse) to redistribute more widely someone else's posting without its author's permission.

Still, it is worth noting that because "the net" is so vast and the number of its users so large, it can be extremely difficult to police it for copyright purposes. Authors who distribute works on the Internet are generally not paid to publish, and receive no royalties. Nor do readers generally have to pay to read items on the Internet. But it is fair to state that many Interact activities are being paid for (or at least subsidized) by Interact participants' employers. Hence, it can be argued that anything posted on the Internet that is work-related is the intellectual property of the employer who provides access to the Internet by paying for the computers and telecommunications infrastructure.

Employers may feel that the value of the information their employees glean from the Internet outweighs the costs of the time to obtain it, but it is unlikely that many employers explicitly make this analysis. In addition to electronic mail and newsgroups, the Internet now supports several innovative services that enable it to function as a distributed digital library with vast holdings. If an Internet site chooses to make some of its information publicly available, a user on another site can use the anonymous FTP (file transfer protocol) mechanism to retrieve it.

Other experimental services, some with fanciful names like Archie, Gopher, and World Wide Web, build upon FTP to provide users with a worldwide index so that they can find sites that offer the information they seek. The WWW service allows users to retrieve what they want even if they cannot directly connect to the site that stores it. These new services are being enthusiastically embraced in the academic and research communities of the Internet, but they pose even more problems for intellectual property rights because they erode the boundaries between public and commercial information sources.

LEXIS ARM WESTLAW

Lawyers have had access to digital libraries of legal materials for well over a decade, thanks initially to the farsightedness of a paper manufacturer, which perceived a market opportunity for providing electronic access to judicial opinions, statutes, regulations, and other legal materials. This manufacturer formed Mead Data Central, whose Lexis data base lawyers use regularly. Like so many other print publishers, the major legal print publisher, West Publishing, did not see the market opportunity for electronic information services until after Lexis had become a major success.

Although a late entrant to the business, West has succeeded in designing a digital library of legal materials that offers some services, particularly the key numbering system that West had long used in print, that give it some competitive advantage. The initial pricing scheme employed by Lexis and by West was similar to that used by CompuServe: usage-based pricing based on connect-time. This pricing strategy worked particularly well because lawyers could typically pass these charges on to clients. Over time, both services developed pricing strategies for institutions, such as law schools, where connect-time charges could not be passed on.

Both services also now permit downloading of electronic versions of legal materials as well as printouts of selected materials. No special charges seem to be levied for these services, although usage-based charging would absorb the costs through connect-time, and institutional subscription pricing would be based on a predicted quantum of such uses. There is no technical reason why these two digital libraries could not become hypertext publishing systems. Their considerable financial success might suggest that this extension would be a natural one, and indeed, at least one author has tried to make them become so.

Professor Peter Martin of the Comell Law School sought to bring about this kind of expansion of legal data base functions by creating a hypertext treatise on Social Security Law on the Lexis system. Because Lexis had no particular incentive to promote its use, Martin eventually negotiated an arrangement by which he could "port" the treatise to a CD-ROM so it could be commercialized. Professor Henry Perritt of Villanova Law School has also proposed hypertext publishing systems built on top of digital libraries of legal materials as a way to produce electronic casebooks.

But except for the work of a few pioneers, such as Professors William Andersen of the University of Washington Law School, William Boyd of the University of Arizona Law School, and Ronald Staudt of the Chicago-Kent Law School, hypertext has yet to come to the field of law. The richly inter textual nature of law makes it a natural field for hypertext applications, and perhaps ways can be found to create them on top of a digital library of legal materials such as Lexis or Westlaw, and make them commercially viable.

THE INTELLECTUAL PROPERTY SYSTEM IN XANADU

The most complete proposal for making digital library or hypertext publishing systems commercially viable has Ted Nelson. For over two decades, Nelson has been writing and talking about a proposed system called Xanadu, which he envisioned as a vast digital library containing all of the world's literature. Because Xanadu would allow users to create new and derivative documents via links, Xanadu is also a hypertext publishing system. Xanadu can usefully be understood as an attempt to create an institution that will be writing environment, publishing environment, library, and bookstore in one.

Despite his visionary reputation, Nelson is practical enough to realise that the commercial success of the Xanadu proposal critically depends on the way it deals with intellectual property issues. The intellectual property system in Xanadu has sometimes been summarized in writings about the Xanadu system in popular magazines, but has been subject to little serious analysis. After a brief description of how Xanadu would deal with intellectual property rights issues, this Part will discuss some respects in which the Xanadu proposal differs from that which is reflected in the existing copyright system.

Xanadu contains some interesting ideas about how to solve certain problems with digital library and hypertext publishing systems, but some aspects of the Xanadu model of author and user behaviour may be unworkable. Nevertheless, Nelson's analysis suggests some respects in which intellectual property systems might have to adapt to make digital libraries and hypertext publishing systems commercially viable.

XANADU'S REVENUE SOURCES AND MECHANISMS

Nelson envisions revenues being generated in Xanadu from two sources: first, from authors who would pay fees for renting space for their documents in the Xanadu system, and second, from users who would pay fees based on their usage of the system. Nelson expects that authors will want to put their documents into the Xanadu system because once the documents are in the system; authors will be able to earn royalties whenever users make use of their documents. Between ten and twenty per cent of usage fees would go to authors whose documents are accessed by users; the rest would go to the system to recoup costs and make profits. Nelson intends for usage fees, and consequently the royalties as well, to be set on a per byte delivery basis for administrative convenience.

Nelson expects that people will pay to use the Xanadu system, because not only will it contain as much of the world's literature as Nelson can get into it, but there will also be legion opportunities in the Xanadu system for users/browsers/readers to make money by adding value to the system through their creative uses of the system. There are two main means by which Nelson intends to let users make money in the Xanadu system. One is by making derivative works of documents already in the system. This would include creating new versions of other authors' documents, creating compound documents consisting of portions of a number of different documents, or creating commentaries on other documents in the system.

By creating derivative documents, users would become system authors themselves, and thereby become able to earn royalties when other users access their derivative documents. No special permission would be needed to make derivative documents from other authors' documents, for Nelson will make it a condition of storing documents in Xanadu that authors agree to allow others to make whatever derivative uses they want of published documents in the system.

Nelson relies on two factors to motivate authors to agree to allowing derivatives to he made of their documents. One is that they will then be able to do to others' documents what others can do to theirs. But more importantly, when a third party accesses the derivative document on Xanadu, the author of the underlying document, as well as the author of the derivative document, will earn a royalty, because the derivative document will be connected to the original document; bytes from both will be called up when third parties access the derivative document.. Hence, both authors will receive royalties.

The second way for users to generate revenues when using the Xanadu system will be by creating links between or among documents in the system. Nelson expects some links to be very elaborate, such as a specialized index to certain classes of documents in the system. Other links may be modest, such as a connector between two documents. User links between documents, in effect, become new documents in the system. Each time other users traverse a set of links, the link author will receive a royalty, as will the authors of the documents on either end of the link.

Although Vannevar Bush was the first to perceive that information trailblazers would be needed for computerized information systems, Nelson deserves credit for recognizing the need to give incentives to information pioneers to cut paths through the invisible contents of a digital library. Nelson's scheme would also provide authors with the opportunity to store private as well as published documents in the Xanadu system. Authors would be able to decide who could have access to private documents and under what conditions. But Nelson envisions that authors of private documents would generally make them available for linking.

Private documents could be withdrawn without difficulty from Xanadu by their authors. The same will not be true for published documents because of the effect withdrawal would have on the interests of authors who have linked to or otherwise built upon the foundation of the published document. Nelson attempts to create a strong incentive for authors to publish their documents ill the Xanadu system by making system royalties unavailable to authors for private documents, even those with unrestricted distribution (*i.e.*, from which derivatives can be made, and to which links can be constructed). Because publication imposes obligations on the Xanadu operator and the author, publication of a document in the Xanadu system is a formal event, requiring a signature of the author on a form affirming the intent to publish the work.

COMPARING XANADU AND THE COPYRIGHT SYSTEM

Nelson refers to copyright in a positive way in a number of passages in his book, and takes care to establish a plausible case that nothing in Xanadu violates existing copyright law. Xanadu gives authors new ways to generate revenues from their works—even some that copyright might not provide—and so aims to create incentives to authorship, revealing a predisposition in keeping with traditional copyright incentives. But the Xanadu system is more different from copyright than might be apparent from a cursory examination.

Compensatian based on Uses, Rather than Distribution of Copies

One difference between the Xanadu intellectual property system and traditional copyright is that Xanadu aims to derive revenues for authors by charging for each and every use of their documents, rather than, as has traditionally been done in copyright industries, on the sale or other commercial distribution of copies of copyrighted works. Many commercial computer data bases do much the same thing. Such arrangements seem likely to become increasingly common for works in digital form.

Blurring the "Idea" and "Expression" Distinction and Eliminating "Fair Use"

A more novel set of differences from copyright flow from Xanadu's treatment of links. Fundamental to the copyright regime is a distinction between "ideas" (which are unprotected by copyright law) and "expression" (which copyright protects). Under the copyright regime, authors generally do not expect remuneration whenever other authors comment on, quote from, use ideas from, or make reference to their work. The statutory fair use provision has been interpreted as allowing even literal copying of copyrighted text if the amount taken is relatively small, especially if the taking is for research, educational, or critical purposes.

Only if other authors take a fairly hefty chunk of "expression" from the protected work do copyright holders expect compensation. In Xanadu, information can be included in a document by linking.

Because of this, Xanadu draws a different line than the print world would about what information to count as a single work. Even if Xanadu had a fair use provision, the lack of separateness among documents would complicate the determination of what constitutes fair use. But Xanadu allows no fair use copying.

Authors in the Xanadu system will get royalties based on how many bytes were linked to-merely for being linked to. This aspect of Xanadu prefigures an intellectual property system that compensates authors without regard to whether chunks of expression have been appropriated. In time, this would seem likely to undermine the "idea/expression" distinction that has been a staple part of the copyright system.

Treating Linking as Authorship

Nelson's decision to treat linking as a kind of authorship-that is, as an intellectual activity that should not only be encouraged, but should serve as the basis for earning royalties when users traverse the links-also seems to diverge somewhat from the traditional copyright model. While an extensive set of links, such as an index, might readily be protectable by traditional copyright law as a compilation, many of the kinds of links that Nelson would treat as works of authorship might be unprotectable under traditional copyright law.

A link between a passage in document A and a passage in document B might, for example, be considered a "discovery" that the statute says copyright cannot protect. Traditional copyright law would also not regard it as a compensable use of a copyrighted work for readers to traverse the links among documents referred to in a printed article. Yet link authors in Nelson's scheme would be compensated for others' traversal of their links.

Use Rights vs. Rights to Exclude

Nelson, like many others who are not lawyers, finds it natural to think of intellectual property rights in terms of what uses of works should give rise to author compensation. This intuitive "rights to do" framework is used by Xanadu. The law tends to define intellectual property rights in a somewhat different way. The law focuses on what rights owners have to exclude other people from doing certain kinds of things with the protected work. Copyright law defines the ownership rights of authors by saying what kinds of activities they can stop unauthorized people from doing.

Chief among copyright's exclusive rights are these: controlling the making of copies and derivative works of the protected work and distributing copies or derivative works. The only exclusive right Xanadu seems to contemplate is whether or not to put a document into the Xanadu system in the first place. Xanadu is more like a compulsory-license system than an exclusive-rights system. While U.S. copyright law does contain some compulsory-license provisions, compulsory licenses are generally an anathema to owners of intellectual property rights because the license fee generally bears little or no relation to the price obtainable if the issue were left to the market.

Unlimited Duration

The Xanadu system seems to contemplate no end to the duration of author rights. As long as authors (or their heirs) continue to pay for storage on this system, Xanadu will continue to pay royalties for uses of the documents. Under the U.S. Constitution, copyright can only be granted to authors for limited times. Upon expiration of the copyright, the work is in the public domain. While Nelson may not have consciously rejected this aspect of copyright in the Xanadu system, his description of the system reveals that he does not intend to reduce usage fees for accessing public domain materials. Royalties from them go into the "author's fund" over which he undoubtedly will exercise some control.

Making Publication an Important Formal Event (Again)

Publication is an important formal event in the Xanadu system. Under previous U.S. copyright laws, authors generally only "copyrighted" their works when the work was published. A formal copyright notice had to appear prominently in all publicly distributed copies of the work, or the claim of copyright would be forfeited. The Copyright Act of 1976 permitted inadvertent omissions of copyright on a small number of copies of the work to be remedied, but extended protection to all original works of authorship from the moment of their first fixation in a tangible medium.

In 1989, in order to bring U.S. copyright law into compliance with requirements of the Beme Convention, the notice requirement as a precondition to protection of published works was dropped. Copyright notices are now important only for incidental purposes, such as foreclosure of a defence of innocent infringement. Publication used to be a very important event in U.S. copyright law, but more recently, this law has made publication into a virtual nonevent. By making publication into a significant event, Nelson's scheme resembles "old" copyright more than "new" copyright.

Nelson's decision to make publication a formal event in Xanadu is necessary because publication in Xanadu would create a contract between the Xanadu system and the author to guarantee the existence of the published document for a period of time. This provides an integrity to links and citations generally absent in the print world, where only law reviews, with their armies of student citation-checkers, assure the reader that the cited document exists and supports the proposition for which it was cited.

Contracting to Permit Derivative Works

Yet another respect in which the Xanadu system diverges from the standard copyright model is in proposing to contract with all authors whose works would be stored in the Xanadu system so that users could make derivative documents from documents in the system. Varying the "default setting" of copyright by contract is not, in itself, a novel thing.

The motion picture industry is an example of a copyright industry that has historically depended for commercial success on contract-based distributions of copies, rather than on the outright sale of copies that has typified most copyright industries. Nelson's scheme is novel in proposing to use a contract-based scheme for commercial distribution of written texts, the prototypical subject matter of copyright, and in seeking to permit the widest derivative uses of documents in the system. Copyright, by contrast, has become rather stingy about derivative uses of anything but abstract ideas from protected works.

A CRITIQUE OF XANADU'S MODELS

CONCERNING ITS MODEL OF AUTHOR BEHAVIOUR

One question raised by Nelson's proposal is whether authors, particularly good ones, will be willing to pay to publish their works in Xanadu. In the print world, some authors do pay to have their works published by "vanity presses," but this represents a small percentage of publications. There might be some authors who would pay to publish documents in Xanadu out of misplaced confidence in the value of their work, just as some authors now post messages of dubious information content to CompuServe or Internet newsgroups. Such authors would get negative feedback at the end of the first rental period when no royalties were credited to their account, and perhaps decide not to renew.

However, some authors might decide not to renew their document rental space in Xanadu if no one linked to them during the first rental period, even though if they had stayed in the system, their documents would eventually have been discovered and made them a fortune. Still other authors might lack confidence in their work or might be too poor to afford the rental fee, which might cause them to withhold from the Xanadu system documents that would have been widely utilized if published there.

Xanadu might benefit from a scheme by which authors could solicit sponsors willing to subsidize the inclusion of their works in Xanadu in exchange for some portion of the royalties. Authors may not, in other words, behave in the way Xanadu's designer might expect them to behave. Authors may prefer the print world's system, which does not require them to pay directly for the privilege of being published. Authors may feel it is quite enough to have had to work hard to write the text in the first place. Some of the trick of authoring is writing something that publishers are willing to risk their capital to publish.

A system that would make authors pay to get published may end up either deterring authorship or sending authors in search of another digital library/hypertext publishing system in which to place their work. Nelson may also have underestimated how reluctant many authors may be about giving other people unlimited rights to make derivatives of their work. Although authors might have no objection to letting Xanadu users link to their documents, many may feel quite differently about allowing any Tom, Dick, or Susan to make new versions of their works. It will be little consolation to such authors that they might get royalties when the revised version is accessed by Xanadu users.

Authors often regard their writings as expressions of their personalities. Any tampering with their texts may be viewed by such authors as a "mutilation" of the work, as objectionable as if someone had the effrontery to walk up to you and cut your hair without your permission. In many countries, authors are expressly granted "moral rights" in their intellectual products, one of which protects the integrity of the work. In the United States, the derivative work right of copyright owners protects authors' economic interests in controlling adaptations of their works, although sometimes unauthorized adaptations affect economic rights of authors as well as moral rights. Nelson, like many in the technical community, seems to have a very positive attitude about the acceptability of making use of someone else's work and building on it to create a better modified version. Nelson seems to have assumed that this attitude is more widespread in the authorial community than may, in fact, be true.

CONCERNING ITS MODEL OF USER BEHAVIOUR AND INCENTIVES FOR USERS TO BECOME AUTHORS

The Xanadu intellectual property system also reflects a certain model of user behaviour. Nelson proposes a number of incentives for people to make use of the Xanadu system for a wide variety of purposes, from research to entertainment to hobby to full-time occupation. Probably his most creative idea about user behaviour is in contemplating the transformation of the digital library part of Xanadu into a hypertext publishing system, and incenting users to become system authors through linking and other derivative uses of documents in the system. The royalty mechanism in Xanadu, however, may create some unfortunate, unintended incentives.

The system would seem to give a special premium to those who are first to mention a particular topic in the Xanadu system, even if the first treatment of the topic were shallow or wrong. This may create incentives to rush documents into the system rather than to craft them to be deeper and more accurate. An example will illustrate one such problem. Suppose a journalist attended the first conference of scientists concerning the just-formed Human Genome Initiative (HGI), that he was an avid Xanadu user, and that at the first break in the conference schedule, the journalist authored a document for Xanadu describing in a shallow but intelligible way what HGI was about.

By virtue of being the first to mention HGI in Xanadu, this journalist's entry might be, for a time at least, the most frequently linked to source on HGI in Xanadu, which would make him the most compensated author on the topic. A naive user of Xanadu, when faced with a decision whether to access the journalist's HGI description or a later much deeper one by a scientist who was a founder of the HGI, might see that the first had been linked to a thousand times, whereas the scientist's document had been linked to only five times in the time it was on the system.

This might cause the user to choose the more frequently cited source over the better but less frequently cited source, again causing more royalties to flow into the journalist's account, and incenting rushed documents over considered documents in the system. In the print world, the shallow first treatment on a topic will tend to be ignored by later authors, but in Xanadu, the first document to mention a subject might always be called up on a user search, and not until the user reads the shallow document (and hence pays the author royalties on it) will the user know to ignore it.

Even creating a derivative document advising users to ignore the underlying document will result in royalties to the author of the underlying document. Suppose further that the journalist's Xanadu document on HGI contained some errors. Other Xanadu users might well notice the errors, and make derivative documents containing the needed corrections. Although this would correct the error, an inadvertent result of the scenario would be that the journalist might make a lot of money from putting out an erroneous document, for every time someone linked to his document or created a revised version of it, the journalist would share in the revenues.

The more and more noticeable the errors in the document, the more Xanadu users would be likely to notice the errors, to link to the journalist's document, and/or to revise it, which once again would generate more revenues for the journalist. This would seem to over-reward the journalist for rushing to get his document on HGI into the Xanadu system and not to deter entry of erroneous information.

Usage-based systems, such as Xanadu, may also have the disadvantage, at least for price-sensitive users, of making those with the most curiosity and tenacity in research pay the highest cost. They are the ones who will presumably use Xanadu for longer periods of time. One might argue that this is fair because those who use the system the most are those who pay most. But some may conceive the issue differently, and think it one of the great virtues of the library systems of the print world that scholars do not have to pay more than casual users for access to the library.

Society has an interest in encouraging deep scholarship. By not making scholars or other deep users pay more for their use of the library, the print world encourages scholarship. Digital library and hypertext publishing systems may also need to find ways to encourage good scholarship and curiosity without making it prohibitively expensive. But a more serious problem perhaps than this may be figuring out how to motivate users to be persistent and creative in their use of the Xanadu system.

When people use traditional libraries, they can walk around and browse until they find something to interest them. In Xanadu, the clock will be ticking and the price will be rising as one browses. Also, digital libraries, because of their invisibility to the user, may be too abstract to be enjoyably browsable. Once again, Nelson may have mistakenly modeled the Xanadu user in terms of his own persistence and creativity, which others may not share.

QUESTIONS ABOUT PRICING INCENTIVES

Perhaps the single most questionable element of the Xanadu intellectual property scheme, in terms of economic incentives, is pricing. If one looks at the universe of copyrighted works in the print-dominated world, one immediately observes that copies are priced according, more or less, to what the publisher/distributor and author/creator think the market will bear for the number of copies that might reasonably be sold or licensed. Xanadu posits a flat fee for Xanadu connect time and a fixed royalty for authors based on per-byte delivery for usage of their documents. This is like mandating that all books are to be priced according to the number of pages they contain and all pages must be priced at the same amount.

The CompuServe example seems to suggest that differential pricing of information is necessary to encourage the development of specialized markets. Unless Xanadu were the world's only digital library and hypertext publishing system, which remains Nelson's vision but which is unlikely', Xanadu will lack the negotiating power to compel authors to accept fixed pricing per byte of their information. People who own copyrights in very valuable intellectual properties simply will not use a system that does not let them make market-based pricing decisions.

The only options authors of very valuable intellectual properties would have in the world Nelson envisions is to put the work in Xanadu as an encrypted private document and contract with users for access to the document, or to withhold the document from Xanadu altogether. While encryption might allow market pricing to occur, Xanadu does not facilitate these transactions. They must be dealt with by private negotiations between the parties, but if Xanadu does not facilitate the transactions, it is difficult to see how they can occur.

The transaction costs of individual negotiations that would have to occur without Xanadu's help in order to access an encrypted document in Xanadu might be inordinately high. Another question we have about Nelson's Xanadu economic model is whether it overemphasizes author and user incentives and underemphasizes the need for some of the value-added services that publishers in the print world provide, particularly as to the promotion of sales of the work, whether by advertising or otherwise. Nelson wants people to use Xanadu, for that's how the system makes money. But Xanadu is indifferent to what they use. The lack of a promotional system for works in Xanadu may lead to underutilization of the system, which in turn may affect its commercial viability.

CONCLUSION

Whether digital library or hypertext publishing systems can be made commercially viable will depend on how they deal with intellectual property rights issues. The traditional copyright model will require adjustments in order to facilitate these new kinds of institutions. Ted Nelson offers one model of how such adjustments might be made. While Nelson's intellectual property scheme for the Xanadu system is bold and innovative, there are a number of respects in which his system can be questioned.

The most uncertain aspects of the Xanadu system are the accuracy of the Xanadu model of author and user behaviour, and the adequacy of financial incentives for authors to put their most valuable copyrighted works in the Xanadu system. A generation of exposure to tape recorders and VCRs—and a raft of new digital technologies for scanning, frame grabbing, and sampling—are making it harder to predict how people will understand and relate to intellectual property.

What is legal, and what is merely technically possible to copy? What constitutes "fair use" of copyrighted works in digital form? Laws that were suited for traditional kinds of copyrighted works no longer seem to fit. More work is needed to develop new models of author and user behaviour and the economics that will yield the right level of incentives for creation of digital library and hypertext publishing systems. The law can be made to conform to these new models, but only after we figure out what the right ones are.

4

Library an Information Policy at the National Level

INTRODUCTION

The establishment of the *National Council for Library and Information Services* (NCLIS) resulted from a long history of *library and information services* (LIS) policy initiatives in South Africa. These initiatives gained momentum during the 1990s to address the continuous challenge of improving access to information for all South African communities.

These and related issues were addressed by several advisory councils since 1990, including the:

* Library and Information Services Research Group of the *National Education Policy Investigation* (NEPI), a project of the National Education Coordinating Committee in 1991-1992;
* LIS Task Team of the *Centre for Education Policy Development* (CEPD) in 1993-1994;
* *Arts and Culture Task Group* (ACTAG) appointed by the then Department of Arts, Culture, Science and Technology (DACST) in 1994-1995; and
* Inter ministerial Working Group (IWG) on the Library and Information Services Function (National Level) in 1996-1997.

It is the work and recommendations of the IWG on library and information services building upon the work of the previous advisory councils that laid the legal foundation for the creation of the NCLIS and presented the mandate for its functions.

The IWG, consisting of academics and other experts in LIS, was appointed by the then Minister of the DACST and the Minister of Education specifically to advise them on:

> "...The mechanisms to ensure good governance of the library and information services system at the national level in South Africa, and to facilitate maximum availability and use of all relevant information sources to advance the Reconstruction and Development Programme".

THE CASE FOR A NATIONAL COUNCIL

The mission of the provincial library services in South Africa has been to raise the quality of life of all citizens by enabling library authorities to provide public library services to the various communities. The reality on the ground, however, is that the majority of South Africans, especially those living in rural communities, still do not have access to LIS as envisioned by the government. Historically, library services in this country have been characterised by fragmentation of information provision to a mainly academic, business and scientific user group on the one hand, and rudimentary or non-existent library provision to the majority of the population on the other hand. The services are stratified along the lines of race, class and urbanization. As the majority of South Africans live in rural communities, it is imperative that these areas be developed if the country is serious about, and committed to a truly democratic and informed citizenry.

The NCLIS had to understand in order to carry out its mandate:

> "It is obvious that, with the disparities in the development of the rural sector of South Africa, there must be a national drive towards the development of rural information services in order to avoid widening the gap between the rural information poor and the urban information rich. While the provincial authorities have a right to develop their own rural areas, the

development of rural information services will be accelerated if guided at the national level. Proper mechanics in the relationship between the national and provincial governance would need to be in line with the whole LIS sector".

The NCLIS was established in terms of the National Council for Library and Information Services Act and was inaugurated on 11 March 2004 in Cape Town.

OBJECTIVES AND FUNCTIONS OF THE COUNCIL

The Act sets out the aims and objectives of the NCLIS as being to advise the Minister of the DACST and the Minister of Education on matters relating to LIS in order to:

* Support and stimulate the socio-economic, educational, cultural, recreational, scientific research, technological and information development of all communities in the country; and
* Provide optimal access to relevant information to every person in an economic and cost-effective manner.

The NCLIS must inform and advise the Ministers on the following:

* The development and coordination of library and information services;
* The promotion of cooperation among LIS;
* Legislation affecting LIS;
* Policies, principles and criteria that should govern the allocation of public funds for LIS;
* Existing adequacies and deficiencies of library and information resources, including literature in African languages and services;
* The effectiveness of education and training in library and information science;
* Service priorities, after consultation with any organ of state responsible for LIS and other interested parties;
* The promotion of basic and functional literacy, information literacy and a culture of reading;

* Ways in which new information and communication technologies should be harnessed to achieve improved integration, equity, cost-effectiveness and quality in LIS; and
* Any other matter relating to LIS which the Council deems necessary, or which any of the Ministers may refer to the Council.

In addition, the Act stipulates that the NCLIS must:

* Coordinate the response of the LIS sector to LIS matters;
* Iiaise and develop synergy with other bodies and councils regarding LIS matters;
* Play an advocacy role in LIS matters; and
* Investigate incentives for donations to libraries.

COMPOSITION AND COMMITTEES OF THE COUNCIL

The NCLIS consists of 12 members appointed by the Minister of Arts and Culture on the basis of their expertise and/or special insight into LIS matters and the management, leadership and economics of LIS. The Council is broadly representative of all sectors in the LIS field.

It is constituted in a manner that takes account of gender, disability and historically disadvantaged per-sons, and ensures a spread of expertise and experience with regard to national, provincial and local interests; the role of information in society; and research, development and education in LIS.

Additional members include one official of the *Department of Arts and Culture* (DAC), one official of the Department of Education, the National Librarian, and one representative of the *Library and Information Association of South Africa* (LIASA). The chairperson is appointed by the Minister and the vice-chairperson is elected by the Council at its first meeting. Members are appointed for a term of three years. At the first (inaugural) meeting of the NCLIS in March 2004, the vice-chairperson was elected and a strategic planning workshop scheduled for 22 May 2004.

Here the vision, mission and strategic goals of the NCLIS were formulated and these working committees were formed according to the stipulations of the Act:

* Executive Committee, with the specific mandate to identify critical partners, address legislative deficiencies in the LIS sector, and source funding;
* Information Awareness Committee, in charge of the communication strategy of the Council;
* Education and Training Committee, responsible for education and training of LIS workers, education and training programmemes, skills audit, the establishment of norms and standards, etc.; and
* Marketing Committee.

The committee structure is supported by the secretariat from the DAC, but has no implementation or executive unit in charge of implementing the decisions of the Council. At present, there is no specific physical facility or offices where the work of the NCLIS is carried out. Whilst the NCLIS embarked on an ambitious programme of action, it soon became very clear that in its current form (even with the excellent committees it had put together) and given the limited budget allocated to its work without an implementation unit, the Council had started off on a disadvantaged footing.

The Council would hold its meetings and make plans, yet fall short of implementing them in an effective manner. In some cases, it was able to source the necessary expertise to get a number of projects off the ground. However, the day-to-day running of the business of the Council still needs to be investigated and proposals made for a ful-fledged structure with staff to implement its plans along the lines of other public entities with executive authority.

The NCLIS has recommended that the Minister reconsider changing the status of the Council from that of an advisory body to an executive one, to allow for the implementation of its decisions in line with other national councils and boards. This matter is currently under review by the DAC. In spite of this drawback a great deal has been accomplished in the short three years of the Council's term of office, which ended in September 2006.

STRATEGIC DIRECTION

The vision of the NCLIS is "to position South Africa as the best informed nation". Its mission is to "provide strategic leadership and advocacy for literacy, a culture of reading and writing, innovation and open access to information". Key strategic concerns are to raise government and public awareness of LIS matters; encourage synergy among stakeholders and strategic partners; address legislative deficiencies in the current LIS sector; improve funding of the LIS sector; and provide education, training and skills development of LIS human resources.

Key activities of the NCLIS from 2004 to 2006 were the following:

* The NCLIS inauguration and first meeting were held at the Centre for the Book in Cape Town on 11 March 2004.
* A strategic planning workshop was held in Pretoria on 20–21 May 2004.
* A value statement workshop was held in Durban on 28 October 2004.
* Presentations were made at the LIASA conferences of 2004 and 2005, the National Heritage Council Transformation Indaba in Durban, and the DAC Parliamentary Portfolio Committee in 2005.
* The DAC and NCLIS jointly hosted two symposia on the cost of a culture of reading, one in Cape Town in September 2004 and the other in Port Elizabeth in January 2005, with the latter focusing more on blind and print-handicapped readers.
* A consultative workshop on the review of national LIS, archives and heraldry legislation and related legislation was hosted jointly by the DAC and NCLIS in Cape Town in June 2005.
* During 2005 and 2006, the chairperson of the NCLIS, Professor Seth Manaka, ad-dressed the Technical Committee on Arts and Culture, the Provincial Members of the Executive Council, the Select Committee on Education and Recreation, LIASA,

and the Heads of the Provincial Library and Information Services.

* Both the chairperson and vice-chairperson of the NCLIS were involved in the tender process to appoint the company charged with the responsibility to develop a funding model for community and public libraries.

Through these activities, the Council has been able to accomplish these outcomes:

* The vision and mission of the NCLIS provides a specific direction and compelling niche for the work of the Council.
* Through the consultative process it has galvanized synergy and brought together all stakeholders working towards the development of an informed South African citizenry.
* The NCLIS has created a platform for national conversation around the issue of a culture of reading and has made recommendations to the Minister regarding the legislative and policy framework conducive to developing the South African information society.

The greatest outcome of the Council's activities thus far has been the funding of community and public library projects, and the subsequent study on the development of the funding model that is being administered by the DAC.

CHALLENGES FACING THE NCLIS

In its infancy, the NCLIS faced many challenges that threatened the success of its work. To begin with, members had to work through their collective understanding and conceptualisation of the work they needed to do, given their different backgrounds and expectations. On the other hand, the LIS community saw the Council as a body appointed to lobby the government about their bread-and-butter issues, including the closing of public libraries, the salaries of LIS workers, provision of LIS in the rural communities, and other issues.

These pressing matters had been on the agenda of the LIS community for a long time and, understandably, they were impatient to see when the issues would be addressed to their satisfaction. Some members of the Council saw their role as that of constituency representatives who would lobby the NCLIS on behalf of those interests. This exercise in clarity on roles took a considerable amount of time to carry out. In the meantime, there were structural issues to iron out, one being the fact that the Council had only committees and the secretariat to work with, but no executive office to implement its decisions.

The funding made available for its work did not take into consideration the projects that needed to be undertaken and the expertise that needed to be sourced. The debate on, and call for, a national council was historically housed and hosted by the Ministry of Education, where national LIS had a home. At the time of the promulgation of the Act, the DAC was still part of the Department of Science and Technology and under one Minister. By the time the Council was launched, the DAC was separated from the said Department.

In order to capture the original thinking that gave rise to the Council, all three Ministries needed to participate equally in its work. (The Minister of Education has a representative on the Council, whereas the Minister of Science and Technology still needs to appoint a representative.) This three-legged representation by government departments is crucial to the information society issues addressed by the Council: education, technology, arts and culture. The three-year term of office for the first Council proved to be very short, as there was much to be accomplished.

In essence, planning took most of the first year before any implementation was seriously off the ground. Just as the identified and approved projects were taking shape, the term ended and the DAC was not ready to have a second Council on board in time to continue with the work. At the time of writing, the second Council had not yet been announced. Additionally, the following issues were identified and confirmed by the consultative process as key challenges to the work of the NCLIS.

CONSTITUTIONAL PROBLEMS

Although public libraries are the exclusive charge of provincial governments, the funding mechanism is a serious problem due to legislative deficiencies in the funding role of these governments with regard to public and community library services. Until Schedule 5 of the Constitution is amended, provision of funding to public and community libraries will remain a challenge.

FUNDING

Funding continues to be a problem even with the recent injection of R1 billion into public and community library development. These funds are for a three-year period and additional funding might be made available, depending on how the initial funds are appropriated. The funding model developed by KPMG will hopefully alleviate this concern and provide a strong foundation for continuous support from the National Treasury in this regard. Issues extend to the funding of school libraries and provision of LIS for blind students.

NORMS AND STANDARDS

The development of public libraries for the majority of South Africans had been so neglected by the previous regime that the need for norms and standards in terms of quality library services, staff and funding remains dire. The NCLIS understands its task to facilitate this process and establish standards and norms for provinces in partnership with lo-cal government bodies.

SKILLS DEVELOPMENT, CAREER OPPORTUNITIES AND REMUNERATION OF LIS SECTOR WORKERS

This issue was at the top of the agenda of the consultative workshop, indicating the threat and risk that this matter is presenting to the work of the NCLIS in assisting South Africa to become an informed nation.

LIS TRANSFORMATION CHARTER

This charter is seen as a transformation vehicle for the LIS sector. The debates and workshops on the charter have begun, and it is hoped that the incoming Council will continue to develop and finally craft a charter that forges ahead the transformation of LIS.

THE FUTURE OF THE NCLIS

The term of office of the first Council expired in September 2006. A call for nominations for the new Council was published in October 2006, and at the time of writing, the process of appointments had not yet been finalised by the Minister of Arts and Culture. The new term of office is from 1 April 2007 to 31 March 2010. The first Council laid the foundation for its work as outlined in the NCLIS Act. It has grappled with issues of common understanding and visioning among its members and stakeholder groups, and has managed to create a platform for engagement and synergy.

The communication channels between the Council and the Ministers of Arts and Culture and Education are open and receptive, and the Council has enjoyed the audience and support of the Portfolio Committee of Arts, Culture and Sports. The R1 billion grant from the Treasury for the development of community and public libraries is a case in point. The strategic imperatives identified by the first Council are still relevant and timely and need to form a critical part of the work of the incoming Council.

These include:

* The need for an implementation unit for the NCLIS;
* Finalisation of the transformation charter process;
* Legislative deficiencies in the current LIS sector;
* Funding of LIS;
* Education, training and skills development;
* Greater focus on school libraries; and
* The continuous need to raise government and public awareness of LIS matters.

The second Council will have to carry the baton and move the work of the NCLIS towards a stage of consolidation by taking advantage of the prevailing conducive environment and synergy. Although the NCLIS in its current form may look very different from the original vision developed in the early 1990s, it is nonetheless a "victory for those who believe that government has a vital role to play in delivering LIS and access to information to South African communities at every level".

In her capacity as the Deputy Minister of Arts, Culture, Science and Technology, Ms Buyelwa Sonjica addressed the inaugural meeting of the NCLIS as follows:

> "As suggested, all recall how important the sharing of information during the struggle years was and how precious information is to sustaining human rights. . . Libraries play a vital role in the freedom of information environment, especially in a developmental sense. Democracy can only be sustained by providing access to all the information necessary for our citizens to take informed decisions...LIS in South Africa should be revitalised from the bottom up, with the Council steering and coordinating new ideas and initiatives for restructuring the LIS sector.

5

Laws of Library Science

LIBRARY RESOURCE SHARING LIBRARY NETWORK

India, the largest democracy in the world with an estimated population of 114 millions has more than 1,00,000 libraries comprising academic libraries, public libraries, special libraries and libraries attached to the research and development institutions, government departments and ministries, etc. There is no denying the fact ICT has brought a paradigm change in the functionality of the libraries in the country but this technological change pattern is not seen uniformly across the wide-section of the libraries in the country.

On one hand the country is proud to have the most sophisticated libraries with ISO certifications and the implementation of modern tools and technologies, on the other hand, we do encounter the challenges of providing a better infrastructure in the form of PCs and Internet connectivity in the libraries that are still striving hard to get the necessary hardware and Internet connectivity in their libraries from their managements. The adoption of standards, retrospective conversion work, the adoption of suitable library software packages continues to remain as the major areas of concerns for the libraries and the library and information science professionals.

In such constraints and hostile conditions, DELNET has been able to establish itself as an effective, operational resource sharing library network in India. The network whose journey started as a city based library network in 1988, emerged as a major operational library network not only in India but in South Asia, connecting more than 1597 libraries in 30 States and UTs in India and seven other countries.

The network is growing from strength to strength, with escalating resources of union catalogues, the wider coverage of libraries from varied disciplines, the growing number of users and the horizontal and vertical expansion in its services to its members. This paper highlights the incredible and pioneering work being done by DELNET-Developing Library Network which is a non-governmental, non-profit making organisation with inputs from the Ministry of Communications and Information Technology, Government of India and located in its own building in the well-known academic environment of Jawaharlal Nehru University at New Delhi.

I would like to reiterate that DELNET do not receive any government funding and is based on a self-sustainable model, it is considered as a role model for the library networks especially of the developing nations. A survey has also been conducted by the author to assess the utilisation of DELNET resources among the member-institutions and is reported in the article. The questionnaire technique was used to get the inputs from the member-libraries. 147 libraries responded to the questionnaire.

THE GENESIS OF LIBRARY NETWORKING IN INDIA

In India during the late 1980s and 1990s there was a movement to establish city and regional-based library networks by NISSAT (National Information System for Science and Technology), a body under Dept of Scientific and Industrial Research (DSIR), Government of India. It provided some financial assistance for the setting up of these library networks.

This has lead to the mushrooming of various city library networks in India including:

* BONET (Bombay Library Network),
* CALIBNET (Calcutta Library Network),
* DELNET (Delhi Library Network which later became Developing Library Network in 2000),
* PUNENET (Pune Libary Network).

The University Grants Commission (UGC) has also developed INFLIBNET (Information and Library Network) in 1991 to network the University Libraries in the country. Only a few networks were able to work on the self sustainable model and continued to exist after the initial phases of implementation and functioning. DELNET, started as a project in 1988 became a national library network in India by the year 2000. UGC continued funding INFLIBNET to provide the support to the University Libraries in the country. The remaining city library networks due to the lack of planning for developing the networked resources and its functions soon perished from the networking scene of the country.

DELNET-DEVELOPING LIBRARY NETWORK

DELNET-Developing Library Network is a major operational resource sharing library network in India connecting more than 1597 libraries in 30 States and UTs in India and seven other countries. DELNET was conceived as a city based library network in Delhi in 1988 and was known as Delhi Library Network, networking the libraries of the Delhi region. It got registered as a society in 1992. With the availability of DELNET services on the World Wide Web, the accessibility soon was transformed from the local dial up connectivity for the Delhi region institutions to the global access through the Web.

This gave a great boost to DELNET and soon DELNET crossed the geographical boundaries within the country and also became accessible outside. It was on 13th September 2000 that the name of DELNET got changed from DELNET-Delhi Library Network to DELNET-Developing Library Network. The main objectives of DELNET is to promote resource sharing among the member-libraries by collecting, storing and disseminating information and by providing networked services to the researchers and scholars to supplement their research activity.

FIVE Cs-FUNCTIONAL PARAMETERS OF DELNET

We would like to mention the five Cs of the Library Networking which is essential for an operational library network and governs its functionality.

These five Cs are:

1. Connectivity;
2. Cost;
3. Computers;
4. Client; and
5. Content.

Connectivity

The connectivity is a life line for the smooth functioning of a library network. There is an availability of the leased-line, wireless, broadband, VSAT and Wifi connectivity in the libraries. The DELNET services are accessible through the World Wide Web by the registered member libraries. The DELNET databases are hosted on Basis Web server and are connected with a 11 mbps RF link offered by National Informatics Centre, Ministry of Communications and Infor-mation Technology, Government of India. The network remains functional on 24/7 basis. The web tracking software installed at DELNET servers gives a day to day picture of the usage of the DELNET services by the member libraries.

It is quite heartening to note that the access to the servers hosting the databases are being made by the researchers and scholars of the member libraries at different times starting from midnight to early morning besides the usual peak hour network access. The survey conducted among the member libraries have shown very encouraging figures regarding the availability of the dedicated links in the libraries. ninety per cent of the respondents have confirmed the availability of the dedicated Internet facility in their libraries.

The University Libraries have the largest availability of the dedicated Internet facility with 95.2 per cent affirmed the availability of the dedicated link, followed by 90.7 per cent in Institutes, 89.7 per cent in Research/Special Libraries and 86.7 per cent in the Colleges. The survey results shows that Internet has been able to penetrate well among the organisations in the country and the libraries have the Internet bandwidth availability with them. It is found that in 97.3 per cent of the organisations, the faculty has Internet facility at their own desk.

It is quite essential to have the direct internet access in order to utilise the library network's resource and services to the fullest.

Cost

The cost of membership to the library network and the resources provided through them are important for the sustainability of a library network. DELNET membership charges are quite nominal, it is T 7500 per annum for the libraries in India and SAARC nations, the non-SAARC members pays USD 500 per annum. The membership fee is kept same for all Institutional Members whether it is a University, an Institution, an R&D organisation, a specialized library or a school library. The democratic approach, an unbias one, helps in promoting the resource sharing. Also it leaves an impression of being equal in their participatory roles in a network for resource sharing.

It is worth reporting that some of the library networks in India could not grow and sustained themselves due to the exorbitant membership charges rates and different categorization of the members on the basis of their collections, etc. DELNET charges for the actual courier charges for sending the books on Interlibrary loan and the member-institutions and their researchers finds it an affordable one. In a developing country like India, Cost of getting the desired material plays a crucial role. Herein, the researchers and scholars for higher research are not being helped financially to a reasonable extent through scholarships, grants, etc. contrary to their counterparts in the Western world.

Computers

In order to facilitate the optimum use of the library network resources and services, the researchers, scholars and faculty of the member institutions should have adequate availability of the computers. Through the survey conducted, it was found that 43.2 per cent of the libraries have upto 10 computers in the library whereas 59.1 per cent of the University Libraries have more than 20 computers in the library and only

32.2 per cent of the respondents have more than 20 computers in their libraries. It is quite evident that the libraries are not better equipped with the availability of the computers in their libraries though there may be separate computer labs or the computer departments but they are not the part of the libraries.

Client (Member-Libraries)

The more diverse the library network has the coverage, the more effective would be the resources of such a library network. In DELNET, the participating libraries are from various disciplines and they pool their resources together and share them across the network. I would like to mention the fascinating scenario of resource sharing wherein a technical book required by a S&T Library will be available in a library specialising in Commerce discipline rather than being available in the best technical libraries.

The resources and the collections becomes more transparent for the act of resource sharing. The survey results have shown that 92 per cent of the member-libraries are aware about DELNET services and 61 per cent are the frequent users of the DELNET services. It would like to mention that DELNET organizes one day orientation programmes in member-institutions located in various parts of the country. This enables in better promotion and spreads awareness about DELNET and helps in popularizing the services among the users, faculty and researchers of the member-libraries.

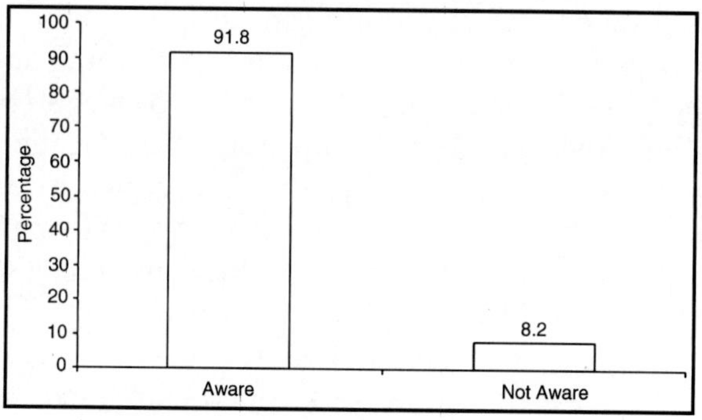

Fig 5.1. Awareness about DELNET Services among the Library Users.

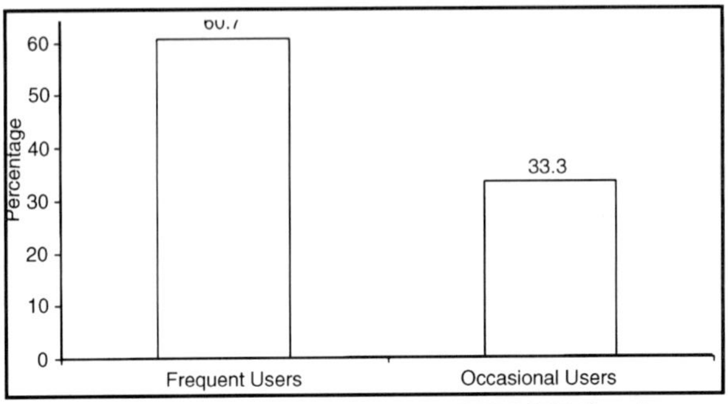

Fig 5.2. How Often do you Use DELNET Services.

Content

Content is a major resource of a library network. The greatest concern for a library network is the consolidation of the resources lying scattered across the member-libraries. This ensures a wider access to information to the information seekers. Since inception, DELNET is actively engaged in developing the union catalogues and union lists which are the major resource strength for any library network. The records in the DELNET databases are growing in size and more and more resources are becoming accessible to the member libraries. These resources are the major source for resource sharing as they carry the locations data wherein physically the information may be available.

The database are collected through the electronic transfer of the exported records through the online facility, e-mail, ftp protocols; the data is physically sent in CDs by the member libraries. I would like to mention that in a country like India, the cooperative cataloguing or cooperative collection building is still not in existence. There is a lot much of duplication efforts in the libraries for cataloguing the same titles in different libraries. The various libraries in the country are using various software packages which ranges from the commercial software packages (Libsys, Alice for Windows, Virtua, etc) which may be adhering to international standards to the inhouse developed software packages developed with the backend on SQL, Access, Excel, Oracle, Sybase, etc.

DELNET collects the records from the member libraries in the default exported format and the conversion programs are being developed to convert the base records into the standard ISO 2709 format before they are finally being merged in the Union Catalogues. I would like to mention that the information is also collected from the prominent libraries of the country who may be non-members since they can always be approached for getting the desired references. There is an online facility for uploading the machine readable records to DELNET by the member-libraries. The bibliographical databases do not strictly adheres to the international bibliographic formats and the library professionals are not much familiar with MARC 21 cataloguing.

DELNET DATABASES AND THEIR SIGNIFICANCE

Union Catalogue of Books

DELNET provides access to more than 8 million bibliographic records of books in English language available with various member libraries located in and outside the country. The databases can be accessed by any of the desired fields including Title, Author, Subject, Date of Publication. The Boolean operators can also be used for refining the search queries. The sorting can be done on the searched results. The searching using Phrase searching, Any Words and includes can be used. The records can also be retrieved using the specific indexes including Title, Author, Subject, etc. The database size grows with each passing day as more and more data from the member libraries are being merged in the centralized union catalogues.

DELNET has developed its own modules on Basisplus software, an RDBMS. The member libraries availing to the Interlibrary Loan facility can place the requests online through the system itself for getting the books on loan. The Interlibrary Loan is one of the most popular services of DELNET, the resource sharing is done not only between the libraries located in India but also outside India. It is quite heartening to note that DELNET has evolved a very successful functional model of Interlibrary Loan/Document Delivery services. Through these services, the users, faculty, researchers and scholars of the member libraries are able to get and refer to the books which are not readily available in their own libraries.

At times the books are out of print and are not even available with the book publishers themselves. The Reference books are also lended out though for fewer loaning period. It is worth mentioning that certain libraries in the country which are reference libraries like Central Reference Library, Delhi University, Indian Institute of Advanced Study, Shimla does lend out books to DELNET. It is only possible due to the mutual cooperation and benefit the libraries generates from the process of resource sharing.

It demonstrates a win-win situation. DELNET charges only for the nominal courier for sending the books on loan and it is the responsibility of the borrowing Institution to return back the book at their own cost. In India wherein the users and also the libraries have the limited resources, through the resource sharing the needs of the information users are fulfilled in most economical ways. I would like to mention that DELNET also serves its member-libraries outside India. DELNET has also created a database of E-books which are available in the public domain.

Union List of Current Journals and E-journals Consortium in India

The journals are a vital source of current information for the scientific research. The information about the availability of the current journals is of great help for the document delivery services. DELNET is maintaining an online union list of current journals available in the fields of Science and Technology, Social Sciences and Humanities. This database has more than 25,000 unique titles of current journals available in member as well as the non member libraries of DELNET. The database is updated continuously by receiving the list of currently subscribed journals and this database contains the information about the journals not only available with the member libraries but also with the major reputed libraries in India which are the non members.

The photocopies of journal articles are arranged from the libraries and are supplied to the requesting libraries. It is also one of the most popular services. In India a major E-journals consortium was formed in 2000 named "INDEST (Indian National Digital Library in Science and Technology Consortium" with a financial contribution of ₹200 million by the Ministry of Human Resource Development (MHRD), Government of India. All India Council for Technical Education (AICTE) has also contributed ₹37.5 million to this. Thirty Eight centrally funded government institutions including the IITs, NITs and NITs and few others are the core members of INDEST.

The private Institutions are self supported. Under the consortium, an access to more than 6500 journals from various publishers and aggregators are provided. The UGC Infonet E-journals consortium covers 4453+ejournals and provides access to nearly 100 Universities of the country. It has been noticed that private institutions who are not able to afford being the member of the consortium is greatly utilizing to the DELNET Document Delivery Services.

Moreover, at times the members of the Consortium also approaches DELNET for the delivery of the journal articles since the desired journal may not be the one covered under the access or the desired specific issues are not available online. There is lot much of speculation about the extent of utilization of E-journals in the Institutions and a large number of studies have been carried out to know about the pattern of accessibility. Moreover it has been noticed that if a Institution ceases to be a member of the Consortium because of the non availability of the digital archiving, the users are deprived to browse the issues for which the Institution had paid to the consortia.

Union Catalogue of Journals

DELNET has also created a database containing the holdings data of the journals available in the member libraries besides containing the other bibliographical information about the journals. At present the database contains 19,289 records of the journals. It is a good resource for tracking down the articles from the rare, old issues of the journals dating back to late 19th and early 20th century. DELNET does receive a number of requests from the libraries for locating the journal articles from the very old issues of the journals. It is a good resource for locating the articles from the rare old issues of the published journals.

Database of Journal Articles

There are a number of libraries, though not many on the network who are involved with the articles indexing in the machine readable form. A large portion of the library budget is annually spent on subscribing to the journals, either in print or in online mode by the libraries but the libraries lack the access to the databases containing the bibliographic details about the journal articles.

For the researchers and scholars it is very essential to know about the latest articles getting published in their specific fields of discipline. This specific database contains more than 800,000 records and is growing in size. For journal articles, the concerned users, researchers send the requests with their bibliography through e-mail and DELNET arranges for the full text delivery. DELNET also helps in providing the list of articles through various other networked sources and the fulltext copies of the selected articles are provided on demand.

Databases of Non-print Materials

DELNET does maintain the databases of CD-ROM, Video recordings and sound recordings available in the member libraries. The non-print materials can not be loaned out from the libraries, however the video recordings and sound recordings are being taken on loan in special cases though for a lesser period of time. The CD-ROMs are used for keyword searching and the concerned bibliography containing the abstracts are provided to the requesting libraries. There are 2,281 records of CDs available with member libraries, 748 sound recordings and more than 5,000 videorecordings listings in the respective databases.

Database of Thesis and Dissertations

This database contains around 45000, Thesis and Dissertations submitted to the various Universities and Institutions. This database contains bibliographic information and since thesis and dissertations are the reference materials available in the libraries, the researchers and scholars use this database to know about the works being carried out in their specific fields.

There has been some projects in India concerning the digitization of the Thesis and Dissertations by INFLIBNET and University of Mysore (Vidyavahini project), but the project has not taken off due to the copyright restrictions.

USEFULNESS OF DELNET UNION CATALOGUES

The access to Union Catalogues created and developed by the library networks remains the most highly used resources by the member-libraries. The locations data available in the union catalogues helps the respective users to find out the availability of the documents in their own regions, state and in different locations of the country and outside.

It is a very effective resource discovery tool and is a great boon to the scholars and researchers of the country. The survey results have highlighted the fact that 85.7 per cent of the member-libraries finds DELNET Union catalogues useful and 86.3 per cent of the library users are getting benefited (Fig. 5.3 and Fig. 5.4).

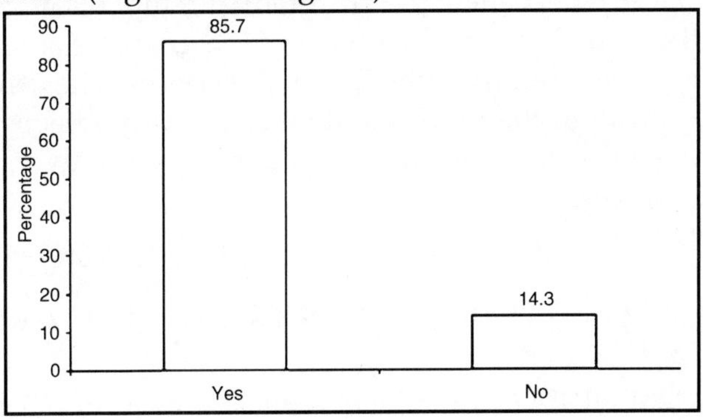

Fig. 5.3: Do you Find DELNET's Union Catalogues Useful.

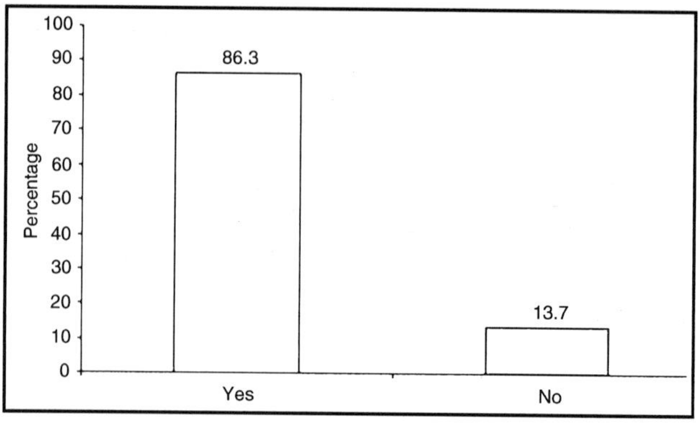

Fig. 5.4: Do you Feel Library Users are Getting Benefited.

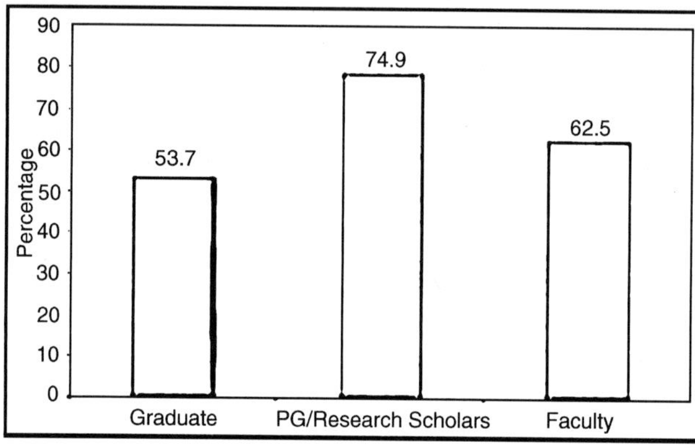

Fig. 5.5: Kind of Users Getting Benefited from the DELNET Services.

While 78.9 per cent of the Postgraduate students, 62.5 per cent of the faculty and 53.7 per cent of the graduate students are getting benefited from the DELNET services. The content available through the union catalogues are very selective in nature since the libraries purchase the titles through a strict selection process.

DELNET SERVICES AND ITS UTILISATION

INTER LIBRARY LOAN (ILL) AND DOCUMENT DELIVERY SERVICES (DDS)

The DELNET's ILL and DDS services are one of the most popular services among the member libraries located in different parts of India as well as outside the country. The requests for the supply of books on Interlibrary Loan or the requests to arrange for the journal articles are received by DELNET through various modes including DELNET Online System (options are available through the online databases), E-mail (one of the most prevalent method used by the member libraries), also through fax and at times through post also.

DELNET promotes the electronic communication since it is more faster and interactive and it facilitate the process of quick and safe delivery of the ILL/DDS items. DELNET has a separate ILL tracking system wherein each and every transaction is recorded and status about its date of dispatch, date of retun, etc. are well recorded.

DELNET is able to reach out to the users of the member libraries located in far-flung, remote parts of the country apart from those from the main stream cities. The material is sent through the insured courier services. It is worth mentioning that DELNET not only provides the ILL/DDS to its member libraries located in various parts of the country but is also engaged with International Interlending.

DELNET sends the books on Interlibrary Loan to the member institutions outside India like Baha Social Sciences, Kathmandu, Nepal and Caledonian College of Engineering, Oman; Waljat College of Science and Technology, Muscat. Also the photocopies of journal articles are provided to the member libraries to NILIS, Sri Lanka, IRRI, Philippines, etc. DELNET is also working towards the implementation of ISO ILL protocols.

The member libraries saves a lot of revenue by availing to the Interlibrary Loan and Document Delivery services of DELNET. It is of great boon to the faculty, researchers and scholars since the expensive, reference books and also out of print titles are made available to the member institutions besides other titles.

The DELNET ILL/DDS services are the heart-line of DELNET. There is a great sense of satisfaction among the member-libraries availing to the services. The timeliness factor is crucial in library services. The survey results supplements the fact that 30.7 per cent of the respondents find the response time of ILL/DDS requests as excellent, while 36 per cent rate it as very good and 33.3 per cent finds the response time as 'good' (Fig. 5.6).

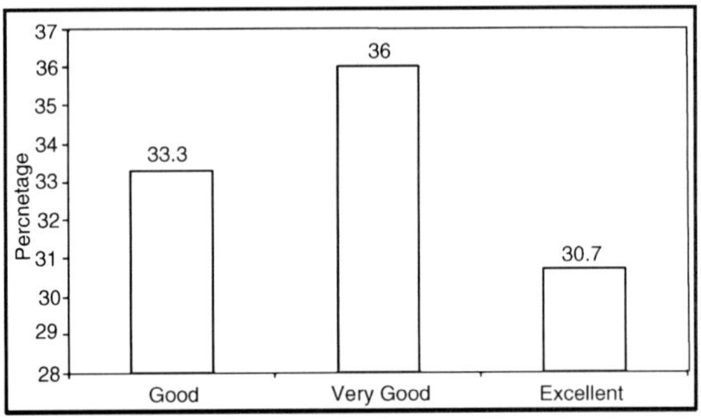

Fig. 5.6: Response Time of ILL/DDS Services.

Regarding the overall impression of DELNET services, 35.3 per cent consider it as 'good', 31.9 per cent founds it to be 'very good' and the rating of being 'excellent' was given by 23 per cent and 2.72 per cent considered the services as poor (Fig. 5.7).

Fig. 5.7: How do you Rate DELNET Services.

DELNET has also opened up a coordination units in Southern part of India i.e in Bangalore (Karnataka). The unit coordinates for the ILL/DDS services as the nation wide catalogue of the member libraries are available on the DELNET system and these it deals on day to day basis with the respective libraries of the region for the ILL/DDS.

Reference Services

DELNET receives a large number of reference queries every day through various modes. DELNET maintains a referral centre which provides reference services to the researchers, scholars and users from and outside India. DELNET is planning to start a national referral centre wherein the reference queries will be saved and accessed by the users on anytime, anywhere basis. It will be based on the question-answering technology.

NETWORKING AHEAD: NEW CHALLENGES

The new challenges posed by the growing Knowledge economy is the need to network knowledge more vigourously and dynamically. DELNET is also chalking out its plans to move with the needs of the time and to gradually move into the knowledge sharing model.

We have listed below some of the immediate plans of DELNET, though they are full of challenges but with its strong networking capabilities in the country, it is confident of moving ahead with the time in a self-reliant manner:

* DELNET intends to network both libraries and knowledge in the integrated network model. National Knowledge Commission of the Government of India has identified DELNET as one of the major library network in India which will network more than 25,000 libraries in the near future in India.
* DELNET is interested to help the libraries in tapping the tacit knowledge available in their Institutions and to contribute for the development of the Knowledge Repositories and networking the knowledge resources.
* DELNET is supporting the establishment of Knowledge Centres in India. The plans are under consideration for establishing a Central Institutional Repository for the member-libraries in order to tap the tacit knowledge available with the researchers, scholars and the faculty members.
* DELNET is interested to open shortly the State Centres in different parts of India and also the

Regional Centres in order to provide training to the library professionals, promote the usage of network resources and also to help the local libraries in the development of the digital content.

* DELNET is wanting that more libraries especially specializing in South Asian studies from different parts of the World should become a part of the network and utilize the services and resources created for their researchers and scholars at much affordable cost.
* DELNET is wanting to implement the social networking tools in order to enhance the user interaction. The DELNET Helpline support is also offered through the YMS. The users of the member-libraries of DELNET interact with the official of DELNET in an interactive mode and it brings the end users closers to DELNET.
* DELNET is launching the Technical Support System for Koha-the Open source ILS in order to help the Indian Libraries for adopting the open source software. An online portal will also get launched soon by DELNET wherein the online audio/video learning material for implementing Koha, including tutorials on MARC 21 will be offered. It will be operational on 24/7 basis against a nominal registration fee.

LIBRARY MOVEMENT IN INDIA

India has a glorious history of 5000 years with a rich heritage of philosophy, language, religion, art and culture. The Nation has 428 languages with 1600 dialects out of which 13 are extinct. These languages have several classical scriptures in their Scripts. These scriptures are scattered and preserved in different libraries of the country. Creating a digital library of available classics and establishing federated look-ups to these collections are burning issues of the day. The Indian Digital Library Initiative (IDLI) has been triggered out of Digital Library Initiative (DLI) of United States. Both the Indian collections and the environment are totally different from the one United States has. A fresh look to the existing problems should be given.

ISSUES WITH INDIAN DIGITAL LIBRARIES

Though there is a huge thrust in India for establishing digital libraries, there are several reasons due to which the whole movement is fallen behind.

Behavioural Issues

The Government of India must look forward to pool the knowledge base of the country. Phase-wise pooling of available knowledge resource of various libraries in the country must be encouraged. This requires funding to various libraries for digitizing the documents of their collection. So far, much of the funding for the purpose is made through United States through Million Book Project. Though, the project has been initiated with novel interest, unfortunately, keeping control over the whole project appeared little difficult. Besides, many of the technological challenges specific to Indian context are new to the American environment need to be addressed. It looks better to initiate test-beds in first phase with the objective to demonstrate technological capabilities.

Some centres can be identified from different language speaking states and accordingly funded for developing technical capabilities in a limited time frame. Unfortunately, the present growth of digital libraries in the country is unplanned which has resulted in bad models or instances with just scanned images. The first phase of the National Digital Library Movement could have been better utilized only to understand the underlying difficulties and the possible solutions. The second phase of the project could have been funded for building the live digital collections for use and receive feedbacks.

The required changes and modifications could be further implemented nationwide. There are several libraries with unique collection of its kind. With the third phase such collection can be digitally preserved as well as universal access to the documents could be insured. It has been observed that many of the libraries having unique and rare collection are scared of going online because they think of loosing the physical presence of users in the library. This behavioural difficulty must be addressed in order to ensure universal accessibility including the digital preservation at national level.

Conditional Issues

A multilingual country like India has several conditional constraints hindering the overall growth of digital libraries in the country. There are representation in the literature from all states and languages. It is easy to map the script due to common origin from Brahmi but it is equally difficult to convey the meaning in different languages. It can be easily observed that in different parts of the country people know more than one language with having one script. For example, it is very common to see Brahmins reciting hymn in Sanskrit (a language) written in their mother script.

In such cases mapping of characters can be very handy. Since writing is known to Indians from 3000 BC and paper is invented only in AD. 104. Apart from that the printing technology reached very late to India. Hence, it was very late when Indians started using paper. Many of the ancient writings are on stones, leaves, clay tablets, tree barks, cloth etc. Anything before, AD 1600 is hand written which is difficult for machines to read. Some of the objects are so brittle that they can only be handled using special means. There is abundance of such material in the country.

Technological Issues

World has witnessed impeccable technological advancements. There are digital library suites can be used directly for creating digital collection. But much of the development is in English and European languages as the computer was first used by them only. But off late, market for other scripts is also felt by IT giants and hence Unicode as character representation standard is introduced. Unicode is still being evolving as it promises to cover all the world scripts and signs. The country has a big share in IT industry of the world. But little has been done for the languages and scripts of India.

An Optical Character Recognitions (OCR) software in any Indian script is yet to be developed. The tests are on the way at Indian Statistical Institute, Kolkata and Centre for Develop-ment of Advance Computing (CDAC), Pune. A product named Chitran-kan by CDAC, Pune is available for use in Devnagari but the product has limited variety of font support and is still in testing phase. The Indic scripts are off child of Brahmi script which is not in practice anymore. The derived scripts of Brahmi like Devanagari and other Indic scripts have complex rende-ring principles when it comes to representation of characters in machine.

Complex character glyphs are rendered depicting features like bidirectional and dynamic composition. It is difficult to create rendering engines of this kind for all the Indic languages but major work has been done in this area. The work is in progress to integrate rendering plug-ins with web browsers for creating websites in Indian scripts. With Devanagari and other major scripts the task has been achieved and now-a-days one can see many websites in regional languages. One of the important problems Indian IT community facing today is about sorting the words of one language. There are scores of examples of same kind in Sanskrit. It is because of these reasons it is very difficult to generate index for any Indic document.

Besides, there are no good corpora available in public domain which can be taken as sample for experimentation and testing. This has also influenced the search algorithm. Unlike search algorithms of English, search algorithms in Indian languages are yet to be evolved. What is available today as Indian language search is only pattern matching. The work is still at preliminary level because of the complexity of the languages. It is easy to work with Sanskrit for the purpose as it has morphological rules for construction of words but addressing the same is difficult with other Indic languages (Hindi, Oriya, Tamil etc.) as they don't have such kind of rules for word construction.

The Stemming algorithms like Soundex and Metaphone are yet to be developed by any of the Indian languages. To get a feel, if one searches for Hindi word (correctly spelt as means Back) in Google, gets only the former Hindi string in search result. An application of stemming algorithm would have brought the correct later one in the search results. Similarly, there are n-gram techniques of string search which are warranted to be tested with Indic text.

Though the metadata is not a potential problem but due to uncontrolled growth there is lot of disparity in use of metadata standards. Many of the libraries have drafted their own metadata set not confirming to the International standard. This has happened in the case of distributed digitization centers at the initial stage. Though, an awareness has been aroused among the professionals to use International standard, but, still it is very difficult to convert non-conforming one's to the standard form.

With the use of codified data a standard metadata scheme can yield an efficient cross-lingual information retrieval. This technique of cross-lingual information retrieval has been demonstrated in the system named "Brass" developed at Documentation Research and Training Centre. Such information retrieval systems can supplement automatic translation projects to some extent, as there is not significant development in machine translation of Indic languages.

INDIAN SCENARIO

India is witnessing a strong move for developing digital libraries around the country. Some are in public domain like LDL of Documentation Research and Training Centre, Bangalore and Digital Library of India. Some are with restricted access like, Nalanda Digital Library of National Institute of Technology, Calicut. As far as, the English literature is concerned there are editable text available over web but when it comes to Indian language only scanned images of the documents are available for display supplemented by metadata. The experiment has been done with many of the Open source software and results are positive. Some test beds can be found at Documentation Research and Training Centre site but still much has to be done.

LIBRARY LEGISLATION IN INDIA

The present information explosion and the direct relation of information to developments in all walks of life emphasizes the need to give greater priority to the planning of systems which give library and information services to the people. Such systems can only be planned at national levels, if the total information resources of the nation is to be pooled together in a federal country like India, and shared between the cons-tituent states to make it available to all the users who require it in an equally and unbiased way at optimal cost.

Such library and information systems are to be founded upon sound legislation, if they are to attain their objectives the Society's information need has become so imperative that, many of the national and international library organizations has started to stress the urgent need for national library systems working together and sharing their services and materials at international level to provide better services to the people. Better can be defined here in quantitative and qualitative terms. Such national level and international level networking and resource sharing between library systems make possible service at lower cost, convenience of access, access to more materials and more rapid availability of materials.

THE MODEL ACT OF S.R. RANGANATHAN

To attain these objectives Dr. S.R. Ranganathan had framed the first model public libraries Act in 1930 which he placed for discussion at the Educational Conference at Banaras. Before framing the Act, this internationally reputed library scientist had travelled through most countries of the world where library legislation existed and had evaluated them and in many countries his ideas helped them to improve the systems.

In his Library Development Plan which he submitted in 1947 to Government of India he had included a union library bill and a revised state library bill also which envisaged the national public library and information system according to the most modern principles. Another model library Act was drafted in 1963 by a committee under the chairmanship of D.M. Sen on behalf of the Ministry of Education, Government of India. In 1966 the Library Legislation Sub Committee of the Planning Commission also prepared a model bill. The library Acts that came into existence in Madras, Hyderabad, Andhra, Karnataka and Maharastra totally or partially accept the ideas of Rang ana than as reflected in his Model Acts and bills. These States became the laboratories where the ideas evolved by Ranganathan were experimented and observed.

In the light of these observations and suggestions contained in the other model bills and Acts, Ranganathan has improved his model Act by rectifying the clauses found to be defective in working and by adding new provisions that seemed essential. This model libraries Act was published in 1972. This is the latest and most advanced Model Act. Ten States out of the 25 States and 7 union territories have enacted library legislation. They are Madras 1948, Andhra 1960, Karnataka 1965, Maharastra 1967, West Bengal 1979, Manipur 1985, Kerala 1989 and Haryana 1989.

Others are Goa and Mizoram. But none of them are considered perfect or efficient. So in this comparative analysis of the essential aspects of State Public Library Acts, the Model Public Library Act, 1972 of Dr. S.R. Ranganathan is taken as the measuring rod or ideal situation with which the State Act is compared. Whenever some notable additional provisions or improvements are found in other existing Acts the same is discussed at the concerned contexts. The Kerala Act to which stress is given in this study and Ranganathan's Model Act of 1972 will be referred herein after as KPLA and Model Act respectively.

PREAMBLE OF STATE ACTS

The preamble of a Library Act should summarise and state the aims and objectives of that Library Act. Even though the preamble of KPLA went on to explain the existing situations and the intentions with which the Act was initiated in an elaborate and vague form, it has given what is to be in preamble just before the preamble in precise and clear words as a long title ofthe Act. This summary or long title of the Act which we have to consider as preamble contains the basic concept of modern public library service which the actual preamble failed to state and the KPLA in its totality failed to support.

Like the Model Act, this summary provides for the establishment and maintenance of a system of public libraries and for the comprehensive development and organisation of all kinds of library and information services required for the people. The long title that follows the title of the Act in KPLA states, it is: An Act to consolidate and unify the library laws in the State and to provide for the reorganisation of the entire library system in the State of Kerala with a view to the development and maintenance of a comprehensive rural and urban library service and for matters connected therewith or incidental thereto.

Ranganathan has laid clear emphasis on legislation for public library service and for the organisation of a comprehensive library system. But all other Acts except KPLA provides for establishment and maintenance of public libraries only. They all cling to the obsolete concept of treating public libraries as independent units in their collection and services. So in this statement of the purpose of the Act, KPLA has accepted the most modern concept of Public Library legislation and the statement is a distinct improvement over those in all other existing State Acts.

STATE LIBRARY AUTHORITY

The concept of the *State Library Authority* (SLA) underwent an evolution from State Library Committee to Minister of Education or Libraries; everywhere in the world. The Model Act recommends that for the purpose of promoting and organising a library system in the State the Ministry for Education of the State shall be the SLA. It shall be the duty of the SLA to provide; for an adequate library and information service in the State and, for the progressive development of the institutions devoted to the purpose and to secure the effective execution by *Local Library Authorities* (LLA) of the national policy for providing adequate library service to the people in every locality.

In the existing' State Acts only Karnataka Public Library Act, 1965 provides and clearly names SLA. Section 3 of the Act provides for the constitution and composition of the SLA.6 SLA shall be a body corporate having perpetual succession and a common seal with power, to acquire, hold and dispose of property and to contract and may by the same time sue and be sued. It consists of twenty members from the fields concerned with information creation, organisation and services, with Minister for Education who shall ex officio be the President and State Librarian who shall ex officio be the Secretary of SLA.

But it is desirable to make only one person, instead of a corporate body to be the supreme authority for providing this very important service, for that gives a unified command from administrative points of view. And this person should not be any person less than the Minister for Education, because he is directly responsible to the legislature and his term of office being limited to a period of five years he is ultimately responsible to the people. Hewit who made a study of the library legislation in India; it will be observed that two kinds of supreme authority are favoured in existing legislation and in the drafts of the model bills framed in India.

One is a body of persons *i.e.,* State Library Councilor Committee and second is a Minister of State. He suggests the second as the better of the two, mainly because a Minister is responsible to his legislature, and through it, to the electors and many be called to account therein. A body of persons even though a Minister may be President or Chairman thereof is not so easily questioned. In any case; so important an activity as the provision for public library and information service to the people fully justifies direct representation in State Legislature.

So all the studies on library legislations and the evaluation of existing legislations throughout the world and especially in third world counties, like that of Gardners's study comes to the conclusion that providing up of a body or a person as SLA and clearly naming and defining its powers and functions is certainly essential for the successful working of library Acts. But KPLA is very vague in this aspect and it fails to name a person or body as SLA.

STATE LIBRARY COMMITTEE

The Model Act provides for a *State Library Committee* (SLC) for the purpose of advising the SLA on all matters arising under the Act. All existing State Acts and Model Bills enacted or drafted in India provide for appointment of such a Committee or Council. KPLA names it as Kerala State Library Council. All Acts of the states except Kerala's have prescribed its membership on somewhat similar lines. All Acts provides that this body will be headed by Minister for Education. Despite differences in nomenclature and composition the function of this committee or council envisaged everywhere is basically the same *i.e.*, to advise the SLA or State Government in all matters arising out of the Act.

Kerala State Library Council (KSLC)

A careful analysis of the Kerala State Library Council (KSLC) in comparison with the SLC as provided in the Model Act or other State Acts will reveal that it is not a councilor committee of advisory nature as SLCs are. KSLC is an SLC and at the same time an SLA by itself. Naming it as a council is a difference in terminology only. Instead of appointing a Minister as SLA as in Mysore it appoints a body as SLA. But the Act fails to name it as SLA. The duties, powers and functions assigned to KSLC is inclusive of all those assigned to SLA and SLC in Model Act.

Sub-section 1 of the Section 3 of KPLA dealing with the constitution and composition of KSLC states9; KSLC shall be a body corporate having perpetual succession and a common seal with power, to acquire hold and dispose of property, both movable and immovable and to enter into contracts and shall by its name sue and be sued. This is an adaptation of the class related to Karnataka State Library Authority of Karnataka Act. No other Act including Model Act has so clearly defined the nature of this body and assigned so much powers as this like the Acts of Kerala and Karnataka. The powers and functions assigned to KSLC includes both the advisory functions of the committees and councils provided by Model Act and other Acts and the duties assigned to SLA by Model Act and Karnataka Act.

Sub-sections of section 8 of KPLA provides that the KSLC may:

* Advise the government of all matters connected with the administration of that Act and . . . the overall library policy of the State.
* Co-ordinate the working of the District Library Councils and Taluk Library Unions and...supervise and direct all matters relating to library service in the state.
* Establish one or more State Libraries . . . at such place or places in the State as may be considered necessary.
* Appoint and control such officers and servants as may be necessary for the efficient performance of its duties and functions under this Act and the rules made there under.
* Give to the District Library Councils and Taluk Library unions directions in the performance of their functions under this Act and . . . they shall not in-the discharge of their functions under this Act depart from directions given by the KSLC.

While we consider these classes and compare them with the parellel sections of the Model Act or other Acts it becomes clear that the classes which assigns the duties, powers and functions of KSLC is a distinct improvement from all others. KPLA has identified most of the functions and duties expected from such a body and very clearly assigned them to it without giving space for doubt and vagueness.

Composition of KSLC

If KSLC is to become able to fulfil such duties and functions expected from it, the composition of the body should be done accordingly. Membership of such a body should include persons who have contributed to the growth of knowledge, who has evolved or developed methods and techniques for collecting, organising and disseminating information and who have wide experience in related fields of activity. It is not the method of representation but the quality of representation that will make possible the efficient functioning of the system.

The sections which prescribe the membership of SLA in Karnataka Act and SLC in Model Act and other State Acts prescribe their membership on somewhat similar lines. Prof. P.B. Mangla in his study of library legislation opines that it should be a body having representatives from various institutions, organisations, government etc. interested in and connected with the growth and development of library and information services in the State.

The Model Act, the opinion of experts and recommendations of committees set for studying library legislation agrees that such a body should include among its members; the Minister for Libraries if there is one, otherwise Minister for Education, then Minister in charge of Local-Self-Government, Director of Libraries, State Librarian, sufficient number of representatives from State Legislative Assembly by election from among themselves, Secretary to Government for Education, representatives elected from Local Library Authorities by rotation to limit size of the body, representatives of associations of library profession and experts with specialization in library and information services and represen-tatives of Universities of the State.

It would be essential that the Minister in charge of Libraries should act as *ex-officio* chairman and the Director of Public Libraries or State Librarian should act as ex-officio secretary of the committee.

The rationale behind such a composition of this body is that it is a body which is to advise the government and discuss continuously on a most important responsibility of the government, that is organisation and dissemination of information required by the society. But disregarding all these principles KPLA provides for constituting a body of members who were not suitable to undertake this work.

The section 3 sub-section (2) related to the composition of the KSLC in KPLA provides: The KSLC shall consist of one member each from Taluks, elected by the general body of the District Library councils, and five members of whom one shall be a librarian, another a person belonging to the scheduled caste or scheduled tribe and another a woman nominated by the government. Library and information service is an intellectual service. It goes without saying that this body as provided in KPLA will not be able to fulfil satisfactorily the purpose for which it is intended.

In these days of information explosion and flooding of vast and varied types of books and other printed materials that originates every minute without wide familiarity of all spheres of knowledge and expertise in handling their information in most effective way at minimum cost the body which heads such a system will be having a mere formal and useless existence. As we have seen in section 8 of KPLA the most important function of KSLC is to advise the government on all matters connected with the administration of this Act and overall library policy ofthe State.

It is not clear how this committee will be competent to render such expert technical advise when it has only persons as members, who has come through election without expertise or knowledge about information work and without even any educational qualifications. Library and information service to the people if provided efficiently will be the continuously active service of government and will require expert advise everyday on many matters.

The KSLC's inability to provide such expert advise will make government's efforts futile and to overcome this, government will be forced to create a continuous chain of Advisory Committees which is also not very practicable. While no hard and fast rule can be laid down about the size of this body it is generally felt that it should not have more than twenty members. The KSLC may remain a supreme body in name only for real powers of the council have been passed over to a smaller body which is the executive committee. But it also becomes an unwieldy body with membership of 25 persons.

Thus KSLC has acquired all the defects existing in SLAs and SLCs into one body. This Executive Committee is a new addition in our library Acts. But the findings of Ashok Mehta Committee and various committees appointed by many State Governments to study Panchayat Raj Institutions advise us against such an elected body like KSLC for organising important service as library and information service to the people. Instead of adopting the constitution and composition of SLA and SLC provided by the Model Act or followed by the other State Acts KPLA gave legal sanction to the organizational set up of an association that was already existing there, that is Kerala Granthasala Sangham.

The constitution and composition of KSLC and its Executive Committee is the same followed by Sangham for its general body and Bharanasamithi. In all other provisions KPLA follows the same pattern of Sangham with some minor alterations. For more than half a century Sangham was pressurizing the Government to give legal sanction to Sangham to be the SLA and to accept its system as it is,as State's Library System.

But experts have continuously pointed out during this period the futility of such a system for library and information service. But Sangham objected government's all other attempts to enact a modern library system legislation and at last come out successful in legalizing its own system. But this in fact totally prevents the State from having an advanced library legislation and developing its library and information services in conformity with the requirements of the time.

LOCAL LIBRARY AUTHORITY

Library and information service is to be rendered locally by thousands of service points spread throughout the state. The State as a whole in view of its large size is not suitable for being considered as a single unit for organizing these services. So it becomes essential to organize this service system on a decentralized pattern. The units of responsibility at different levels, their nature, functions and relation with other levels should be clearly specified in the Act. In the Model Act Ranganathan recommended two types of Local Library Authorities; District Library Authority in a district and City Library Authority in a city.

The KPLA improves the scope of decentralization of services; providing a three tier system that is after State level at District and Taluk levels parallel to Government's Administrative machanism. The District Library Councils (DLC) and Taluk Library Unions (TLU) are miniature forms of KSLC.

Their constitution, composition, powers and functions are all the same as KSLC; limited within the geographical area of its coverage. DLC and TLU shall elect their Executive Committee which will elect the office bearers very much like in KSLC. All the defects of KSLC are reflected in these bodies also. The Act does not provide for City Library Authorities. It is the duty of the Taluk union to organize and administer the library and information service to the people living in cities and villages.

DEPARTMENT OF PUBLIC LIBRARIES AND OFFICIALS

It is generally emphasized that in order to develop a system of public libraries in a State or country on proper lines, it is essential that a separate department of public libraries be created at par with the department of education and that the former should not be a part of the later or any other' department. The Acts of Andhra, Maharashtra, West Bengal and Karnataka prescribe for the creation of separate department of Public Libraries.

Director of Public Libraries

Most of the recommendations related to public library system legislation emphasizes that the department of Public Libraries should be headed by a Director of Public Libraries (DPL), whose rank must be equivalent to that of Director of Education. He must be a person with qualification and experience in Library and Information Science. Emphasis on his being a professional is laid because it is he to whom the whole public library system in the State would look for guidance and inspiration and his professional outlook would normally greatly help the development of the system on desired lines.

The first public library Act in this country; the Madras Public Library Act, 1948 provided for the appointment of DPL. Andhra, Maharastra and West Bengal also prescribes for the creation of DPL. In Madras and Andhra the Director of Public Instruction is made the ex-officio Director of Public Libraries also.

The disadvantages of such an administrative set-up are quite obvious. The Department of Public Libraries becomes an additional burden to the Director of Public Instruction. This new department will be looked upon as an uninvited guest. A. R. Hewit has rightly pointed out that many of the duties of Director of Public Libraries would require technical knowledge and skill in librarianship. So professional experts only can undertake this responsibility efficiently.

State Library

All the Acts except KPLA which is not providing for these offices, combines the responsibilities of developing and managing the State Central Library Superintending and directing all matters related to the State library system in a single person called State Librarian or DPL.

The Model Act also recommends this pattern. But the Sinha Committee report suggested the creation of two separate posts for this purpose when it said "The DPL may have the overall responsibility to organize develop and supervise the public library system as the Head of the Department of Public Libraries.

The State Librarian should have the responsibility to manage supervise and develop State Central Library and should be the Chief Technical Advisor of the DPL, with no responsibility for the administration of the service in the State. This responsibility should be entirely that of DPL. But in KPLA there is no provision for appointing a Director of Libraries or

State Librarian. While the class by class discussion of the Bill was going on in Assembly Mr. V.M. Sudheeran; member presented an amendment to add a new clause in the Act providing for appointment of a Director of Libraries. But was not considered.

Administration

For the administration of public libraries all the State Acts have created a department or directorate of public libraries. It is put under the charge of Director of Libraries or State Librarian who is to be the *ex-officio* Secretary of SLA. The functions of these posts as prescribed by all Acts including the Model Act are: to supervise and direct all matters relating to public libraries, to direct and control the working of LLAs, submit reports to Government and deal with schemes and plans relating to libraries. Many of the highly technical and specialized works of State Central Library also is to be supervised by them.

So it is clear that these posts which are carrying heavy responsibility concerning various matters-financial, advisory, administrative, technical, supervisory and so on-under the Act would require technical knowledge and skill in library and information service. So the Secretary or High Officer of this body should be a whole time officer having the prescribed qualifications to practice the library profession. Disregarding all the facts KPLA assigns all these duties and powers to a Secretary elected by members of the Executive Committee ofKSLC.

Section 3 sub-section (5) of KPLA provides that the elected members of the Executive Committee shall elect a President, Vice-President, Secretary and Joint Secretary from among themselves to be the President, Vice-President, Secretary and Joint Secretary respectively of the State Library Council and of the Executive Committee. Their term of office will be for three years.

KPLA assigns to the Secretary of KSLC the duties and powers which other State Acts assign to State Librarian or Director of Libraries. Section 9 Sub-section (1) States: the

Secretary of the State Library Council shall be Chief Executive Authority of KSLC.

The nature of the office of Secretary of KSLC requires professional knowledge and experience as well as continuity of office for the successful operation of the Act, so it is inevitable that this provision will prevent KPLA from fulfilling the objectives for which a modern library legislation should exist. This serious defect of the Act has been pointed out by many members during the discussion of the bill.

Dr. M.Kuttappan has brought to the notice of the Assembly that such an important system like that for library and information service requires qualified government officials as their secretaries at State, District and Taluk levels. The period of an elected non-official member may be over by three years and if he misappropriates government fund allotted for library development it will not be possible for the government to take action on him. Sri Ishac Kurikkal suggested an amendment to the Bill to provide that the Secretary of the SLC shall be appointed by the Government on the advice of the Kerala Public Service Commission.

Another member Sri Kodiyeri Balakrishnan opined that the Secretary of KSLC should be appointed by Government and the Act should specify the qualifications and method of appointment for this post. Sri Ramesh Chennitthala presented an amendment to add the following sub-clause in KPLA namely: The Secretary shall be a person not below the rank of a Joint Secretary to Government appointed by Government from among persons qualified and competent to hold such post. But all these suggestions were rejected and principles were disregarded to maintain a democratic system for constituting the SLA.

State Central Library

The existing State legislations and the Model Act provide for a State Central Library (SCL) as an integral part of the Public Library Service. The SCL is normally the copy right collection. It should collect as far as its resources allow, expensive work and literature published abroad, material for which the local public library would have little need and could not afford. All the countries of the world possessing adequate library systems, have national library systems and all have national central library as distinct from the other libraries in the system, but is accessible to all through any library of the system.

The same role of National Central Library to the National system is done by SCL to the State system. Usually the library legislations designate the biggest collection available in the State as SCL and makes its resources and services available to the system. Even though various Acts and Model Act give different names to SCL like State Service Library, etc. in a public library system only one such library will be maintained and its resources will be shared by all participating units. Maintaining more than one SCL is unnecessary duplication of work and waste of resources.

Most of the State Acts and Model bills drafted, designate the biggest public library existing in the State as SCL and adopts it to the system and shares its resources among participating units. But instead of designating Trivandrum Public Library, the oldest and biggest collection in the State as SCL, the KPLA deems it to be one of the many State libraries it will establish.

The Act provides for no SCL in its system. Instead it provides that KSLC shall establish one or more state libraries at such place or places in the State as may be considered necessary. The relation of State libraries with other state libraries and different level service units and the purpose of more than one such institution is not defined in the Act.

Library Co-operation

To make the best possible use of the document resources not only in the public library system but also in other types of libraries in the State such as universities, special libraries etc, a system of inter library co-operation needs to be developed in the state as a whole. It would also be useful and economical if centralization of different aspects such as acquisition programme, technical processing etc. of documents should be introduced at State level or at different levels of the system. The KPLA gives no such provision for co-operation or centralized processing and the institution which is to give leadership in such activities that is SCL is absent in KPLA.

State Library Service

State Library Service brings the manpower of the State in one pool and thus avoids the waste of time and money involved in filling up posts that would otherwise involve, if every Local Library Authority were to appoint the staff independently. A State Library Service further avoids the influence of members of the Local Library Authority in day-to-day management of libraries. Mysore Act has created a special state library service and it ensures proper administration and economy through State Library Service. But KPLA gives to KSLC and Local Library Authorities that is DLC and TLU the powers to appoint and control required officers and servants.

FINANCE

For the growth and development of a public library system in a State, there must be a specific provision in the Act for required financial support. Since education is an essential responsibility of a welfare State, public library system should obviously be established and maintained at the expense of the State.

The Model Act of Ranganathan, the suitable sources for this purpose are:

* Library cess,
* Grants from the State Governments, and
* Grants from Central Government.

In the provisions related to finance; KPLA accepts all the generally accepted principles. The Act provides that the KSLC shall levy a library cess in the form of surcharge on building tax or property tax collected by local bodies at the rate of five paise for whole rupee. The cess shall be paid to the KSLC by local bodies. The government may also make every year a grant to the KSLC of a sum which shall not exceed one per cent of the budget for education. This amount of grant is insufficient.

Ranganathan's Library Development Plan, the documents on National Policy on Library and Information Science and Indian Library Association suggests that six per cent of the Education budget of the State should be set apart for libraries. The Act also provides for a State Library Fund from which all expenses of KSLC, DLC and TLU shall be met. Grants of State and Central Governments to KSLC, contributions by persons, bodies or authorities etc. to KSLC and other funds transferred to it shall be credited to State Library Fund. KSLC shall distribute from State Library Fund such amounts as required for each DLC and TLD. Against creating such Library funds as suggested by Model Act and some State Acts at State and local levels; these provisions of KPLA related to finance providing a centralized fund are truly a notable improvement.

LIBRARY SERVICES

The libraries have transformed drastically from storehouses for books and journals to the powerhouses of knowledge and information since the middle of the 20th century. The information and communication technology is responsible for this revolution. The very existences of libraries are dependable on users' satisfaction. Users are getting satisfied when the library is able to rise to his or her expectation or meet the actual needs. A quality service is said to be one, which satisfy the users' expectation resulting a good experience.

Throughout the history, libraries were mainly concerned with collection development and processing. The library professionals gave less concern to quality in product and services, never checked whether the users were satisfied or not. Gradually the social and economic changes have prompted the libraries to develop services. The staff has a vital role in the satisfaction of users. The library being a service organization, its prime objective is to provide the right documents, information and services to its users. Only the users' satisfaction survey will facilitate the assessment of their satisfaction with products and services offered. There are various methods, tools and techniques to measure, control and improve the quality of library services. Quality measurement and evaluation assumes great importance in modern libraries, as it brings immense benefits to the library as well as user community. Different methods such as collection of data for measuring the performance and quality of libraries; The SERVQUAL method, a multiple item scale to measure service quality; The LibQUAL, a tool developed on SERVQUAL for measuring the quality of library products and services.

WHAT IS QUALITY

The word 'quality' has several definitions. The conventional definition is " One that wears well, is well constructed will last for long time" and the strategic definition is "meeting customers' requirements."

* According to Juuran 'The quality is fitness for purpose'.
* According to Robinson, "Quality is meeting the requirements of customer-now and in the future."
* According to Sarkar "Quality of a product or service is the ability of the product or service to meet the customers' requirements.

QUALITY CONCEPT IN LIBRARY SERVICES

The library is an organization to offer reference and information services to its users. Library service is the combination of the services-process and its delivery. In a library, the service offered from acquisition section, technical section, maintenance section etc. are the processes carried out there and thereafter delivered to the users. The quality should start from the acquisition section, which should be carried uniformly to circulation section. A user who had an unpleasant experience from the library will tell it to many people, but a good experience will be told to very few. Therefore it is very necessary for librarian to understand the users, what they want, how they want, and when they want the documents and information.

HOW TO IMPROVE THE QUALITY IN LIBRARY SERVICES

In this information age it is very easy to make a quality based library if the parent body or concerned authority assist financially as well as collectively. It is very necessary for the librarian and its parent body to look forward for the present and future generation to cope up with international phenomena. A user must be educated with proper technology to use the library effectively.

He or she should have knowledge of what facilities and services are available in the library and information centre and how to access those efficiently and effectively. To improve the service quality the user satisfaction survey is a tool that provides both quantitative and qualitative data. It is an important part of libraries for process and performance measurement.

Main steps to measure users' satisfaction are:

* Conducting sample survey.
* Data collection.
* Process and analysis of data.
* Interpret and present the data.
* Finding out result.

With the help of the result the librarian can take new steps for development of library. The regular survey will enable the library to understand the changes in users satisfaction and to plan the services accordingly.

The Users' Satisfaction is based on Many Factors Like

* A source of up-to-date information, knowledge, accessing facilities and assistance.
* The library should organize its facilities visible to the users; otherwise they may not have it and get dissatisfied.
* *Accessibility:* The library resources and services should be easily accessible. Books should be arranged in shelves in proper classified order, so that the users can locate books quickly. In case of electronic library the electronic database like OPAC

will help the users to find out the books in stacks.

* *Tangibles:* The tangibles of libraries, namely the building, furniture and other physical facilities, collection, staff, machines etc. should be sufficient and appropriate and useful for the users.
* *Courtesy/Friendliness:* The library staff should be very courteous and friendly with the users.
* *Physical Appearance/Atmosphere/Cleanliness/Comfort:* The appearance of library, its facilities, collection, staff and services should be attractive and pleasant. A Welcoming atmosphere should be must. Furniture, floor, racks, documents etc. should be neat and clean.
* *Process-Reliability/Communications:* The processing part of the library should be dependable and efficient that suffices the expectations of the users. The way of communication, assistance and guidance also greatly affect the satisfaction of the users.
* *Some Useful Criteria to Measure Users' Experience in a Library are:*
  - Speed of services delivery (Access time, location, processing, etc.);
  - Value added services such as Xerox service, CAS, SDI etc.; and
  - Technology used.

It is observed that if something goes wrong that can be very easily learned from the users, so the users' complaints can be taken as good measure of user satisfaction.

Steps for Staff to Meet the Users' Needs

* Being responsible for the total service quality to the users both the Technical staff and frontline staff in the library should serve the users.
* Services must be provided to the users in a most effective way.
* Providing maximum benefits to the users form collection and facilities.
* Stay close to users: Library can not understand users'

needs, tastes, interests etc. without listening to them, and services without users' interest will be a mere wastage.

* Users must be treated well, informed well and acknowledged well about the services to the users.

IMPACT OF RANGANATHAN'S FIVE LAWS IN QUALITY SERVICE

The five laws of Ranganathan help in quality improvement of service as those are concentrated to the users very seriously. The laws directly advocate towards libraries' collection development, speedy processing, maintenance and quick retrieval of information by users.

The First Law

"Books are for Use" is a direction for measuring the quality of a library; quality in terms of contents, accessibility and availability as and when needed.

The Second Law

"Every reader his/her books" implies needs of users. In order to meet this law the library has to index all micro and macro documents so that every reader can find out his or her requirements.

The Third Law

"Every Book/Information its reader" implies the importance of book/information selection in a library. The law advocates scientific document selection, subject based organization, advanced and in depth indexing, efficient and effective searching and locating tools, Staff assistance, open access, extension services, publicity programs etc.

The Fourth Law

"Save the time of Reader" indicates the importance of fast and efficient services to the users with the advanced technologies, method, techniques and tools. Open access, digital services, classified arrangement of documents in shelves, location and directing guides, excellent searching tools, and techniques *i.e.* Online public Access Catalogue (OPAC) in an automated library, Xerox facility, Online Information services, qualified and experienced staff will ensure fast service to the users.

The Fifth Law

"The Library is a growing organism" implies collection development, changing of all components of a library.

Everyday the world of documents and information is changing tremendously. Now the information is recorded not in papers alone, to many media, the latest being the electronic and digital form. So in today's world the library may called as information and knowledge house of world as a whole if it is supported by advanced information and communication technologies.

MEASURING QUALITIES OF LIBRARY SERVICES

The important measuring tools and techniques are:

* TQM (Total Quality Management).
* SERVQUAL.
* LibQUAL.

The TQM is one of the techniques used for the improvement and maintenance of quality or performance of the library. It is to provide the right information to the right users at the right place and time and also at the right cost.

The most important components of TQM in a library are:

* Benchmarking.
* Performance Measuring and Monitoring.
* Qualification and experience of staff.

Benchmarking is a process of comparing the operations, products and services of a library with a library doing quality processes and offering quality products and services to the users. Performance measurement is necessary to identify the problems, if any and find out new ways for improving the products or services. It requires both qualitative and quantitative data.

The major performance indicators of the library functions are:

* *Acquisition:* Efficiency, effectiveness, cost productivity.
* *Classification:* Accuracy, Time factor, cost.
* *Cataloguing:* Efficiency, Time effectiveness.
* *Technical Processing:* Efficiency, effectiveness, cost productivity.
* *Collection Management:* Efficiency, ease, accessibility, effectiveness.

Quality of service depends on quality and experience of staff. The TQM supports user education, sufficient and convenient technical infrastructures. SERVQUAL is the most popular assessment tool of service quality. It is designed by the marketing research team of Berry, Parasuraman, and Zeithaml. SERVQUAL evolve a set of five dimensions to assess the service quality-

* *Tangibles:* Appearance of physical facilities, equipments, personnel, and communication materials.
* *Reliability:* Ability to perform the promised service dependably and accurately; giving correct information asked.
* *Responsiveness:* Willingness to help users and provide prompt service making new information available.
* *Assurance and Empathy:* Knowledge and courtesy of employees and their ability to convey confidence to users. It involves politeness, friendliness, skill to provide information.
* *Access:* It means there are adequate staff and equipments as well as hours of operation. Location of library is central and convenient.
* *Communications:* It involves understanding the users' needs precisely, provision of user education, teaching library skills to users, the use of language understandable to different categories of users.
* *Security:* It involves physical safety within the library, and keeping library dealings secured.

LibQUAL + is a library service quality measurement tool based on the SERVQUAL models of assessing service quality. It is standard survey instrument used in many libraries.It is a tool measuring users' perception of service quality and identifies gaps between desired, perceived and minimum expectation of services. LibQUAL +TM 2002 is the latest version to listening the users

USERS' EXPECTATIONS: QUALITY OF SERVICES

* Modern building and furniture are required for a good library.
* A good library provides excellent facilities and services.
* Required books and journals in adequate number will be available with attractively displayed in a good library.
* In a good library, the staff will assist the users for locating a document.
* Accurate information and proper records will always be available in a good library.
* The staff of a good library will have sufficient knowledge to answer user's questions.
* Easy accessing and convenient working hour should have in a good library.

USERS' PERCEPTION: QUALITY OF SERVICES

* My library has modern building and furniture.
* My library provides me excellent facilities and services.
* Necessary books and journals in adequate number are available displayed attractively in my library.
* My library assists the users for locating the documents needed.
* Accurate information and proper records are always kept in my library.
* The staff of my library has proper knowledge to answer my question.
* My library is easily accessible with convenient working hours.

FACILITIES IN A QUALITY BASED LIBRARY

Physical Facilities:

* Good library is easily accessible.
* Good layout for a good library.
* Sufficient Space, lighting and ventilation.
* Clean, tidy and hygienic.
* Cozy and comfortable furniture.

Library Collection:

* Good collection of textbooks, journals, reference books, online journals, ebooks, etc. is needed in a good library.
* Good library displays new arrival of books in separate shelves.
* Good library offers open access to the collection.

Library Staff:

* Staff in a good library should be experienced with knowledge of modern technology.
* Staff should help the users to locate the documents needed and do their works in time.
* Sufficient staff to run the library.

Technical Processing:

* Good library acquire new documents in time.
* Shelf arrangement and rectification is a never ending process in a good library.
* Good library has proper catalogue or database for collection (OPAC etc.).
* Good library has prompt processing, charging and discharging system.

SERVICES IN CENTRAL LIBRARY, IIT GUWAHATI

The Central Library, one of the important central facilities of the Institute, currently has about 85,000 volumes, including textbooks, reference books, conference proceedings, back volumes, standards, and non-book material such as CD-ROMs, audio tapes, video tapes, slides. The Library also subscribes to about 484 current periodicals. All operations of the Library are automated with the help of an integrated library software package (LIBSYS). The database for the entire collection has been created and available through On-Line Public Access Catalogue (OPAC) to the users via campus network. Now this facility is also available through Institute's Intranet as a Web enabled OPAC.

The Library is a member of INDEST consortium (Indian National Digital Library in Science and Technology Consortium), under the aegis of the MHRD, provides online access to few important science and engineering abstracting database services, such as COMPENDEX and INSPEC, MathSciNet, SciFinder Scholar, Web of Science etc and several full-text journals and Indian Standards. The Central Library Intranet Page provides the IP based online accesses to these resources. Opening hours is from Morning 8 a.m. to 11 p.m. Average number of users in library is 200 per day.

LIBRARY AND INFORMATION SCIENCE EDUCATION IN INDIA

THE STRUCTURE AND LEVELS OF LIS EDUCATION

Professional higher education in library and information science (LIS) in India, now nine decades old, is centred in universities. Exceptions are two national institutes, namely, the Documentation Research and Training Centre (DRTC) in Bangalore, and the education section of the Indian National Scientific Documentation Centre (INSDOC) in New Delhi. These two institutes concentrate on the training of professionals for special and industrial libraries and information centres. Their course contents are biased towards information science and technology.

These two institutes are a class apart from other programmes in their environment and products. There are some regional library associations conducting certificate courses of a few months duration and women polytechnics offering post-masters twoyear diplomas in library science to train paraprofessionals.

At the university level, the Master's degree in library and information science is earned in two yearlong (or, in some places, four semesters) courses after 10+2+3 years of education in any faculty. Of late there are two streams: the majority of the universities conduct two separate courses for the Bachelor's degree followed by the Master of Library and Information Science of one year (or two semesters) duration each. In recent years, some institutions have offered two years of integrated courses in four semesters. This integrated approach affords space for a cohesive and non-repetitive syllabus. Indeed syllabi in such schools are quite modernised. Students have the advantage that they do not have to reseek and compete for admission to master degree courses. In some of the places admission to the Master's degree course could be a competitive ordeal.

CURRICULUM

The University Grants Commission (UGC), a statutory body to plan, co-ordinate, audit and partially finance (non-technical) higher education in India, has from time to time recommended the broader outlines of courses to be taught. The latest effort has been through a UGC Curriculum Development Committee. Every university being autonomous is free to frame its own course of studies. Debate has been going on whether we should go in for a uniform syllabus at least at regional levels. But there seems no obvious advantage to this drab uniformity. In fact there is no co-ordinating body to do this.

Verbal pleas and repeated seminar resolutions to have some national level accrediting body (as the American Library Association in USA) have not borne fruit. The classes taught at the bachelor level are the library in society; cataloguing and classification (theory and practice); reference service and sources; library operations and management; and introduction to information systems and retrieval techniques. There are more variations at the Master's level.

The basic set of courses includes universe of knowledge and research methodology; sources of information and bibliography in social/natural sciences/humanities, etc.; information retrieval systems and techniques; library systems in public/academic/special libraries; computer applications in libraries; and a small research project to be completed before the commencement of examination.

In principle there are many optional classes available to the students. But due to the shortage of teachers most students have to opt for a topic for which a teacher is available. Syllabi are not very relevant and no worthwhile effort has been done at the national level to do research on the relevance of the curricula. There is an urgent need to widen the scope of studies available and to respond to the market forces.

INTAKE AND TEACHING METHODS

There is always a rush for admission. The number of admission seekers is more than the seats available. This is despite the opening of many distance education programmes that rarely disappoint the admission seekers. But the intake of students is generally of poor quality. Library science courses are never the first option of the majority of students. Most of the students turn to library science after having failed to secure admission to other prestigious courses of study. Thus, it is a career of the mediocre at best.

Teaching is predominantly by the lecture method. In some central states, Hindi is also allowed as a medium of examination as a general policy of the state government. Only a few schools have apprenticeship programmes for the students–otherwise classroom teaching with blackboard and chalk is the norm. Dictation of notes and their cramming by students are still popular. Neither class discussion nor questioning by students is encouraged. New methods of teaching are not tried. Use of educational technology in teaching is rather rare.

It can be easily inferred from one of the recommendations of the 15th IATLIS Seminar (1997):

* It is observed that majority of LIS schools are lacking adequate infrastructure facilities to teach/train LIS students in IT. Hence it is recommended that the UGC should provide special financial assistance to develop adequate need-based IT infrastructural facilities in LIS schools.

INFRASTRUCTURE

About a dozen universities have introduced the M.Phil. Degree, predominantly an intermediate research degree. During the last decade there has been a mushrooming of LIS courses available through correspondence courses or by the more respectable nomenclature of distance education. Except for one, most of such open schools are ill equipped for LIS education, though they have proved money minting machines for the parent universities due to higher enrolment. Some such schools do not have even full-time or regular teachers–good libraries or workshops are not even considered. There is always a cry for improvement or for closing of such courses–but they go on thriving.

PROLIFERATION OF LIBRARY EDUCATION

At present about 107 institutions, mostly university colleges and polytechnics, have library science education courses. Of these, the M.Lib.I.Sc. course is being offered by 67 universities; 11 universities offer the M.Phil. though this degree has no value in the job market. Today 32 Universities have Ph.D. research facilities.

One University recently awarded a D.Litt. that it claimed to be the first such degree in library science all over the world. It may not be an odious comparison that up to 1986 only 38 universities had master programmes; and 18 universities provided doctoral research facilities though not all these 18 universities had master programmes then. The words of the eminent librarian, former President of the Indian Library Association, and former President of the *Indian Association of Teachers of Library and Information Science* (IATLIS), P.N. Kaula, starkly hold true today.

A decade ago, Kaula said:

> "It has been observed that more and more institutions and libraries are opening library science courses without having even the minimum facilities for teaching. Even with poor libraries and funds they have started M.L.I.Sc. Programmes. In some

universities there are not full time teachers to teach B.L.I.Sc. courses and yet some of them have also started M.L.I.Sc. programme. Open universities have also started [M/]B.Lib. Sc. programmes. Some private colleges have been conducting large number of C Lib. Sc. programmes with little or practically no facilities for books and libraries. This uncontrolled growth has bought down the standard of the courses. Library associations have also been having large intake of students without accessing the employment opportunities of the products.

Another problem with library schools has been a lack of public relations and marketing of their images and products.

The late C. G. Vishwanathan, a veteran librarian, aptly wrote:

> "At present library schools and professional training centres in India are yet to receive a kind word from any section of the public... Even the academic world still does not believe that there can be anything like education for librarianship and curriculum of studies for library science. But at the same time everyone wants library service to be first rate.

THE BEGINNING OF RESEARCH IN LIBRARY AND INFORMATION SCIENCE

The roots of research in our profession are not very deep. Research in library science is a twentieth century occurrence ushered in by the library school of the University of Chicago in mid-1920s. The visionary efforts of the Chicago School bore abundant fruit and offered leadership to the world in library science research.

The pace of library research is picking up everywhere today due to social pressure as well as inspiration. In justifying the Ph.D. programme in our profession, it has been urged that "if librarianship aspires to become a profession, it should depend upon research to develop its knowledge base and its theoretical framework".

THE INDIAN CONTEXT

In India following British tradition and American precedent as established by Asa Don Dickinson, Librarian, Panjab University, Lahore, 1915-1916, library schools for advanced professional education have remained attached to universities. The growth of universities in Independent India ensured their constant growth. In a university, apart from teaching, a teacher is expected to do and guide research. The third function of a university, namely service and consultation, has always remained weak in India despite many newly established universityindustry linkage programmes.

RANGANATHAN'S WORK

The credit for the formal institution of the doctoral degree programme in library science in India goes undeniably to Dr. S.R. Ranganathan. In 1951, he started one at the University of Delhi surmounting many difficulties and facing personal ridicule. The University of Delhi awarded the first de jure degree in library science in 1957 to D.B. Krishan Rao who worked on a faceted classification for agriculture. Doctoral research remained in the wilderness when Ranganathan shook the Delhi soil off his feet in 1955. The *Documentation Research and Training Centre* (DRTC) in Bangalore, founded by Ranganathan in 1962, is technically not empowered to award the Ph.D.

Therefore, for the rest of his life, from 1962 to 1972, Ranganathan only advocated solo and team research with stress on quality, relevance and basics. No big research projects were taken up at DRTC though individual teachers and students maintained both the quality and the tempo of research. Since the death of Ranganathan almost the entire DRTC faculty has earned Ph.D.s from other Indian universities on topics of research relevant to DRTC. Now the DRTC teachers are approved Ph.D. guides in many Indian universities, and they have already produced many Ph.D.

GROWTH OF DOCTORAL RESEARCH IN INDIA

Elsewhere in India other individual librarians and library science teachers eager to earn doctorates were hampered by the non-existence of programmes. In the 1960s and 1970s some doctorates on library-related topics were earned by library professionals from some other faculties such as sociology, history, law, economics, management, and the like.

The mantle of reviving and furthering doctoral research facilities was assumed by J. S. Sharma, then the university librarian and head of the library science department of the Panjab University, Chandigarh. Under his guidance the second *de jure* Ph.D. in library science was awarded in 1977 after a gap of full two decades. Thereafter, there was no looking back. Many universities followed with mostly individual efforts and enthusiasm. Doctoral research got a fillip in the 1980s. India maintained its Third World leadership in library research as well as in library education and literature. Ph.D. programmes have rather mushroomed even despite the lack of facilities or adherence to standards.

FACILITIES FOR RESEARCH

A conscientious university teacher is always in a dilemma over how to divide the time between teaching and research. Teaching is a primary compulsive and urgent duty to be performed. Students expect their teachers to give them time and personal attention. There may be appreciation in good teaching but the rewards lie in research. The university expects its teachers to do research for its prestige and fame lie therein. But when it comes to supporting of research many universities in India are neither generous nor unambivalent.

Ordinarily piecemeal research, especially in social sciences, is not supported financially. Internal support for research trickles through a tedious and off-putting bureaucracy and political manoeuvring. Colleagues are unsupportive. They are unappreciative, intolerant and jealous. Library facilities are poor. Thus most of the teachers are driven to the passivity of guiding doctoral research instead of doing postdoctoral work.

THE DETERIORATION OF STANDARDS

The University Grants Commission (UGC) preconditions for faculty employment and promotions have prompted many library professionals to acquire Ph.D. degrees, though many may not have the aptitude and the intrinsic ability to do research. Standards have not only been diluted but have been kept at abeyance. Supervisors and the examiners have become obligingly compromising. The cut-off date of December, 1992 for obtaining the Ph.D. degree to get an exemption from the national level test for teaching jobs in universities/colleges has done incalculable damage to research standards.

An eminent academician has corroborated the ill effects of this policy:

> "They were required to submit their theses before the deadline regardless of the date of registration. Some of the candidates on whom Ph.D.'s were conferred were not fully acquainted with the contents of their dissertations. In some cases even the supervisors were innocent of any knowledge of what the theses were about. The incitement came from the UGC".

Programmes for Ph.D. research have been introduced and expanded mindlessly. As a result, there has been a bit of doctoral boom – a spectacular rise in Ph.D. awarding universities and awardees – though many institutions lack utterly the resources of people or material or both. A 1987 bibliography listed 41 Ph.D. theses written from 1957 to 1985. In a recently published bibliography of doctoral dissertations in India from 1950 to March 1997 about 340 titles have been listed. This record of 340 dissertations, though not wholly authentic, is reliable by and large. In productivity the Panjab University, Chandigarh, led up to the mid-1980s. Thereafter, it lost the number game to the universities of the south.

The universities that have so far awarded up to ten degrees are ranked below:

* Karnatak University, Dharwad 44
* Jiwaji University, Gwalior 27
* University of Rajasthan, Jaipur 26
* Andhra University, Visakhapatnam 25
* University of Delhi 17
* University of Pune 16

* Gulbarga University 15
* Utkal University, Bhubaneswar 11
* University of Burdwan 10

The universities in Bangalore, Banaras Hindu University in Varanasi, and Nagpur University are picking up in research.

RELEVANCE OF RESEARCH

In a developing country like India, there could not be a dearth of research problems to be investigated. But there seems a lack of perception to visualise and identify valid problems for research. A cursory glance of the topics worked on will at once reveal that the topics chosen do not have a problem or hypothesis but merely survey the state of the art or the existing conditions. The popular areas for research have been, in order of popularity: university libraries, bibliometrics, library use and user studies, information seeking behaviour, information systems, classification and indexing, special libraries, library history, reference service and sources, and library science education.

Document selection and procurement, cataloguing, and experimental designs in library management are the least popular topics — though these seem practical and relevant to present day needs. That basic research is the most neglected area is endorsed by other surveys of doctoral research. Library automation, library software, networking and information technology are just emerging. There is need to revive research in classification especially in context of OPACs, information networks and the electronic information environment in general. The Curriculum Development Committee (CDC) on Library and Information Science of the University Grants Commission rehashed the importance of research, though it did not dwell at length on this aspect in its report.

The blue document listed some areas for research, which are no less broad than the current courses being taught at the Master's level:

* Structure and development of knowledge.
* Classification, cataloguing and indexing.
* Infometric studies.
* Computer applications.

* Historical studies.
* Social and economic aspects of librarianship.
* Library and Information management and systems analysis.
* Applications of techniques of library and information science to evaluate other disciplines.

The list could have been more specific. Though not much revered, the report rightly lays emphasis on standards in research. It uncompromisingly asks for a clear declaration from Ph.D. candidates that the "work is based on the discovery of new facts by the candidate or the new relations of facts . . . and how the work tends to the general advancement of knowledge". While it is normally expected of every completed piece of research, yet it rarely happens. The evaluation process, however formal, is easily manipulated without qualms. Examiners are obliging on a reciprocal basis.

In a small profession like ours this interplay of mutual usability comes in easily. It is often said jocularly that the degree is recommended more for the supervisor than for the candidate. We must admit that the library profession has failed to lure the best brains and even more to retain them. Mediocrity thrives; hypocrisy reigns. But this is not to overlook the genuine research and researchers. Apart from not so relevant topics, theses have contributed little towards pushing the frontiers of knowledge; few are models of methodology. Indian library research seems to have no moorings in the prevailing realities.

Topics are ideal, superficial and bookish. Even experienced librarians keen on earning the Ph.D. degree rarely come with an important problem for research. The supervisor who shies from controversial topics usually suggests the topic. Criticising individuals in formal black-and-white mode or exposing harmful tendencies of a class are not for them. Even a mild and healthy criticism is not tolerated in India. Feudal norms still lie deep in the Indian social ethos.

In addition, there is a dire paucity of data archives and reference works. Collecting data and information is considered a satisfactory end to the job — the goal of the research exercise.

It is very difficult to collect data by questionnaire in a vast country like India. Each researcher has a bag full of woeful tales to tell. Library associations at all levels seem to have washed their hands of the research responsibility. These do not even collect and compile statistics of the professional activities pertaining to their areas. Their libraries are poor. They have no research budget. For quite a time professionals have been talking, writing and conferencing about library education and research in India.

Every year the Indian Association of Teachers of Library and Information Science (IATLIS) holds a seminar on topics of library education and research. That it is the most popular topic with the teachers and librarians can be gauged from the fact that the FID/ET seminar was the largest of all the 49th FID pre-conference seminars held in India. The literature on library education and research is enormous, though repetitive and inflated. We have given lip service to the change of curricula and the raising of standards of research. But the needed change has not come through. The blame is wholly put on the lack of infrastructure and unavailability of funds. That is not the entire reason. The lack of effective collective efforts to safeguard the standards seems no less major cause.

THE CONTRIBUTIONS MADE BY RESEARCH

Contrary to expectations, dissertations are not fountain heads of the rest of the literature to grow and mature. These primary sources of information are distanced from relevance. The National Social Science Documentation Centre systematically procures one copy of each research dissertation in social sciences to preserve and make them available to researchers for consultation within the premises of its library. Retrospective bibliographies of LIS dissertations in India are available.

The latest information on theses awarded, Ph.D. degrees and Ph.D. research in progress is available in the featured column of the weekly University News of the Association of Indian Universities, New Delhi. It is a major source to keep track of the dissertations awarded Ph.D.

degrees by Indian universities in all disciplines. In spite of availability, other researchers do not adequately use these dissertations; nor are these works cited or quoted by teachers or textbook writers.

Working librarians rarely use research results to solve their professional problems. There is no precedent of a library inviting a library school to do research on a problem confronting them. At the risk of calling attention to a red herring, it is worthwhile to have this idea corroborated from a veteran library leader.

Professor P.N. Kaula candidly observed:

* That LIS departments have little or no understanding and cooperation with the central library . . . The problem is more psychological than academic . . . Much harm has been done to the teaching of library science by the disharmony....

Librarians go in for local, *ad hoc* and *pro-tem* solutions for their practical problems. Researchers consult a teacher or a fellow researcher for a topic of research rather than a practitioner. It is not only true in India but elsewhere too. Thus research has become divorced from reality–a theoretical exercise at best. This seems a universal phenomenon in our profession. Carl Keren doubting the value of research in information science daringly suggests that "It would be worthwhile to find out how much of it has really contributed to our body of knowledge and to the methods used by practitioners." He himself understands that "As suggested, probably be rather disappointed".

American teacher Margaret Steig endorses this notion:

* Research done by library and information science educators seems to receive little respect from professionals, and if they do not find it of value one has to wonder who will.

6

Library Associations

INDIAN LIBRARY ASSOCIATION

Indian Library Association (ILA) was established on September 13, 1933, on the occasion of the First All India Library Conference held at Calcutta. The ILA is the largest and renowned professional body in the field of Library and Information Science in India with a membership of more than 7000.

OBJECTIVES

The main objectives of the Association are:

* Promoting library movement in the country,
* Developing Library and Information Science education,
* Training and research, betterment of library personnel,
* Cooperation at the national and international levels,
* Promotion of standards, norms, services and guidelines, and
* Providing a forum for professionals and publication of materials.

CONFERENCES

Its 53rd Annual conference was held in Hyderabad in 2007. Its 54th Annual conference was held in Mumbai in 2008.

AMERICAN INDIAN LIBRARY ASSOCIATION

The American Indian Library Association (AILA) is an affiliate of the American Library Association (ALA), and is a membership action group that focuses on the library-related needs of American Indians and Alaska Natives. The organization's members consist of both individuals and institutions that are interested in improving library services to Native American people in any type of library in the United States.

HISTORY

The American Indian Library Association was officially established in 1979 as a result of the Indian White House Pre-Conference of 1978 on Indian Library and Information Services On or Near Reservations. This Pre-Conference took place in Denver, CO, and its focus was on the amelioration of library services and resources to American Indians. The individuals who attended the meeting represented a number of Indian tribes from different parts of the United States.

The initial *idea* of such an organization began in the early 1970s, however. In 1971, at the ALA's Annual Conference in Dallas, TX, Lotsee Patterson, Charles Townley, and Virginia Matthews formed a Task Force on American Indians within the Social Responsibilities Round Table and held an initial meeting. Around the same time, the ALA Advisory Committee in the Office for Library Service to the Disadvantaged created the Committee on Library Service for American Indian People, in which Charles Townley served as the first chair.

Additional issues that influenced the creation of the organization were the implementation of tribal libraries and changes in United States federal law that reflected the increasing concern regarding the inadequacy of library services to American Indians. The AILA held its first meeting as an individual entity in New York during the ALA's 1980 Annual Conference, its constitution was passed the following year during the Annual Conference in San Francisco and, in 1985, the ALA Executive Board finally approved the AILA as an affiliate during the ALA Annual Conference in Chicago, IL.

MEMBERSHIP

Annual membership costs $40 for organizations, while individuals must pay $20 and students must pay $10.

Membership includes a subscription to the *American Indian Libraries* Semi-Annual Newsletter and *AILA-L*, a discussion group for all AILA members.

GOVERNING STRUCTURE

The AILA is governed by an Executive Board, which meets annually and delegates to the Association's committees. The Board enables those committees to both develop and implement programs and activities that are in accordance with the Executive Board's policies. The current 2008-2009 President and Vice-President of the Association are Susan Hanks and Liana Juliano, respectively.

COMMITTEES

Current ad hoc AILA committees include the Budget and Finance Committee, By-Laws and Constitution Committee, Children's Literature Award Committee, Communications and Publications Committee, Development and Fundraising Committee, Distinguished Service Award Committee, Nominating Committee, Programming Committee, Subject Access and Classification Committee, and the Scholarship Review Board.

GOALS

Loriene Roy's "Retaining Cultural Identity in a Transformed Future: The American Indian Library Association Response to ALA Goal 2000," as excerpted onto the AILA's official website, the American Indian Library Association:

* "Promotes the establishment, maintenance, and upgrading of Indian libraries on or near reservations and in other rural and urban areas;
* Develops criteria and standards for Indian libraries, and works for their adoption by other associations and accrediting agencies;
* Provides technical assistance to Indian tribes on the establishment and maintenance of archival services;
* Builds support for the development of Indian information networks, facilitating the exchange of

information among Indian tribes, and also among these groups and major institutions maintaining Indian archives;

* Educates legislators, public officials, and the general public about the library/information needs of Indians communities;
* Brings together those interested in Indian libraries and cultures at ALA conferences and other library and educational conferences;
* Helps members of individual Indian communities to gain access to and use existing libraries to their best advantage;
* Works to enhance the capability of libraries to assist tribes and individual Indian authors in writing tribal histories and other Indian-related works;
* Encourages and helps to coordinate and plan the development of courses, workshops, institutes, and internships on Indian library services;
* Develops grant proposals and conducts fund-raising activities to support these and other Indian library projects; and
* Helps develop awareness in the majority society that Indian people desire library information resources to help unlock their potential."

ACTIVITIES

The AILA participates in a multitude of programs, awards, outreach services, conferences, and publications.

Programme

* *American Indian Library Association Book Ring:* The AILA Book Ring's goal is to connect people with extra items with those who would be glad to accept them.

Awards

* *American Indian Youth Literature Awards:* These AILA awards are also known as the Native American

Youth Services Literature Awards, and are given to books in three categories: picture book, middle school, and young adult. The awards were first presented in October 2006 during the Joint Conference of Librarians of Colour, and they attempt to "identify and honour the very best writing and illustrations by and about American Indians." Winners of the awards are given $500, in addition to a commemorative plaque. The most recent award in the young adult category was given in 2010 to native Hawaiian author Lurline Wailana McGregor for her *Between the Deep Blue Sea and Me.*

* *Honouring our Elders:* This is a Distinguished Service Award that honours either active or retired AILA members. The award was established in 2003; Lotsee Patterson was the first recipient. To be considered, an individual must have demonstrated "significant and continuous service to the ongoing operations and growth of the American Indian Library Association; service to Indian communities and exceptional progress in his/her career development that has resulted in specific and extraordinary service to the American Indian Library Association; [and] work for the improvement in library and information services for and to American Indian people."
* *Library School Scholarship:* This AILA Scholarship is an annual, $500 award that was officially created in July 2000, yet first awarded for the 2002-2003 academic school year, in order to encourage librarianship among American Indian students. One reason for the award is the idea that there "needs to be American Indian library professionals to help guide information seekers to the facts about American Indians-past, present, and future, and to incorporate American Indian perspectives in those institutions that mandate how people are taught and what they learn." To be eligible for the scholarship award, an individual must be either an American

Indian or an Alaska Native that lives and works within the Indian community, who is either currently enrolled or will soon be enrolled in an accredited Masters of Library and Information Science graduate programme. Preference is given to individuals who are employed in a tribal library or another library serving American Indian populations. This scholarship is particularly necessary and relevant considering the fact that, per a 2004 report by the Association for Library and Information Science Education (ALISE), American Indians only made up about 0.3 per cent of all the graduates from library-related undergraduate, graduate, and doctoral programs in the preceding academic school year.

Outreach

American Library Association Office for Literacy and Outreach Services

* The AILA is one of five ethnic groups affiliated with the ALA-the other four being the Asian/Pacific American Librarians Association (APALA), the Black Caucus of ALA (BCALA), the Chinese American Librarians Association (CALA), and the National Association to Promote Library and Information Services to Latinos and the Spanish Speaking (REFORMA). As such, it works closely with the ALA's Office of Literacy and Outreach Services (OLOS). The goal of the OLOS is to "[serve] the Association by identifying and promoting library services that support equitable access to knowledge and information stored in...libraries." The OLOS also has a Subcommittee on Library Services to American Indians, which focuses on the following three objectives:
  - Developing information networks and facilitating the exchange of information between Native American communities and institutions, especially those with Native American archives,

- Through education and programming, raising awareness in the public and the library profession about the library/information and literacy needs of Native American communities as underserved populations, and
- Coordinating and planning the development of workshops, institutes and meetings to promote library services in Native American communities and providing forums at ALA and other library conferences for those interested in tribal and Alaskan Native village libraries and other Native American libraries.

Conferences

* *American Library Association Conference:* Aside from its annual business meeting that takes place during the ALA's annual meeting, the AILA co-sponsors the ALA's popular Annual Conference.
* *International Indigenous Librarians Forum:* The AILA supports this conference, which takes place every two years, in order to address major issues and concerns facing libraries and other organizations that deal with indigenous information. The conference also focuses on the similarities of the Native experience within the Library and Information Science profession, in addition to encouraging the discussion of different indigenous viewpoints. The upcoming 2009 conference will take place in Aotearoa, New Zealand from February 1–4, 2009. Past conferences have been held in New Zealand, Australia, Sweden, Canada, and the United States.
* *Joint Conference of Librarians of Colour:* In 2006, the AILA participated in the first Joint Conference of Librarians of Colour (JCLC), titled "Gathering at the Waters: Embracing Our Spirits, Telling Our Stories." This conference took place between October 12–15 in Dallas, TX, and took the five ALA ethnic associations representing librarians of colour roughly

eight years to coordinate. The participants-who included library directors, library staff, ALA leaders, and others-totaled over 1,200. As one of the ethnic affiliates, the AILA sponsored the event and contributed $2,000. A second, highly-anticipated conference was hoped for soon, but all five ethnic caucuses had to agree on how to arrange it. Two proferred ideas were (1) to implement a five-year timeline for "JCLCII," or (2) to have the second meeting in conjunction with a future ALA annual conference. Most recently at the 2008 ALA Annual Conference in Anaheim, CA, however, the five ethnic associations began officially planning for the future "JCLC2012;" the location for the upcoming conference has yet to be decided.

Publication

* *American Indian Libraries Newsletter:* The AILA's Newsletter, *American Indian Libraries*, is published quarterly and informs its readers about decisions made during the AILA's business meetings, in addition to containing information on "programs, projects, grants, and resources relating to American Indian culture and library and information services." The publication also features book reviews, job announcements, and other pertinent information regarding the Association's goals. It has been edited since 1996 by Rhonda Harris Taylor, Ph.D.

AMERICAN LIBRARY ASSOCIATION

The American Library Association (ALA) is a non-profit organization based in the United States that promotes libraries and library education internationally. It is the oldest and largest library association in the world, with more than 62,000 members.

HISTORY

Founded by Justin Winsor, Charles Ammi Cutter, Samuel S. Green, James L. Whitney, Melvil Dewey, Fred B. Perkins and Thomas W. Bicknell in 1876 in Philadelphia and chartered in 1879 in Massachusetts, its head office is now in Chicago. During the Centennial Exposition in Philadelphia in 1876, 103 librarians, 90 men and 13 women, responded to a call for a "Convention of Librarians" to be held October 4–6 at the Historical Society of Pennsylvania. At the end of the meeting, "the register was passed around for all to sign who wished to become charter members," making October 6, 1876 to be ALA's birthday.

In attendance were 90 men and 13 women, among them Justin Winsor, Charles Ammi Cutter, Melvil Dewey, and Richard Rogers Bowker. Attendees came from as far west as Chicago and from England. The aim of the Association, in that resolution, was "to enable librarians to do their present work more easily and at less expense." The Association has worked throughout its history to define, extend, protect and advocate for equity of access to information. Library activists in the 1930s pressured the American Library Association to be more responsive to issues put forth by young members involved with issues such as peace, segregation, library unions and intellectual freedom.

In 1931, the Junior Members Round Table (JMRT) was formed to provide a voice for the younger members of the ALA, but much of what they had to say resurfaced in the social responsibility movement to come years later. During this period, the first Library Bill of Rights (LBR) was drafted by Forrest Spaulding to set a standard against censorship and was adopted by the ALA in 1939. This has been recognized as the moment defining modern librarianship as a profession committed to intellectual freedom and the right to read over government dictates.

The ALA formed the Staff Organization's Round Table in 1936 and the Library Unions Round Table in 1940. The ALA appointed a committee to study censorship and recommend policy after the banning of *The Grapes of Wrath* and the implementation of the LBR. The committee reported in 1940 that intellectual freedom and professionalism were linked and recommended a permanent committee — Committee on Intellectual Freedom. The ALA made revisions to strengthen the LBR in June 1948, approved the Statement on Labeling in 1951 to discourage labeling material as subversive, and adopted the Freedom to Read Statement and the Overseas Library Statement in 1953.

In 1961, the ALA took a stand regarding service to African Americans and others, advocating for equal library service for all. An amendment was passed to the LBR in 1961 that made clear that an individual's library use should not be denied or abridged because of race, religion, national origin, or political views. Some communities decided to close their doors rather than desegregate. In 1963, the ALA commissioned a study, *Access to Public Libraries*, which found direct and indirect discrimination in American libraries.

In 1967 some librarians protested against a pro-Vietnam War speech given by General Maxwell D. Taylor at the annual ALA conference in San Francisco; the former president of Sarah Lawrence College, Harold Taylor, spoke to the Middle-Atlantic Regional Library Conference about socially responsible professionalism; and less than one year later a group of librarians proposed that the ALA schedule a new round table programme discussion on the social responsibilities of librarians at its next annual conference in Kansas City.

This group called themselves the Organizing Committee for the ALA Round Table on Social Responsibilities of Libraries. This group drew in many other under-represented groups in the ALA who lacked power, including the Congress for Change in 1969. This formation of the committee was approved in 1969 and would change its name to the Social Responsibilities Round Table (SRRT) in 1971). After its inception, the Round Table of Social Responsibilities began to press ALA leadership to address issues such as library unions, working conditions, wages, and intellectual freedom. The Freedom to Read Foundation was created by ALA's Executive Board in 1969.

The Black Caucus of the ALA and the Office for Literacy and Outreach were set up in 1970. In June 1990, the ALA approved "Policy on Library Services to the Poor" and in 1996 the Task Force on Hunger Homelessness, and Poverty was formed to resurrect and promote the ALA guidelines on library services to the poor. The ALA archival materials, non-current records, are currently held in the University of Illinois archives. These materials can only be used at the University of Illinois.

MEMBERSHIP

ALA membership is open to any person or organization, though most of its members are libraries or librarians. Most members live and work in the United States, with international members comprising 3.5% of total membership.

GOVERNING STRUCTURE

The ALA is governed by an elected council and an executive board. Since 2002, Keith Michael Fiels has been the ALA executive director (CEO). Policies and programs are administered by various committees and round tables. One of the organization's most visible tasks is overseen by the Office for Accreditation, which formally reviews and authorizes American and Canadian academic institutions that offer degree programs in library and information science. The ALA's current President is Molly Raphael. Notable past presidents of the ALA include Theresa Elmendorf, its first female president, Clara Stanton Jones, its first African-American president, Loriene Roy, its first Native American president, Michael Gorman, and Roberta Stevens..

ACTIVITIES

The official purpose of the association is "to promote library service and librarianship." Members may join one or more of eleven membership divisions that deal with specialized topics such as academic, school, or public libraries, technical or reference services, and library administration. Members may also join any of seventeen round tables that are grouped around more specific interests and issues than the broader set of ALA divisions.

Notable Divisions

* ALA Editions (book publishing).
* American Association of School Librarians (AASL).

* Association for Library Collections and Technical Services (ALCTS).
* Association for Library Service to Children (ALSC).
* Association of College and Research Libraries (ACRL).
* Library Information Technology Association (LITA).
* Public Library Association (PLA).
* Reference and User Services Association (RUSA).
* Young Adult Library Services Association (YALSA).

Notable Offices

* Office of Intellectual Freedom (OIF).
* Office for Accreditation (OA).
* Office for Literacy and Outreach Services (OLOS).
* Office for Information Technology Policy (OITP).

Notable Sub-organizations

In 1970, the ALA founded the first lesbian, gay, bisexual and transgender professional organization, called the "Task Force on Gay Liberation", now known as the GLBT Round Table. On July 23rd, 1976, the Committee on the Status of Women in Librarianship was established as a Council Committee of the ALA on recommendation of the Ad Hoc Committee with the same name and of the Committee on Organization.

The Committee on the Status of Women in Librarianship works to "officially represent the diversity of women's interest within ALA and to ensure that the Association considers the rights of the majority in the library field; to promote and initiate the collection, analysis, dissemination, and coordination of information on the status of women in librarianship; to coordinate the activities of ALA units which consider questions of special relevance for women; to identify lags, gaps, and possible discrimination in resources and programs relating to women; in cooperation with other ALA units, to help develop and evaluate tools, guidelines, and programs designed to enhance the opportunities and the image of women in the library profession, thus raising the level of consciousness concerning women; to establish contacts with committees on women within other professional groups and to officially represent ALA concerns at interdisciplinary meetings on women's equality; and to provide Council and Membership with reports needed for establishment of policies and actions related to the status of women in librarianship; and to monitor ALA units to ensure consideration of the rights of women."

In 1979 the Committee on the Status of Women in Librarianship received the Bailey K. Howard-World Book Encyclopedia-ALA Goal Award to develop a profile of ALA personal members, known as the COSWL Study. In 1980 the Committee on the Status of Women in Librarianship was awarded the J. Morris Jones-World Book Encyclopedia-ALA Goals Award with the OLPR Advisory Committee to undertake a special project on equal pay for work of equal value.

National Outreach

The ALA is affiliated with regional, state, and student chapters across the country. It organizes conferences, participates in library standards development, and publishes a number of books and periodicals. The ALA publishes the magazines *American Libraries* and *Booklist*. Along with other organizations, it sponsors the annual Banned Books Week the last week of September. Young Adult Library Services Association (YALSA) also sponsors Teen Read Week, the third week of each October, and Teen Tech Week, the second week of each March.

Awards and Honours

The ALA annually confers numerous book and media awards, primarily through its children's and young adult divisions. The children's division ALSC administers the Caldecott Medal, Newbery Medal, Batchelder Award, Belpré Awards, Geisel Award, and Sibert Medal, all annual book awards; the Odyssey Award for best audiobook and the (U.S.) Carnegie Medal and for best video. There are also two ALSC lifetime recognitions, the Wilder Medal and the Arbuthnot Lecture.

The young-adult division YALSA administers the Margaret Edwards Award for significant and lasting contribution to YA literature, a lifetime recognition of one author annually, and some annual awards that recognize particular works: the Michael L. Printz Award for a YA book judged on literary merit alone, the William C. Morris Award for an author's first YA book, the new "YALSA Award for Excellence in Nonfiction for Young Adults", and the "Alex Award" list of ten adult books having special appeal for teens. Jointly with the children's division ALSC there is the Odyssey Award for excellence in audiobook production.

The award for YA nonfiction was inaugurated in 2012, defined by ages 12 to 18 and publication year November 2010 to October 2011. The first winner was '*The Notorious Benedict Arnold: A True Story of Adventure, Heroism and Treachery* by Steve Sheinkin and four other finalists were named. Beside the Alex Awards, ALA disseminates some annual lists of "Notable" and "Best" books. The annual awards roster includes the John Cotton Dana Award for excellence in library public relations.

From 2006 the ALA annually selects a class of Emerging Leaders, typically comprising about 100 librarians and library school students. This minor distinction is a form of organizational outreach to new librarians. The Emerging Leaders are allocated to project groups tasked with developing solutions to specified problems within ALA divisions. The class meets at the ALA Midwinter and Annual Meetings, commonly January and June. Project teams may present posters of their completed projects at the Annual.

Conferences

The ALA and its divisions hold numerous conferences throughout the year. The two largest conferences are the annual conference and the midwinter meeting. The latter is typically held in January and focused on internal business, while the annual conference is typically held in June and focused on exhibits and presentations. The ALA annual conference is notable for being one of the largest professional conferences in existence, typically drawing over 25,000 attendees.

POLITICAL POSITIONS

The ALA advocates positions on United States political issues that it believes are related to libraries and librarianship. For court cases that touch on issues about which the organization holds positions, the ALA often files amici curiae briefs, voluntarily offering information on some aspect of the case to assist the court in deciding a matter before it. The ALA has an office in Washington, D.C., that lobbies Congress on issues relating to libraries, information and communication. It also provides materials to libraries that may include information on how to apply for grants, how to comply with the law, and how to oppose a law.

Intellectual Freedom

The primary documented expressions of the ALA's intellectual freedom principles are the Freedom to Read Statement and the Library Bill of Rights; the Library Bill of Rights urges libraries to "challenge censorship in the fulfillment of their responsibility to provide information and enlightenment." The ALA Code of Ethics also calls on librarians to "uphold the principles of intellectual freedom and resist all efforts to censor library resources."

The ALA maintains an Office for Intellectual Freedom (OIF) headed by Barbara M. Jones, former University Librarian for Wesleyan University and internationally known intellectual freedom advocate and author. She is the second director of the Office for Intellectual Freedom, succeeding Judith Krug, who headed the office for four decades. OIF is charged with "implementing ALA policies concerning the concept of intellectual freedom," that the ALA defines as "the right of every individual to both seek and receive information from all points of view without restriction.

It provides for free access to all expressions of ideas through which any and all sides of a question, cause or movement may be explored." Its goal is "to educate librarians and the general public about the nature and importance of intellectual freedom in libraries." The OIF compiles lists of challenged books as reported in the media and submitted to them by librarians across the country. In 1999, radio personality Laura Schlessinger campaigned publicly against the ALA's intellectual freedom policy, specifically in regard to the ALA's refusal to remove a link on its web site to a specific sex-education site for teens.

Sharon Presley said, however, that Schlessinger "distorted and misrepresented the ALA stand to make it sound like the ALA was saying porno for 'children' is O.K." In 2002, the ALA filed suit with library users and the ACLU against the United States Children's Internet Protection Act (CIPA), which required libraries receiving federal E-rate discounts for Internet access to install a "technology protection measure" to prevent children from accessing "visual depictions that are obscene, child pornography, or harmful to minors."

At trial, the federal district court struck down the law as unconstitutional. The government appealed this decision, and on June 23, 2003, the Supreme Court of the United States upheld the law as constitutional as a condition imposed on institutions in exchange for government funding. In upholding the law, the Supreme Court, adopting the interpretation urged by the U.S. Solicitor General at oral argument, made it clear that the constitutionality of CIPA would be upheld only "if, as the Government represents, a librarian will unblock filtered material or disable the Internet software filter without significant delay on an adult user's request."

Privacy

In 2003, the ALA passed a resolution opposing the USA PATRIOT Act, which called sections of the law "a present danger to the constitutional rights and privacy rights of library users". Since then, the ALA and its members have sought to change the law by working with members of Congress and educating their communities and the press about the law's potential to violate the privacy rights of library users.

ALA has also participated as an *amicus curiae* in lawsuits filed by individuals challenging the constitutionality of the USA PATRIOT Act, including a lawsuit filed by four Connecticut librarians after the library consortium they managed was served with a National Security Letter seeking information about library users. After several months of litigation, the lawsuit was dismissed when the FBI decided to withdraw the National Security Letter.

In 2007 the "Connecticut Four" were honoured by the ALA with the Paul Howard Award for Courage for their challenge to the National Security Letter and gag order provision of the USA PATRIOT Act. In 2006, the ALA sold humourous "radical militant librarian" buttons for librarians to wear in support of the ALA's stances on intellectual freedom, privacy, and civil liberties. Inspiration for the button's design came from documents obtained from the FBI by the Electronic Privacy Information Center (EPIC) through a Freedom of Information Act (FOIA) request. The request revealed a series of e-mails in which FBI agents complained about the "radical, militant librarians" while criticizing the reluctance of FBI management to use the secret warrants authorized under Section 215 of the USA PATRIOT Act.

Copyright

The ALA "supports efforts to amend the Digital Millennium Copyright Act (DMCA) and urges the courts to restore the balance in copyright law, ensure fair use and protect and extend the public domain". It supports changing copyright law to eliminate damages when using orphan works without permission; is wary of digital rights management; and, in ALA v. FCC, successfully sued the Federal Communications Commission to prevent regulation that would enforce next-generation digital televisions to contain rights-management hardware. It has joined the Information Access Alliance to promote open access to research. The Copyright Advisory Network of the Association's Office for Information Technology Policy provides copyright resources to libraries and the communities they serve.

INDIAN ASSOCIATION OF SPECIAL LIBRARIES AND INFORMATION CENTRES (IASLIC)

Indian Association of Special Libraries and Information Centres (IASLIC): Three leading librarians from Calcutta, J. Saha, A. K. Mukherjee and G. B. Ghosh convened a meeting of librarians and documentalists on June 25, 1955 at Indian Museum, Calcutta.

OBJECTIVES

The objectives of IASLIC are to

* Promote the quality of Library and Information Services;
* Coordinate the activities;
* Foster mutual cooperation and assistance among the special libraries, scientific, technological and research institutions, learned societies, commercial organizations, industrial research establishments as well as centres of studies in social sciences and humanities;
* Improve the technical efficiency of the professionals;
* Act as a centre of research and studies in special librarianship and documentation techniques; and
* Act as a centre of information in scientific, technical and other related fields of LIS in pursuance of the aforesaid objects.

ORGANIZATION

The general body of the members of IASLIC biennially elects 14 office-bearers and 20 members of the Council, which is the highest organ to formulate the policies and programmes of work. The Council appoints from among its members the Executive and Finance Committee consisting of 8 office-bearers and 4 members to manage the regular activities. Six Divisions are also constituted by the Council for each term.

They are:

* Documentation Services;
* Education;

* Publication and Publicity;
* Library Services;
* Documentary Reproduction and Translation; and
* Cooperation and Coordination of Libraries.

MEMBERSHIP

IASLIC is composed of four kinds of members, namely Honourary Membership, Donor Membership, Institutional Membership, Individual Membership.

FUNCTIONS AND ACTIVITIES

* *OCLAI:* To bring about mutual co-operation and unified action on matters of common interests, IASLIC mooted the idea of forming the Joint Council of Library Associations of India (JOCLAI) especially of those at national level. The JOCLAI meetings take place during the national meets of each IASLIC and ILA. It has formulated a Code of Ethics for the library profession in India.
* *Documentation, Documentary Reproduction and Translation Services:* The IASLIC undertakes compilation of bibliographies and English translation of documents from Russian, German, French, Chinese, Japanese, etc. and also undertakes imaging of documents for archiving. All these services are provided on non-profit basis.
* *Library Consultancy Service:* The Association undertakes consultancy services like creation of computerized bibliographic databases, retrospective conversion of records, preservation and conservation of documents, cataloguing, classification and stock verification in public and private organizations on non-profit basis.
* *Publication:* Its publications include IASLIC Bulletin, IASLIC Newsletter, Different books, Monographs, Directory, IASLIC Proceedings, IASLIC Annual Report, etc.
* *Seminars, Conferences, Workshops and Training:* The

Association in its continuing education programmes conducts short term courses, workshops, round tables, seminars etc. It holds a biennial seminar and a conference in alternate years.

* *Mailing Lists and Forum:* IASLIC Council created Special Interest Groups (SIG) to bring together persons of common interests. SIG Group meetings are held during IASLIC Conference of common interests. The SIG includes SIG on Industrial Information; SIG on Social Science Information, SIG on Computer Application, SIG on Humanities Information, SIG on Informetrics, and SIG on Library and Information Science Education.
* *Others:* The IASLIC conducts study circle meetings for discussion on various issues of interest concerning LIS. It also conduct Ranganathan Memorial Lecture which has been held since 1993 on any topic of Library, Information and Communication science by leading personalities of the profession. Besides, it also conducts Annual Special Lecture and celebrates the Librarian's Day every year.

LIBRARY, ARCHIVE, AND MUSEUM (LAM)

RISING FROM THE RENAISSANCE

The achievements of the modern world are a direct consequence of coming to know and understand the world. Coming to know the world has required systematic creation of order from confusion. We see order in the maintenance of civil society, in the transport of people and cargo, in the maintenance of currency and credit, in the global network of communications. Nevertheless, there is still much confusion to testify to the emergent nature of knowledge. Confusion arises at the intersection of the known and the unknown, and is an essential feature of the expanding frontier of knowledge.

Knowledge is created by managing the ambiguity inherent in the unknown. The more effectively ambiguity is managed, the more rapidly and effectively knowledge is acquired and progress is sustained. Ambiguity in the creation of knowledge arises when one doubts or is uncertain regarding the interpretation or meaning of some piece of information. The centrality of ambiguity in knowledge creation is evident throughout the history of epistemology, but it can be seen in stark clarity through the work of key individuals in the late Renaissance who leveraged the institutions of their time to frame what we now recognize as modern scholarship.

This work is far too short to recount the history of western intellectual development, but a few key points are worth noting to frame our discussion of the role of the LAM in building the knowledge-based world we know today. The essential elements of the story are the slow departure of western philosophical thinking from the tradition of scholasticism that dominated intellectual development for centuries.

The scholastic construct was built on the writings of Aristotle and elaborated through the patristic writings of the western Christian church. A key point in this departure was the work of Thomas Aquinas in the 13th century. Aquinas adopted the view of the 12th century Arabian scholar Ibn Roschd (Averroes) that Aristotle's philosophy required the separation of religion and philosophy into two different spheres of mental endeavor. In intellectual enquiry reason must prevail in exposition of faith.

Aquinas argued successfully that intellect is a legitimate force in the construction of theology, and by extension, all vital realms of human endeavor. This argument sowed the seeds of the Renaissance by establishing intellectual enquiry as a kind of piety, even when the enquiry appeared to challenge prevailing religious beliefs. The importance of this break-through is seen directly in the work of two philosophers of the early 17th century, Rene Descartes and Francis Bacon, who helped lay the foundations of modern scientific enquiry. Descartes' 1641 *Meditations Concerning First Philosophy* was addressed to the faculty of theology at the University of Paris.

Descartes dwelt at length on Aquinas' arguments regarding the need to exercise reason in theology, but went beyond to argue that use of reason in addressing all problems of knowledge was a kind of worship that must not be suppressed in ill-considered defence of the faith. In the realm of ideas, Decartes' major contribution was a refutation of the particularist effort to build general epistemic understanding from *prima facie* intuitions about particular items of knowledge. He argued that *prima facie* intuitions are unstable and unreliable, and recommended instead the use of method to develop settled and reflective intuitions that would allow credible claims about particular knowledge.

The resulting Cartesian revolution vaunted reason as the means to resolve ambiguities that arise when empirical facts do not match *a priori* assumption. Descartes' work is remarkable in that it survived the scrutiny of the Church even as the Church was reeling from the revolution begun by Martin Luther at the turn of the 16th century. Paris in the early 17th century was in the grips of the counterreformation led by Francis de Sales and Vincent de Paul. It is clear that Descartes was well aware of the gravity of his endeavor.

His *Meditations* was actually a letter to the Church hierarchy presenting a meticulous apology for importance of preserving reason above all in the work of the pious scholar. His success in this opened the door for the triumph of the rational in the Roman Catholic realm following the Reformation, and in so doing, established a common scholarly bond with the Reformed realm. Francis Bacon's 1623 work, *The Great Instauration or Renewal of the Sciences,* was also addressed to church leaders who might regard it as a threat to the faith, but his tack was fundamentally different from that of Descartes.

Bacon worked from an England already swept by the Reformation, and the introduction to Instauration reads very much like Descartes' introduction to his Meditations. Bacon takes great care to show that the scholarship and science he advocates are in the service of God and not a threat to faith. Unlike Descartes, however, Bacon argued that fundamental questions about the nature of the world could not be explained through rationality alone.

Moreover, he explicitly links his philosophy to Aristotle's logic, naming the second part of his *Instauration* the *New Organon,* after Aristotle's *Organon*. Bacon argued that ambiguity in understanding of the material world could only be resolved through systematic empirical investigation, and through the application of what would in time be called inductive reasoning. While Bacon's philosophy never achieved the status of Descartes in the realm of the mind, his work had a profound practical influence on the conduct of scholarly enquiry. This is especially true in what we now call the natural sciences, where Bacon was arguably the most powerful advocate of getting out and looking at things instead of only ruminating about them.

An essential contribution of both Descartes and Bacon was the recognition that knowledge could only be achieved by the application of *method,* a systematic protocol abstracted from the effort to understand any given thing, but applicable to the effort to understand many things. The methods of reason and empiricism are complementary and are often used iteratively on the path to knowledge. The quest for ultimate knowledge is the establishment of concrete, global understanding from the evidence of the particular.

The effect of the Cartesian and Baconian traditions was the separation of the realm of faith from that of knowledge, and the establishment of systematic method using reason and investigation as the tools by which knowledge is created. The LAM played a critical role in the evolution of these traditions from the early 17th century onward. In time, they became fundamental institutional mechanisms facilitating knowledge creation and sharing.

The LAM provided a distributed and consistent mechanism whereby the important questions of the time could be exchanged among scholars, and the means for answering those questions would be made accessible. We do not mean to imply that the LAM were nonexistent prior to 1600. Archives, for example, are an ancient phenomenon.

The American Heritage Dictionary of the English Language defines an archive as "a place or collection containing records, documents, or other materials of historical interest. Often used in the plural: *old land deeds in the municipal archives.*" The retention of "old land deeds" and similar records related to property characterizes archives from the earliest eras.

It has been a practice for millennia record upon birth an individual's given name and location of birth, usually accompanied by attributions of parentage, each person born into a locale. Property and identity records are needed to maintain the social order. Nevertheless, the LAM as we know them today emerged mainly during the Enlightenment and the Industrial Revolution. Equally important for our story, the modern LAM were *causes* of the Enlightenment and the Industrial Revolution, and the subsequent material progress the world has enjoyed as a result.

THE RISE OF THE MODERN LAM

We combine the history of libraries and archives for our investigation of the rise of the modern LAM. We begin with museums because they are most directly tied to the revolution in thinking of the early 17th century. We then extend this discussion to libraries and archives to illustrate the depth of institutional embeddings with which the LAM have become epistemic infrastructure in the knowledge-based economy.

The Rise of "Wonder" and the Creation of the Modern Museum

It seems obvious to the modern observer that the public display of interesting items has great value in the education and enlightenment of the population. That was not evident prior to the Enlightenment. The museum as we know it today grew out of a form of entertainment that slowly evolved into a deliberate practice of collecting. The recognition of the scholarly utility of collecting was contemporaneous with the revolution in thinking illustrated by Galileo, Erasmus of Rotterdam, Descartes, Francis Bacon, Newton, Spinoza, Rabelais, Montaigne, Voltaire, Rousseau, Locke, Hume and others.

Nevertheless, the roots of collecting arose not from the realm of philosophy or natural philosophy, but in the practical quest for novelty and utility in agriculture and medicine. A useful case for illustrating the rise of the modern museum is found in the history of the Ashmolean Museum, part of Oxford University since the late 17th century.

The museum is regarded as the oldest in the UK, and it might well be the oldest surviving museum in the world. However, its antiquity is only part of what makes the Ashmolean useful as an example.

The history of the Ashmolean traces the very concept of the museum from the tradition of the private collections of individuals that arose in the 16th century. The Ashmolean arose from the collection of the John Tredescants, a father and son both named John who built their collection between 1610 and 1662. Both Tradescants were master gardeners by profession, and their most extensive collecting was done in the realm of plants.

The elder John's service as gardener to various noblemen required him to make numerous journeys to Holland and France to collect plants. His service to Edward, Lord Wotton, at Salisbury House near Canterbury, also brought him into contact with global traders and promoters of settlement in the recently established British colonies. He entered the service of Sir Dudley Digges of the East India Company, in whose employ he made a trip to Russia in 1618 and accompanied the British fleet in its mission to quell the Barbary pirates in 1620.

During these missions he began collecting artifacts and recording information about his collections in a journal. Tradescant's fortunes changed dramatically in 1622 when he became gardener to the powerful George Villiers, First Duke of Buckingham, and began landscaping New Hall in Essex. Tradescant collected in earnest on behalf of Buckingham, at one point directing Edward Nicholas, Secretary of the Navy, to instruct all merchants engaged in trade in the New World to be on the look out for a long list of rarities, concluding with the admonition to bring "any thing that is strang".

Tradescant also began aggressive collecting for himself, and by the time of Buckingham's assassination in 1626, had amassed one of the best collections in Europe. Shortly after Buckingham's death, Tradescant was appointed gardener at the royal palace at Oatlands in Surrey, which further established him in the upper echelon of royal society. He also established residence in South Lambeth, across the Thames from London at Westminster. Several rooms of his Lambeth House were dedicated to display of his collection, which became widely known as John Tredescant's Rarities.

Tradescant opened his collection to the public under the name The Ark, and apparently charged admission. On his death in 1638, his son John took over as gardener at Oatlands, and also became the keeper of the collection. The younger Tradescant expanded the collection significantly, and personally visited the Virginia colonies to acquire artifacts. In 1850 the younger Tradescant met Elias Ashmole, a successful lawyer who had studied a variety of subjects at Oxford and had grown attached to the institution.

Ashmole was one of the most learned astrologers and alchemists of his time, and had written an historical anthology of alchemy that had gained him renown. He was also an early member, and some argue a founder, of The Royal Society, and was fascinated by the emerging practice of scientific discovery. Through Ashmole, the younger Tradescant obtained service as gardener of Oxford's medicinal garden. Ashmole grew close to the Tradescant family, and recognized the importance of the collection. In the early 1650's, with Tradescant's consent, Ashmole and a colleague, Dr. Thomas Wharton, began documenting the entire collection.

The document was published as the *Musaeum Tradescantianum* in 1656. The end of the document names over 100 contributors to the collection, providing a fascinating picture of the Tradescants' social networks among the most learned people of England at that time. By 1559 the younger Tradescant was concerned about the future of the collection. He had no heir, and no obvious means of keeping the collection together after he and his wife died.

In fact, he was forced to close The Ark in 1661 under pressure from a corrupt and grasping courtier named Sir Henry Herbert, the King's Master of the Revels, who attempted to tax the establishment as an entertainment. Under the influence of Tradescant's friends, the King reversed the order, but The Ark never reopened. John Tradescant the younger died in 1662. In a series of disputes with Tradescant's widow over various versions of wills her husband left, Ashmole managed to gain legal control over the entire collection. He obtained the full physical collection by the early 1670's and was showing them to learned colleagues, although not to the general public as the Tradescants had done with The Ark.

In 1683 Ashmole dedicated the entire collection to Oxford University, whereupon it evolved over the next century into the Ashmolean Museum. The evolution of the Ashmolean was not a unique event. Throughout Europe from the middle of the sixteenth century onward a remarkable synthesis began in which gardeners active in the collection of plants expanded their collecting to include other natural creations and man-made artifacts. The movement first took shape in Italy in the collections of Francesco Calceolari, Ulisse Aldrovandi, Michele Mercati and Ferrante Imperato.

None of these collectors were from the aristocracy, but rather were learned members of the emerging middle class who had climbed the social ladder through the apparatus of the university. Calceolari and Imperato owned pharmacies and depended on botanical medicines that they grew; Mercati was a physician and keeper of the medicinal garden in the Vatican; Aldrovandi was a professor of natural philosophy at Bologna and keeper of its medicinal garden.

Two of these collections were meticulously documented: Calceolari's by 1584 and Aldrovandi's by 1594. The resulting catalogs were shared among collectors in manuscript form, creating a discourse independent of the physical specimens, but nonetheless grounded by the specimens. The practice of collecting expanded in Italy through the collections of Manfredo Settala, Lodvovico Moscardo and Ferdinando Cospi, each with published catalogs that were widely circulated. The travels of the aristocracy, many of whom were taken with these collections as a kind of entertainment, spread the word on collecting throughout Europe.

Collecting became a popular activity resulting in what became known in German as Wunderkammeren, or Wonder Cabinets. By the early 17th century Wunderkammern were becoming common in the Netherlands, and often contained exotic specimens drawn from the rapid expansion of Dutch exploration. Among the most important Dutch collections were those of the brothers Jan and Gerard Reynst and of Fred-erickRuysch, both in Amsterdam. Ruysch's collection, in particular, was important because it contained the most extensive set of preserved human and animal organs and body parts yet assembled.

Olaus Worm's collection in Copenhagen was also a vital anatomical collection, and with Ruysch's, had a significant influence on the development of anatomical medicine. Universities played a key role in the rise of the modern museum. As already shown in the case of the Tradescants, it is likely that their collection would have been dissipated and destroyed had it not been acquired by Ashmolean and given to Oxford. But the role of universities had already emerged clearly in the rise of the medicinal gardens and the focus on the collection, identification, classification and testing of plants in medical treatment.

The first known medicinal garden in Europe was in Pisa, established in 1543. By the end of the century the Pisa garden was accompanied by a gallery for display of preserved specimens and a growing collection of interesting artifacts brought back from the orient by travellers. The University of Leiden established a gallery attached to its medicinal garden and another attached to its anatomy laboratory by the late 16th century.

The establishment of collections in universities spread quickly through the 17th century, but many of these were haphazard affairs that were not systematically documented or preserved. The evolution of the modern museum for scholarly enquiry was also inspired by a society of learning that called upon the "invisible college" of scholars distributed throughout the world to collaborate through meetings and correspondence.

This was The Royal Society of Great Britain, established by Robert Boyle, John Wilkins, John Wallis, John Evelyn, Robert Hooke, Christopher Wren and William Petty, most of whom were affiliated in some respect with the Tradescants' collection. The Royal Society created what it called a "Repository" under the supervision of its Curator of Experiments in 1663, built largely around the cabinet of Robert Hubert. By 1665 the Repository had a printed catalog. Though a smaller collection than the Tradescants', it was almost entirely devoted to natural objects.

Most significant for our purposes was The Royal Society's decision in 1669 to collect all natural objects to be found in the British Isles that were not yet contained in the Repository, and the subsequent decision to use the Repository as the chief resource in constructing a universal taxonomy of natural objects. Although the effort to create the universal taxonomy failed, it established within the society the goal of systematically building a coherent natural science that remains the mission of The Royal Society that continues to this day.

The subsequent life of the Repository itself was less glorious. It became a burden on the Society and its maintenance suffered steadily over the decades until the residual collection was given to the British Museum in 1779. In reflecting on the emergence of the Wunderkammer as precursors to modern museums, we see three crucial elements in the rise of modern science and scholarship.

The first was the essential role of collections in stimulating efforts to comprehend and understand the natural world. Collecting, to use Lugli's term, was a form of enquiry: a means of creating a didactic resource that not only made sense to the collector, but that could be shared among collectors to create a common knowledge. This new knowledge revealed in graphic terms the inadequacies of the Aristotelian accounts of the natural world. It began a protracted effort of clarification and correction of that record, and its expansion to previously unknown realms. This was a vital step in the abandonment of scholasticism and the rise of modern scholarly and scientific enquiry.

Through the existential act of placing natural objects on display, the observer was required to try to explain the existence of such a thing in light of old beliefs. The initial purpose of these collections was simply to elicit wonder, but the act of wondering led soon to enquiring and theorizing. In a way, Master of the Revels Henry Herbert was not far wrong in attempting to cast The Ark as an entertainment. Wonder at the objects in The Ark spread its fame, and it was entertainment that eventually established museums as a public educational experience.

The political and social ramifications of this merger of entertainment and public education were soon seen in the displays of the skeleton of the dinosaur *Iguanadon*, discovered in 1822 in southern England. The museum patron was compelled to ask where such a thing came from, since it obviously was not like anything anyone had seen. The display of dinosaur skeletons over a quarter of a century to untold numbers of British citizens paved the way for widespread alarm at the publication of Darwin's *Origin of the Species* in 1859.

Darwin put the idiosyncratic fossil record square in the path of the literalist version of Creation from Judeo-Christian tradition, and offered instead a mechanistic model of the emergence and diversification of life. It seems doubtful that Darwin's work would have elicited the public reaction it did had the stage not been set by tradition of the Wunderkammern. The second element of the Wunderkammern was their role in the rise of systematic method in the sciences.

To move beyond naïve enquiry and into deep understanding of complex relations among natural objects requires careful, repeated observation. The collections evolved from being somewhat haphazard and random, following the fancy of the collector, and towards a much more focused and systematic pursuit of all examples of the class. This was particularly true in the case of the collectors of natural objects, who increasingly sought to obtain as many different kinds of birds, beetles, shells or whatever objects of collecting caught their attention.

When the collections became large enough to permit careful comparison of morphology among the specimens, the first efforts at taxonomy construction and classification got underway in earnest. A lively trade in travel among collections by collectors emerged, permitting first-hand comparison of specimens and argument over classification. This practice shifted the discussion of the natural order away from the scholastic reflection on God's intention in the creation and the moralistic medieval ascription of anthropomorphic traits to animals, and towards the empirical facts resident in the specimens themselves.

Science was no longer driven by how the investigator thought things ought to be, but rather by things as they clearly are in the state of nature. The third major element of the Wunderkammern was the corollary documentation of the collections, as in the Musaeum Tradescantianum. These catalogs allowed the collections to circulate in a kind of virtual form, greatly aided by the advent of printing. Scholars in disparate places could compare their local collections with the catalogs of other collections, identifying discrepancies and questions that could be resolved through further correspondence, discussion, and examination.

In this way the effort to identify, classify, and compare all of nature first took shape and moved forward. As the experience of The Royal Society's universal taxonomy revealed, the problem was larger and more difficult than it appeared. Nevertheless, books based on collections, especially when illustrated, played a major role in moving forward what became in time systematic biology. The effort to systematically classify natural objects went back to Aristotle, but little progress was made on the matter until the advent of systematic collecting and documentation in the 17th and 18th centuries.

Martin Lister's 1686 *Historia Conchylorium* systematically compared over 1,000 mollusk shells rendered in plates, and

Georg Rumphius' 1711 *Thesarus Cochlearum* expanded on that effort. These and other illustrated catalogs of collections of natural objects laid the groundwork for the masterpiece *Systema Naturae* first published in 1738 by Sweden's Carl von Linné upon which all subsequent biological taxonomy was built. The Wunderkammern were thereby the progenitors of scholarly and scientific collaboration on which knowledge required for the industrial revolution was built.

The details of the processes by which the Wunder-kammern became the institutionalized museums of today are beyond the scope of this paper, but a few indicators are useful. The British Royal Library founded in 1471 was combined with the newly purchased Sloane, Harleian, and Cotton libraries in 1753 to become the nucleus of the British Museum. The museum added collections of artifacts and natural objects in the ensuing decades, and became a major institution of learning by the time its key buildings were completed in the 1830's.

The Royal Botanical Gardens at Kew originally were private gardens of the monarchy, similar to those tended by the Tradescants at Oatlands, but took on new importance for science under the direction of the avid naturalist Sir Joseph Banks in 1772. Although the gardens suffered major decline following Banks' tenure, they were revitalized and turned into a major center of learning with the establishment of the garden's department of economic botany in 1847. The French Jardin des Plantes, founded as a medicinal garden by Louis XIII in 1626, expanded greatly under the direction of Georges-Louis LeClerc between 1739 and 1788.

LeClerc raised funds for the garden and, following the initial publication of his influential *Histoire Naturelle* in 1749, began a number of large collections that became the French National Museum of Natural History. By the turn of the 19th century the museum was an internationally important center of study, engaging figures such as Jean-Baptiste Lamark, Bernard Germain and George Cuvier who had a great influence on the evolution the natural sciences. The 19th century was the golden age of museum expansion and stabilization.

Philadelphia's Academy of Natural Sciences opened in 1812. The Peale Museum opened in Baltimore in 1814. The National Museum of Denmark was established in 1816. The ethnographic museum of the Academy of Sciences in Petrograd opened in 1836. The Smithsonian Institution got going in 1846. The British Great Exhibition of 1851 had a major influence on the relationship between display of collections and emerging industrial enterprise. Harvard University established museums for botany, zoology, and anthropology between 1858 and 1866. The Deutsches Museum opened in 1903.

Since that time, museums have become common fixtures in all developed countries and can be found in many developing countries. Many museums today are major centres of research, but they also play an important role in shaping social discourse regarding contemporary controversies. Part of this influence occurs through the very act of selecting what will be displayed, and how those displays will be presented. Most museums have collections far larger than their space available for display, so what gets displayed can make a statement.

For example, a display of artifacts of Southern Pacific island societies might be read as a statement about what has come to be called "Polynesia". This kind of labeling is more explicit in instances such as the US National Museum of the American Indian or the numerous Holocaust Museums. The very idea of the "American Indian" originates with a mistaken assumption by early European explorers who thought they had reached India, and extends to the lumping together of a large number of highly specialized cultures who were as different from one another as Danes and Italians.

Similarly, the vast majority of the holocaust museums understandably place the extermination of Jews in the foreground, even though Nazi cruelty extended to other classes such as the mentally ill and the politically rebellious. Museums, almost without intending to do so, provide a political context for their collections that affects public perception. The contextual commentary included in the narratives about displays offers yet another means by which museums affect the public's understanding of collections and what they mean.

A museum of technology such as the Deutsches Museum in Munich can display a combination of train locomotives, trucks, and automobiles to signify forms of land transport, or to signify progress in the design of propulsion technology. Only the explicit guidance of the curator will construct a consistent frame of mind in the visitor. Such explicit guidance often escapes notice because the underlying disputes are not in the public consciousness. However, from time to time the commentary can cause extraordinary controversy, as in the case of the Enola Gay exhibit at the Smithsonian Institution's National Air and Space Museum in the mid-1990s commemorating the dropping of nuclear weapons on Japan in WW II.

In one of the most celebrated public fights over a museum exhibit in U.S. history, curators found themselves locked in a struggle between those who wished to foreground the difficult choices to be made in the bombing, and those who wished to commemorate the heroism of those whose efforts brought the U.S. victory over Japan. As Tom Crouch, curator of the museum put it, "Do you want to do an exhibit intended to make veterans feel good, or do you want an exhibition that will lead our visitors to think about the consequences of the atomic bombing of Japan? Frankly, I don't think we can do both." In the end, Crouch was proved right, and the exhibit was constructed to make veterans feel good.

Museums provide a good example of the emerging discussion of the construction of "narratives" in collection and display. Narratives are the means by which artifacts are pulled into the foreground or pushed into the background in ways that create a story for the visitor that cannot emerge simply from the presence of the artifacts themselves. As in the case of the Iguanadon, the narrative did not need to be more than the simple display of the artifact. The emerging tension between strictly biblical accounts of creation and the apparent contradictions of the geological record was evident to all who saw the exhibit.

The Iguanadon skeleton was unavoidably a gauntlet thrown at the feet of the strict creationists, with the challenge, "Explain *this*." Explanation was not easy. The ready response that the fossil bones were merely those of some great creature destroyed in the biblical flood of Noah's time raised questions about why Noah did not rescue such creatures along with all the others recounted in the story of the Ark. There was nothing fictional about the fossils. Their concreteness threw into ambiguity the accepted narrative of the time.

Similarly, the Enola Gay exhibition at the National Air and Space Museum queried whether it was possible to have a master narrative that could speak simultaneously to multiple audiences, enlightening all and offending none: could the master narrative be controlled in an "objective" manner, or was it inherently subjective and perhaps overtly biased? The facts of the Enola Gay, the war, the bombing, and the aftermath were never in dispute by any of the antagonists. At the heart of the argument was the question of what it all *means*.

In other words, the difficult challenge was to wrap up the iteration between the unambiguous and the ambiguous in a manner that yielded knowledge acceptable to the observers. We close our discussion of museums with the observations of Susan Leigh Star and Jamie Griesemer from their study of the museum of systematic biology at the University of California, Berkeley.

They recognized the museum as a site very much dedicated to the generation of knowledge, but they also noted that the key participants in the museum world–collectors, curators, and the scientists who used the museum–each saw different purposes for the museum.

They coined the phrase "boundary object" to denote the role of the museum, which was explicitly to bring together a highly heterogeneous group of people around a shared interest in flora and fauna that constituted a knowledge community. Boundary objects are concrete to each specific user, but plastic enough to be interpreted differently by different users. They are devices for mediating the disagreements that lie at the heart of the role of LAM in the realm of knowledge.

Libraries and Archives

We combine the history of libraries and archives for our investigation of the rise of the modern LAM. Although archives and libraries often are used for somewhat different purposes and are commonly separated institutionally, they are fundamentally similar in their objectives. From the perspective of an epistemic infrastructure of knowledge communities, the similarities between libraries and archives are more central to our argument than are their differences.

We argue that the articulation of libraries as collections of published works and archives as repositories of unpublished primary sources is a relatively recent aberration that developed as a consequence of industrial rationalization and specialization and that is increasingly difficulty to sustain in light of the potential for digital convergence. The origins of libraries and archives are intertwined with the emergence of writing, the development of commerce and accounting, the establishment of the rule of law, and the genesis of scholarly discourse.

The earliest physical evidence of repositories of clay tablets in the Near East suggests that documents were created, collected, and stored to serve pragmatic purposes. Records commonly found in ancient archives include the laws of the land, evidence of administrative transactions, financial and accounting records, and documents that enforced ownership and control over property and people, reflecting constants in records creation regardless of the nature of governmental, religious, and economic institutions.

Recent scholarship suggests that written documents from the ancient and classical period, as well as the institutions that housed them, served many purposes beyond bureaucratic accounting. Stone tablets inscribed with laws and proclamations were erected in public places to inform citizen/subjects of their rights and responsibilities. Inscriptions on pottery and bronze may have played a role in deification, religious practice, and commemoration.

Ancient collections from the seventh and eighth centuries B.C.E. contain a mixture of administrative, spiritual, and literary texts. We can only speculate about the reasons why ancient and classical societies assembled collections of documents and artifacts and built temples to house them. Most scholars agree that ancient libraries and archives were intended to assemble documents in central locales where their owners, and in some cases a broader public, could consult, analyse, and compare multiple texts.

As collections grew in size and complexity, their custodians developed methods for organizing and managing large bodies of texts, using titles to readily distinguish one text from another, creating inventories and catalogs to keep track of what was in the collections, and imprinting documents with seals to assert authenticity.

Collections were housed in purpose-built structures or in fortified portions of royal palaces to protect them against fire, theft, and pillage. Libraries and archives also served as commanding symbols of authority and power. The legendary Library of Alexandria fulfilled more than the purpose of assembling all the world's known texts in a single monumental structure. By acquiring ancient texts and then translating them into Greek, ancient scribes and curators contributed to the hegemony of the Greek language, culture and worldview.

In an ancient context, that particular library enshrined a consciousness of community spread across time and space. To seek out all of the books in the wider world showed a consciousness of that world and a sense of meaningful communication within it.

The later Roman achievement was even greater, spreading Roman culture and law over a much vaster territory with lasting effects on language, social organization, and politics. Nevertheless, we have to deal with the fact that the Alexandrian Library was destroyed, that no library of Greek or Roman antiquity survived, and that the tradition of assembling collections and imposing order on them disappeared for nearly a millennium.

In the canonical interpretation of the history of Western civilization, the loss of organized institutions to collect, preserve, and share written texts equates to "the Dark Ages"-a period of primitive orality and personal autocratic rule enforced by might rather than the rule of law. Were it not for the "molding of Christian monasticism around the preser-vation and veneration of the written word," most ancient texts-both sacred and secular-would have vanished from human knowledge.

During the Middle Ages a veritable industry of salvaging, copying, and translating texts flourished in the monasteries of a Catholic Western Europe awakening from centuries of intellectual impoverishment. Historians of writing and literacy find many connections between the introduction of printing, the spread of Enlightenment thought, and the scientific revolution. Elisabeth Eisenstein treated the printing press as "an agent of change" in early modern Europe and attributed to new modalities of communication that enabled both the Reformation and the Scientific Revolution.

Although subsequent historians have questioned the extent to which Eisenstein ascribes causality to the technology of printing, her basic contention-that the availability of multiple, identical, and relatively inexpensive copies of texts had a profound impact on the circulation of ideas-remains largely unchallenged. In ways that we are only beginning to appreciate fully, the circulation of printed works fundamentally altered the transfer of knowledge between religious and secular cultures, from expert to novice, from academy to academy, from scientists to artisan, and across generations.

Latour refers to these knowledge-bearing objects as "immutable mobiles" which have the properties of being mobile but also immutable, presentable, readable and combinable with one another. Latour is less interested in the impact of printing technology on the history of ideas *per se*, than in the ways that scientists and bureaucrats manipulate texts, documents, and objects to convince and mobilize others to see the world the same way they do.

The advantage of the printing press for philosophers, scientists, and clerics was that it provided a means for those who were successful at mobilization to circulate their ideas and dominate on a larger scale. Latour's notion of immutable mobiles as knowledge-bearing objects that can be mobilized to spread ideas helps to explain the emergence or re-emergence of libraries, archives, and museums in the modern era as social projects intended to persuade and convince ever-expanding publics to perceive the world as coherent and knowable.

Libraries, archives, and museums, with their increasingly sophisticated systems for organizing and classifying monographs, scholarly journals, administrative documents, manuscripts, and physical specimens emerged as critical institutions, not only for collecting and organizing knowledge-bearing objects, but as sources for innovation and new ideas and vehicles for enhancing the circulation of ideas. These were not the only institutions that engaged in scientific enquiry and humanistic endeavors.

Libraries, archives, and museums grew hand-in-hand with the private publishing and the book trade, the emergence of modern the university, the maturation of scholarly societies, and the rationalization of the administrative apparatus of modern states. These forces worked together to further accelerate the production of books, administrative documents, maps, journals, reports, and the like and the collection of physical evidence that flowed into private and public collections.

The quest for a universal library was reinvigourated during the 17th and 18th centuries, not as an end in itself, but as a means of unearthing collections from private, princely, and ecclesiastical libraries and assembling all known works as the foundation from which new knowledge could be generated. In one of the earliest books on library design, Gabrial Naudé stressed the value of a comprehensive library containing all the principal authors who have written on a diversity of subjects and arranged for use of the public.

Naudé's *Advis pour dresser une Bibliothèque* was addressed to the president of the Parliament of Paris, himself a great book collector. Naudé's *Adivis* took aim at the cabinets of curiosity or *cabinet chosi,* distinguished mainly by their small collections of rare and precious works that nobles and wealthy aristocrats collected and assembled for display and personal satisfaction.

Naudé argued that:

> "It is more useful to and necessary to have, for example, a great quantity of books well bound in ordinary fashion than to fill only some small, pale, gilded, decorous room or cabinet enriched with all matter of little oddities [*mignardise*], luxuries, and superfluidities".

During the eighteenth and nineteenth centuries, libraries and archives grew in number and scope using a variety of means to assemble vast collections. Private collectors, who had gradually opened their "cabinets of curiosity" for viewing by privileged elites and for research by qualified scientists, began donating collections to fledgling libraries and archives in universities, major municipalities, and provincial towns. Progressive monarchs donated their private libraries to the citizens forming the early instances of royal libraries. During the French Revolution, the *Bibliothèque du Roi* became the *Bibliothèque Nationale*, vastly expanding its holding by adding an estimated 250,000 books, 14,000 manuscripts, and 80,000 engravings that were confiscated from the Church, emigrants, and the former nobility.

By 1800, national libraries existed in 20 different countries, including the United States which passed legislation establishing the Library of Congress that year. Most library and archival institutions built up their holdings by acquiring pre-existing collections through purchase, donation, and legal decree. During the 19 century, libraries and archives not only expanded their collections, they were transformed into modern institutions and instruments of industrialization, modernization, knowledge generation, and civic engagement.

The establishment of the *Archives nationale de France* immediately following the Revolution offers one particularly compelling example of the transformation of archives from private and parochial to public and national. Within a day of the storming of the Bastille on July 14, 1789, the municipal government of Paris dispatched guards to protect the prison archives from looting and pillage, beginning the long process of building a national collection of documentary sources.

Within a year, the National Assembly began planning for a universal bibliography of every book in every depository in the country.

By 1793, the government had confiscated thousands of ecclesiastical libraries and archives and seized the archives of exiled nobles, convicted counter-revolutionaries, the academies and scholarly societies of the Old Regime, and pre-revolutionary estates. The amassing of vast collections of books, archives, and manuscripts from pre-revolutionary institutions immediately raised questions about the purpose, value, uses, and organization of archives and libraries. Successive regimes in France between 1790 and 1870 proposed new approaches to the organization of French archives and libraries and questioned the purposes to which they ought to be put.

Throughout the 1790s, revolutionary leaders debated whether the archives of the Old Regime should be preserved as evidence of false ideas, as common heritage, and as rich treasures to be enjoyed by the citizens of the Republic; or whether they should be purged because they were no longer useful and risked poisoning the French citizenry with traitorous ideas. Historian Lara Moore, whether revolutionary leaders favoured destruction or preservation of the pre-revolutionary archives they agreed on two key points: that "the bibliographic and documentary legacy of the Old Regime was strongly connected to the French national identity... [and] that national collections ought to be publicly accessible." But just what did accessible to the public mean? This question took decades to resolve, not only because of the turmoil caused by successive changes in government, but because the notion of "publicly accessible archives" was so novel.

By 1839, it was obvious that simply confiscating archival and library collections and distributing them in to system of repositories did little to make the collections usable or useful. Early efforts to select critical documents, establish their authenticity, transcribe, translate and then publish them in documentary editions failed primarily because of the chaotic condition of pre-revolutionary archives and ambivalence on the part of public officials about opening the collections to the public. During the late July Monarchy the focus of attention shifted from detailed analysis of small corpora of documents to the organization of entire archives and libraries.

Departmental archives were the central focus of organization and classification activities guided by instructions from the Royal Archives that introduced a new principle for classification of archives, *respect des fonds,* or the principle of provenance. A *fonds* is the "whole of the records, regardless of form or medium, organically created and/or accumulated and used by a particular person, family or corporate body in the course of that creator's activities and functions." *Respect des fonds* implores archivists to maintain aggregations of documents based on the person or entity that accumulated the records or to restore such order if it has been lost.

Although a detailed discussion of the application of the principle of provenance is beyond the scope of this paper, the significance of this new classification approach should not be underestimated. It not only helped archivists overcome a variety of pragmatic problems that had plagued previous attempts at classifying French archives; by the late nineteenth century it emerged as the core principle for organizing modern archives and it remains the basic tenet of archival science today. Previous efforts to organize and classify French archives had used a variety of approaches; such as time periods or epochs, subject matter, strict chronology, author, location, and even size, shape and colour.

Not only was it impractical to sort large caches of documents by analysing each of them separately, such classification schemes were considered arbitrary and often controversial. The principle of provenance, in contrast to earlier criteria, was considered a reflection of the natural order of things. By keeping archives together as the originator has organized and used them, archivists preserved a larger context for their future interpretation and use. This approach to organizing archives spread to other parts of Western Europe, North America, and regions of the world under colonial domination. If we credit French archivists with developing an epistemic regime for archives, then we have to turn to the Library of Congress to find the origins of systematic classification standards for library materials.

The Library of Congress was established in 1800, when the seat of government was moved from New York to the new capital city of Washington. In 1802, President John Adams approved an appropriation of $5,000 to purchase "such books as may be necessary for the use of Congress." The first books, ordered from London, arrived in 1801 and were stored in the U.S. Capitol. The collection consisted of 740 volumes and three maps. After Washington was burned by the British during the War of 1812, Thomas Jefferson reestablished the Library by selling his own personal collection of 6,487 volumes to Congress in 1815.

At the time, Jefferson's library was considered the finest in America. When Jefferson sold his multifaceted, multilingual collection to Congress, he felt the need to defend its diversity by stating that there was "no subject to which a Member of Congress might not have occasion to refer", establishing a precedent for a comprehensive national collections. Progress towards the comprehensive collection that Mr. Jefferson had favoured was interrupted in the middle of the nineteenth century. In 1851 a fire in the Capitol destroyed 35,000 volumes of the 55,000 in the collection at the time, although Congress responded quickly by appropriating the funds to replace the lost books.

The fire was followed in 1859 by a repeal of the law providing for copyright deposits at the Library. U.S. copyright activities became centralized at the Patent Office, which meant that LC and the Smithsonian Institution no longer received copies of the books and pamphlets deposited for copyright under the 1846 law providing for the enrichment of library collections through copyright deposit. Efforts to build the collection resumed in the 1860s. For example, the Library acquired the 40,000 volumes from the Smithsonian's library in 1866. And by 1870, Congress had passed laws establishing the U.S. Copyright Office as an arm of the Library, thereby centralizing all copyright activities.

As in other countries with mandatory deposit of copyrighted works, the U.S, copyright laws were intended primarily to help the Library develop a comprehensive collection of printed books.

The influx of materials following the creation of copyright deposit laws in 1870, required both more space to refine ways of managing its collections. In 1896, just before the actual move to the new Jefferson Building, the Joint Library Committee held hearings about "the condition" of the Library and its possible reorganization. The hearings provided an occasion for a detailed examination of the Library's history and present functions and for a review of what new functions the Library might perform once it occupied the spacious new building.

The American Library Association sent six witnesses, including future Librarian of Congress Herbert Putnam from the Boston Public Library and Melvil Dewey from New York State Library. Members of Congress listened with great interest to the testimony of Putnam and Dewey, who argued that the national services of the Library should be greatly expanded. Dewey felt that the Library of Congress now had the opportunity to act as a true national library, which he defined as:

"a centre to which the libraries of the whole country can turn for inspiration, guidance, and practical help, which can be rendered so economically and efficiently in no other possible way".

In 1897, when the new Jefferson Building was occupied, the staff increased from 42 to 108, and separate divisions were formed for serials, maps, music, manuscripts, and graphic arts. Although the Library of Congress is most renowned for its large and diverse collections, its key role during the early twentieth century in the area of cataloging is most germane to our analysis of LAM. By the end of 1901 the Library of Congress, the first American library to reach one million volumes, had started organizing its enormous collections of recorded knowledge for public service. Library classification schemes were a nineteenth century invention.

Sir Anthony Pazinni, a librarian at the British Museum from 1831 to 1867 developed his 91 rules for cataloging in 1832. Jewett, 1853; Cutter, 1876 Melvil Dewey introduced the Dewey Decimal System in 1876 while he was librarian at Amherst College and expanded it at the New York State Library. In 1901, the Library of Congress published its first volume of a completely new classification scheme, based on the Library's own collections. The LC classification scheme, was not so much a methodological innovation in the field of library cataloging as a precursor for the development of uniform standards for organization and classification of library materials. This was accomplished in part through the development of the Library's card distribution services that sold and distribution of printed catalog cards to other libraries.

By 1900, there we . . . university libraries, . . . public libraries, and . . . other special libraries in the US which could purchase preprinted library cards for their catalogs rather cataloging their collection just as to idiosyncratic and institution-specific practices. For two thirds of a century the cataloging system was supported with the distribution of printed cards. In the late 1950's LoC began investigating the application of computers to library cataloging and eventually led the development during the 1960s of the machine-readable cataloging (MARC) format for identifying and exchanging information about bibliographic materials, which became a national standard in 1971.

During the 1970s, new inter-institutional consortia, such as OCLC, began to offer competing services for distribution of on-line cataloging services. The extension of the Library's classification and cataloging schemes to the rest of the nation led to a uniformity of cataloging across libraries subscribing to the service and some structures to support standard cataloging procedures. This epistemic infrastructure became further refined during the mid-twentieth century when LoC developed standard classification schemes and cataloging rules for subjects, names, titles, and an expanding variety of new media types. As part of a consortium that included the American Library Association and British participants, it helped develop the Anglo-American Cataloging Rules (AACR), first published in 1967, and eventually leading to a broader international agreement on uniform bibliographic description under the auspices of the International Federation of Library Associations (IFLA).

Discussion of classification: Although we tend to take the distinction between libraries and archives for granted and assume that libraries acquire and circulate printed resources while archives collect and preserve unique unpublished documentary sources, this distinction has never been that sharp. The distinction between libraries and archives evolved gradually as popular and public libraries emerged to support and channel the reading interests of an increasingly literate working class and archives defined themselves as repositories for the scholarly and scientific study of the past.

Public libraries, with small collections of recent and popular collections, and national archives, with large holdings of administrative documents accumulated by modern bureaucratic states, lie at two extremes of the archive-library spectrum. Along this spectrum, however, are many hybrid institutions that hold books, serials, manuscripts, maps, and archival collections. The book collection at the Library of Congress is the largest in the world, but it comprises only a portion of the total holdings which includes million of maps, photographs, motion picture films, newspapers, and manuscripts.

The manuscript division holds 50 million items in 11,000 different collections. The papers of many of the nation's founding fathers, including George Washington, Thomas Jefferson, and James Madison were transferred from the State Department archives to the Library's Manuscript Division in 1903 in part because the United States did not establish a National Archives until 1934. The British Library was part of the British Museum until 1962. Most major university libraries maintain not only general collections of books and serials used for teaching, but also many special collections for exploitation by researchers.

COLLECTING AS LEARNING AND KNOWING

The foregoing histories of the LAM provide strong evidence that collections played a crucial role in the establishment of knowledge communities.

No better summation of this can be found than Francis Bacon's own musing on the essential apparatus of the gentleman scholar in his 1594 Gesta Grayorum:

* First, the collecting of a most perfect and general library, wherein whatsoever the wit of man hath hitherto committed to books of worth, be they ancient or modern, printed or manuscript, European or of other parts, of one or other language, may be made contributory to your wisdom. Next, a spacious, wonderful garden, wherein whatsoever plant the sun of diverse climates, out of the earth of diverse molds, either wild or by the culture of man, brought forth, may be, with that care that appertaineth to the good prospering thereof, set and cherished; this garden to be built about with rooms to stable in all rare beasts and to cage in all rare birds, with two lakes adjoining, the one of fresh water, the other of salt, for like variety of fishes. And so you may have in small compass a model of universal nature made private. The third, a goodly huge cabinet, wherein whatsoever the hand of man by exquisite art or engine hath made rare in stuff, form, or motion; whatsoever singularity, chance, and the shuffle of things hath produced; whatsoever nature hath wrought in things that want life and may be kept, shall be sorted and included. The fourth, such a still-house, so furnished with mills, instruments, furnaces, and vessels as may be a palace fit for a philosopher's stone. Thus, when your excellency shall have added depth of knowledge to the fineness of your spirits and greatness of your power, then indeed shall you be a Trismegistus, and then when all other miracles and wonders shall cease, by reason that you shall

> have discovered their natural causes, yourself shall be left the only miracle and wonder of the world."

Two centuries after Bacon wrote his laundry list of scholarly needs the world had undergone profound changes that brought previously unimaginable individual opportunity and wealth. The rise of the institutionalized LAM paralleled both the Enlightenment and the Industrial Revolution.

Daniel Webster captured the power of this change and the centrality of knowledge in the change in a speech given on June 17, 1825 at the groundbreaking for the Bunker Hill monument in Massachusetts:

> A chief distinction of the present day is a community of opinions, and knowledge, amongst men, in different nations, existing in a degree heretofore unknown. Knowledge has, in our time, triumphed and is triumphing over distance, over differences of language, over diversity of habits, over prejudice and over bigotry... The whole world is becoming a common field of intellect to act in. Energy of mind, genius, power, wherever it exists, may speak out in any tongue, and the world will hear it. There is a vast commerce of ideas. There are marts and exchanges for intellectual discoveries, and a wonderful fellowship of these individual intelligences, which make up the mind and opinion of the age. Mind is the great lever of all things; human thought is the process by which human ends are ultimately answered; and the diffusion of knowledge, so astounding in the last half century, has rendered innumerable minds, variously gifted by nature, competent to be competitors, or fellow-workers, on the theatre of intellectual operation. From these causes important improvements have taken place in the personal condition of individuals. Generally speaking, mankind are not only better fed and better clothed, but they are able also to enjoy more leisure; they possess more refinement and selfrespect.

These two excerpts illustrate the profound shift from Bacon's enquiring gentleman to Webster's broad marketplace of ideas. In the relatively short time between these statements the pursuit of knowledge had emerged from the pastime of the curious individual and into the widespread creation of knowledge communities vital to society. Moreover, the industrial revolution had emerged from trial-and-error experimentation in the tradition of artisans and entered an era in which scientific and engineering knowledge was being systematically applied to accelerate the pace of progress.

By Webster's time this had already resulted in the refinement and application of the steam engine to ship and rail transport, the start of mechanistic agriculture through the cotton gin, the discovery of vaccination against viral disease, and the use of artificial fuel coal gas in the lighting of cities. Within the next fifty years Henry Bessemer revolutionized the making of steel, the railroad industry invented operations management, the telegraph was in regular use, Pasteur pioneered profound changes in human health, and warfare reached a harrowing level of carnage through new weaponry such as the machine gun.

On the social side, by the time of Webster's speech the world had seen the weakening of the British monarchy in favour of Parliament, the American and French revolutions, and the establishment of what would become modern democratic institutions. Within the fifty years following Webster's speech slavery was abolished and compulsory education was established in the industrializing countries of North America and Europe, a in the U.S. the Morrill Act and the establishment of the Land Grant tradition created a radical expansion in availability of higher education. The nineteenth century was the golden age in the evolution of the LAM.

This period saw the creation of nearly all of the world's great museums of natural history, art, and culture, the rise of the great state libraries, the establishment of many academic libraries, and the beginning of the public library systems. Industrialization, urbanization, and mass literacy added to functions to the LAM, and created further pressures to transform private collections of information and artifacts into public goods. During the latter half of the nineteenth century, private benefactors founded and provided resources for countless museums, galleries, historical societies, and libraries so that a broader public could appreciate and learn from collections of treasures that had accumulated over the centuries. These institutions often were steeped in a broader mission that went beyond building collections and preserving knowledge.

Many benefactors and the rapidly growing staffs of professional librarians and curators embraced the social mission of supporting universal education, providing citizens with the information and tools to make informed decisions, and teaching new urban residents how to make intelligent use of their leisure time. Libraries, historical societies, and museums also contributed to nation building by assembling documents and artifacts that provided a basis for a shared sense of the past and a common national and cultural identity.

During the industrial era, libraries, archives and museums assumed a series of functions that extended beyond simply collecting and organizing books, documents, and objects. These institutions brought together objects and specimens that could be examined sideby-side, and amassed large collections that were more valuable in the aggregate than they were dispersed in their natural environment. Experts in organization, classification, and taxonomy imposed an epistemic order on collections, explicitly for efficient management and tacitly to mobilize collections in the service of scientific discovery, an enlightened citizenry, and aesthetic discrimination.

Specialization and selection were the hallmarks of professionally managed institutions. During the industrial age, bibliographers, archivists, museologists, and scholars developed highly refined notions of physical formats and intellectual forms to distinguish publications from manuscripts and to separate documents from three-dimensional objects. These forms and genres defined the natural home for different types of cultural artifacts. Works of art belonged in art galleries, three-dimensional objects belonged in museums, books belonged in libraries, and unpublished, original documents belong in archives.

Libraries, archives, and museums further specialized by country, language and region, by topical area or discipline, and by audience. Within these specialized domains, classification systems and taxonomies drifted from idealized notions of organized universal collections of knowledge to highly refined collections tuned to particular audiences or user communities. The counter trend was the parallel development of the great national libraries, museums, and archives that attempted to collect comprehensively by building national bibliographies and erecting monuments for national treasures. Whether collections were highly refined or comprehensive, selection was instrumental in establishing institutional identity and ensuring the quality and legitimacy of sources.

The imprimatur of an established library, museum or archives bestowed on its contents a mark of authenticity, legitimacy, and authority. The naturalist seeking physical specimens, the historian searching for documents, or the private citizen looking for uplifting fiction could trust these institutions to provide the best evidence and the highest quality resources. Libraries, archives and museums also provided a means to accumulate and preserve knowledge over time. As sources for continuity, their function emerged as the accumulation of knowledge and its perpetual, care even when knowledge-bearing objects had become obsolete, outdated, or irrelevant.

The preservation function reinforced a conservative ethos in libraries, archives, and museums and forced them to balance continuity with change. Libraries, archives and museums often became reluctant to change their practices for classification and exhibition of objects, and tended to resist pressure to discard or limit access to information deemed subversive, dangerous, or unpopular politically. Despite the pull towards conservatism in collection development and practice, libraries, museums and archives adapted to a variety of social, cultural, and economic pressures during the post-war period.

On the social and cultural side, established institutions faced dwindling audiences for exhibits that were viewed as elitist and shrinking communities of users for collections that reinforced conservative, nationalistic, and bourgeois master narratives. From the late 1960s to the 1990s, many museums redefined their role and image from a temple for passively viewing clearly interpreted objects to a forum for interaction, learning, and open-end interpretation.

Public libraries built new facilities in rapidly growing suburban areas, actively targeted young readers, and expanded services such as outreach programs and organized events that helped to integrate libraries into neighbourhoods and communities. In response to a growing interest in social history, local history, and genealogy, many archives reassessed their collecting policies and aggressively sought materials on women, ethnic and linguistic minorities, popular culture, and social movements. At the same time, minority communities began to form their own cultural centers to support research, exhibition, and teaching, and to reinforce a mutual sense of identity.

Often poorly funded and staffed by volunteers, these new institutions, nevertheless, emerged as vibrant catalysts for community formation and as competitors to conservative, established institutions. Economic pressures also forced changes in policy and practice. Facing declining public subsidies and rising costs, cultural institutions, especially museums, have been compelled to assume more market-oriented strategies such as increasing admission prices, introducing museums shops and cafeterias as profit centers, and seeking corporate sponsorship for capital campaigns and high profile exhibits.

In response, critics have questioned whether corporate sponsorship exerts undue influence over the themes and interpretations in museums and whether revenue-generating requirements force curators to produce exhibitions that are popular and trendy rather than critical and thoughtprovoking. It is also worth noting that museums, which emerged from the Wunderkammern entertainment tradition, then evolved in to efforts to collect and organize physical evidence for scientific research with limited public display, reversed course and began to place most of their emphasis on exhibition, outreach, and education.

Libraries and archives have faced similar economic constraints of rising costs and declining public revenues, but both tradition and practice have limited their marketoriented options. Requiring patrons to pay for services that traditionally have been free runs counter to both users' expectations and professional goals of mitigating disparities in citizen's access to information. Libraries and archives have responded to economic constraints primarily through internal structural changes.

Research libraries, under the pressure of rising acquisition costs for books and scholarly journals, have reduced acquisitions and began to develop networks for sharing expensive, but little used, items. Archives have also adopted more focused and judicious criteria for selecting material for long-term preservation. They have turned increasingly to private foundations and competitive public funds, such as the Andrew W. Mellon Foundation and the National Endowment for the Humanities in the United States, the Heritage Lottery Fund in the United Kingdom, and the Riks Bank Jubileum Fund in Sweden, as sources for "venture capital" to support innovation.

THE LAM IN THE KNOWLEDGE ECONOMY

The LAM are arguably the oldest examples of knowledge organizations. Societies have built and sustained institutions to collect, organize, preserve, and provide access to knowledge-bearing objects for more than two millennia. It would seem that these quintessentially knowledge-based organizations would serve as models for other organizations making the transition to a knowledge-driven economy.

In fact, the LAM are facing a period of deep uncertainty at the dawn of the new era due to economic pressures, competition from alternative service providers, changing expectations from consumers of their services, and a fundamental shift in their material base from tangible objects to digital representations. These factors are difficult to distinguish from one another, and as suggested, attempt to do a point-by-point assessment of them.

Instead, as suggested, raise a number of emerging conditions that illustrate the interwoven nature of the challenges, and that raise central questions about the missions and continuing relevance of the LAM and their core functions. The challenges facing the LAM are not new; they have been evolving as part of a larger constellation of changes for some time. However, some contemporary conditions bring the challenge facing the LAM into sharp focus. The advent of the World Wide Web has amplified the long-standing role of radio and television in the competition for attention, and has extended it into competition for information access in ways heretofore impossible.

Through the Web, the LAM are facing serious competition from alternative service providers, possibly for the first time in their history. The Web can be thought of as a global substitute for the LAM because it allows a globally distributed population to publish and access information easily. Of course, the Web is weak on some traditional strengths of the LAM, such as legitimation and authentication of information, and in the persistence and structure provided for information access.

Nevertheless, there are some striking stories to tell about the Web's competition with the traditional LAM. For example, the on-line bookseller, Amazon.com, has an extensive on-line database, not unlike a library catalog, listing several million book titles, 250,000 CD titles, and data about 250,000 motion pictures and entertainment programs from 1891 to the present. Amazon probably compares well in the ranking of research libraries conducted by the Association for Research Libraries. For some kinds of information, the Amazon databases are more comprehensive and more current than the on-line catalogs of large libraries.

Moreover, Amazon competes with other on-line book-sellers by adding services that mimic some of the selection and legitimating functions that libraries traditionally performed, such as alerts and recommendations based on user profiles and past purchases, and opportunities for readers to post and read book reviews. It seems reasonable to ask whether Amazon represents a first step in the migration of traditional LAN functions into a new model based on a commercialized Web infrastructure.

The advent of commercial services such as Amazon causes a subtle but important shift in the political and economic ecology of the LAM. For most of the last two centuries the LAM have operated as a kind of public good in which a patronage structure of universities, governments, and non-profit philanthropies provided funds, and the LAM carried out their missions as best they could. This arrangement never required a very robust means for judging the economic value of the LAM. To the extent that the measurement of value-added was attempted at all, it tended to be built around a crude input/output model in which the raw materials of the LAM were considered inputs and the outputs were the number of patrons served or the number of reference questions answered.

Several important factors were missing from the middle of this model. For one thing, there was very little cost accounting to show how the LAM functions of selection, organization, curation, content delivery, and so on contributed economically to the services delivered. For another, the model provided no way to determine the value of the actual work being done by the users of the LAM's materials. It was therefore not possible to determine how any particular input led to any changes in a user's welfare. This was fine as long as the patrons accepted the idea that the LAM were an important public good and they had to be funded at the appropriate level.

The rise of examples such as Amazon call that idea into question, and the LAM have no useful measures of costs and benefits to fall back on. Amazon provides proof that something like a library can be built and provided on a commercial basis. This proof can refocus the discussion of the social welfare provided by the LAM in a critical way. The welfare model of the traditional LAM started with the aggregate welfare of society and worked backward. As Webster's suggests, the benefits of the "vast commerce in ideas" was the society at large — mankind, to use his term. Of course, the specific contributions that create these benefits were individual in origin, but the appropriate focus was not on the individual.

In the traditional LAM, especially as they evolved in the 19th century, individual contributions arose through the provision of socially organized affordances. The society provided the LAM for use by individuals, and at least some individual users leveraged those affordances into important new discoveries or creations that benefited society. Prosperous societies had robust LAM infrastructure, and any society that wanted to be prosperous should create such infrastructure through collective action. Amazon offers a fundamentally different economic model in which the starting point is individual welfare.

Individuals perceive a need for LAM-like services, and individual investors put up the resources and create the capacity to meet that demand. The individual users pay for the services, and presumably receive the welfare they paid for. As the welfare of individuals rises from use of the services, social welfare rises as well. In the realm of knowledge such as provided by Amazon, society might also benefit from the discoveries or creations of individuals who were able to leverage the knowledge they gained from the services.

Amazon, simply by its existence, raises the question of why the society should support the LAM when the services provided by the LAM might be had through private enterprise using the Web as infrastructure. Fortunately for the traditional LAM, such questions are not yet challenging the heart of the enterprise.

But the questions suggest that the LAM cannot depend indefinitely on the rationales that have held their patronage structures together for the past two centuries. While some strict traditionalists within the LAM world might try to hold back the tide of changing arising from the Web, many are beginning to follow their user community into the Web world in order to leverage the power of the Web in ways constructive to the traditional LAM.

A study of the online habits of 2,000 American college students conducted by netLibrary found that:

* 82% of the students surveyed own a computer and virtually all of them use the Internet.
* 93% claimed that finding information on-line makes more sense than going to the library.
* 83% said they were frequently unable to get the materials they need for the library because of limited library opening hours.
* 75% said they do not have enough time to go to the library.
* 75% liked the convenience and 71% liked the time saved by finding information on line any hour of the day.

Another recent study amplifies on the importance of these data:

"[b]ecause of easy access to the Web, undergraduates are using library collections and services less than in the past and, in the absence of quality information and tools on the surface, they may imperil the quality of student learning".

A transformation is already under way among users of the LAM, but it is not yet clear how social welfare will be affected by the trasnformation. Those who care for the traditional LAM are challenged to decide whether and how they will try to shape that transformation. That challenge should begin in recognizing that the LAM and the Web cannot substitute for one another. They are complementary, and must be developed in a complementary manner. We see four areas in which key complementarities appear: access, information quality, social memory, and information property.

Access

An important complementary role of the Web and the LAM is in improving effective access to information for all strata of the population. The "digital divide" usually refers to disparities in access to Information and Communications Technologies (ICTs). People without access to ICTs have few opportunities to participate in on-line discussions and debates, to use e-mail to communicate with friends and family, or to post their own content on the web. ICTs alone are only part of the problem, however.

Equally important is the development of the information and skills infrastructure necessary to exploit the availability of ICTs. Libraries have long served as equalizers in disparities of access to information by providing free access to materials that individuals cannot afford to purchase, and most have extended their efforts to providing computers with Internet access and licensing access to databases on behalf of their users. Libraries are still relatively new at this, and they are finding that their service provision models based on circulating physical items such as books do not map neatly to the demands of a the digital environment. Users can take a book home and use it at their leisure, but those who do not have a computer and an Internet connection can gain access at a library facility only during its opening hours.

Nevertheless, libraries are providing a vital complementary role in leveraging the Web among those who would otherwise not have access at all. An equally vital complementarity of the Web and the LAM is in the co-location of physical collections and the information necessary to learn from them. Museums can be used to illustrate this in two ways. The consolidated physical location of a museum's collections is beneficial for those who can visit the museum in person, especially for an extended period of time. Unfortunately, the same consolidation makes the museum's collections inaccessible by anyone unable to visit.

Using the Web a museum can make significant portions of its collections available to distant users through images of objects and text information about the objects. Of course, there is much lost in the experience of seeing a photograph of a dinosaur skeleton compared to actually being there to walk around and look at the skeleton. Still, even limited access can be far better than none, especially for scholars who have intimate knowledge of the class of objects being studied and who have need to review items spread across a large number of collections.

Even if some on-site investigation is required, preliminary reviews of on-line collections and commentary can dramatically narrow the search space and provide structure to the study. Another way the co-location of objects and information becomes valuable is in the provision of information at varying levels of depth at the location of the physical object itself. For many museum visitors the information contained on a plaque next to the exhibit is sufficient. But for many visitors, the ability to gain deep access into the records on a given object can be essential for study.

Such access is usually provided for scholars by museum staff allowing entry into areas of the museum not permitted to regular visitors. With Web based technology, the entire holdings of information on each object could be made available at will to any visitor using a hand-held wireless device like a PDA. In this example of a museum it is possible to see that the LAM are a source of the authenticated information available to a distributed audience over the Web, and the Web provides unparalleled access to information about museum collections for visitors on-site at the museum.

Information Quality Assurance

Taken together, the LAM and the Web permit easy access to authenticated information. The Web is easy to use and provides fast access to a vast amount of information. Unfortunately, it is inadequate for teaching and research where definitive and high quality information resources are instrumental for critical analysis, innovation, and new knowledge generation. A great deal of the information in the Web is not accessible through the large search engines, and thus is not available to most Web users. Recent studies of the architecture of the Web distinguish between the surface Web and the deep Web, or what is also called the dark or hidden Web.

Search engines index mainly the surface Web of unrestricted, static Web pages, and no single search engine indexes more than 16% of the surface Web. All of the search engines combined are estimated to index less than half of the surface Web. The "deep" Web is estimated to be 500 times larger than the size of the surface Web, and it is growing faster. There is no question that the Web makes huge amounts of information accessible, and for many applications this is a genuine boon.

However, the Web and search engine package currently available falls short of the infrastructure required by knowledge communities now provided by the LAM. A more serious quality assurance problem with search engine dependence on the surface Web is the comparatively substandard quality of the information there. The deep Web's resources are typically superior in quality, organization, and structure to surface Web resources. Deep Web resources tend to be curated, meaning they have been selected, indexed, and controlled for quality and authoritativeness by subject experts or editors.

Deep Web resources tend to be narrower and richer in content than surface Web sites, and oriented towards specific domains or disciplines. Scholars who rely on Internet search engines might locate substantial information in the surface Web while remaining completely unaware of the better content in the deep Web. Even if their search skills and their ability to judge the comparative quality of resources available are highly developed, they will miss much of the best information. At the very least, this constitutes a major opportunity loss. The co-evolution of the objects, data, and meta-data of the LAM was not accidental. It was an integral and necessary part of the knowledge communities that evolved with and were sustained by the LAM.

The full utility of collections of objects and documents was unattainable until the full set of complementary assets was available. Those complementary assets were the experts on the content in the collections–the librarians, archivists, and curators–and the tools they developed over time in the form of meta-data tools such as indices, catalogs, and reference works. The vital need for those assets was made strikingly evident shortly after the heroic success of the expansion of the US public library base with the Carnegie library endowments.

Most of the . . . Carnegie libraries had been built by 1920, but the benefits were as yet elusive. The Carnegie foundation commissioned a report by . . . Williamson to investigate the matter. In 1923 Williamson's report argued that the investments in bricks and mortar and collections would never pay off until many more professional librarians were deployed to manage the collections and help the public use them. Most US schools of librarianship were established in the decade thereafter, and their graduates made the public library an essential part of the nation's epistemic infrastructure.

In a similar vein, the Web and associated tools such as search engines will not be adequate by themselves to achieving the full potential of the emerging epistemic infrastructure. Librarians and other professionals of the LAM provide essential expertise in information management quality assurance that is badly needed in the world of the Web. The complementary nature of the traditional LAM and the emerging Web is illustrated by the LAM-like services increasingly available on the Web.

These services are tied to large LAM collections, and the services are managed by LAM experts who know the collections intimately. The public's interaction with the collections is intermediated by LAM professionals, providing substantially greater benefits than non-expert users could hope to gain on their own. A good example of this is seen in the experimental on-line library services such as the Internet Public Library. The IPL began in 1996 as a student experiment to create an on-line service providing features of a public library.

Since that time the IPL has demonstrated that essential library services such as reference can be provided on-line to a globally distributed user base from a globally distributed set of reference specialists. The primary user base of the IPL is now students in elementary and secondary school who use the collections and reference services to do assist with their schoolwork.

The IPL infrastructure and concept has been extended to the American Indian Higher Education Council Virtual Library that has made it possible for a number of tribal community colleges to achieve accreditation for programs that was previously denied due to lack of library resources.

The key to such services is their information quality: the content is authenticated by experts who know both the subject matter and the patterns of user demand for the content. The IPL and the AIHEC Virtual Library marry the traditional strengths of the LAM with the distributed access benefits of the Web to create a cost-effective form of epistemic infrastructure not possible before. These examples can be augmented by many others, and suggest that the future of the Web intersects with rather than departs from the traditional LAM.

Social Memory

The LAM provide socially vital core functions that are largely invisible and that cannot be provided by existing Web-based collecting and dissemination mechanisms. A key function in the knowledge-driven economy is the integration of widely distributed objects and collections. This requires a rich set of knowledge and skills in organization and classification, as well as a critical eye towards the epistemic regimes that systems of knowledge organization impose on the worlds they describe. That skill has been built up over two centuries, and is a key part of the role of the LAM in the global epistemic infrastructure. The Web in its current form cannot provide this infrastructure.

The Web provides access to a global user base, but custodianship of information in the world of the Web is largely in local communities, specific disciplines, and private content providers. This is good in the sense that the most intimate expertise resides at such levels, but over-dependence at this level reinforces parochialism and limits the potential for knowledge integration across space and over time. The LAM are not free from such parochialism: the institutional distinctions between libraries as sources of published works, archives as repositories of unpublished documents, and museums as storehouses for three-dimensional objects is artificial and inhibits knowledge generation. But at least across

the subdivisions of the LAM a rich ecology for maintaining integrative knowledge has evolved.

Libraries cooperate closely with one another through shared cataloging and other mechanisms, and similar cooperative arrangements reinforce the shared missions of archives and museums. Effective knowledge integration requires a careful balance between local, subject, and domain knowledge as well as broader principles for rich representation. This remains a challenge for both the LAM and the world of the Web, but the LAM are much farther along than the Web in developing the means to achieve the right balance. An essential function of the LAM is the accumulation and preservation of knowledge that might someday be of vital importance.

Libraries, archives, and museums maintain collections over the course of centuries. The LAM are the most important form of longterm social memory. Preservation experts in the LAM fight a constant battle to maintain documents and objects from destruction and deterioration in the belief that losses inhibit future potential. This tradition is well established, and has found a respected place in all advanced societies. The Web reveals another side, in which loss of information is massive and routine. No social institutions equivalent to the LAM currently take responsibility for collecting and preserving digital objects.

Many of these objects are generated without much consideration beyond their first-order uses, and in complete disregard for their long-term potential for manipulation and repurposing. They are seldom collected and organized the way paper documents have been for the past centuries, and in some cases it is not clear whether anyone is going to keep them at all. This represents a major departure from the past, in which the physical and economic realities of publication made it more likely that knowledge would be collected and preserved. And even in the print world, the idea of "comprehensive collection" has largely disappeared.

No single library on Earth collects everything that is published, and it is virtually impossible to ascertain the

fraction of total global titles held in all the libraries taken together. It is almost certain that a large amount of material disappears forever each year, even as librarians and archivists presume that other libraries are preserving those items. There is no way to tell whether the material being lost is of long term value. The situation in digital information is much more problematic because there are almost no reliable standards or technologies for long-term preservation.

A number of publishers provide full text digital databases made from content they physically own and manage. Libraries purchase access to this content, but they do not actually store or preserve it. Even if copyright laws and license agreements permitted such replication, most libraries would not do so because they figure the publishers will preserve their digital content in perpetuity. But publishers are not in the business of archiving and preserving they content they produce, and there is no reason to assume they will assume this responsibility. Libraries and publishers have not come to sustainable agreements regarding digital archiving responsibilities.

Some publishers pledge to preserve their digital into the foreseeable future; others do not. In any case, it seems that libraries, and especially legal deposit libraries, would be better equipped to perform this function over the long run. In most countries, laws covering mandatory deposit of published work ensure that the majority of published material at least has a chance of preservation. Legislation regarding mandatory deposit of published digital works varies widely from country to country, and the deposit libraries are not yet ready to accept and manage such works. Many Web documents are critical sources of information and important cultural artifacts, but there are few tools to capture and preserve these documents and almost no market incentives for Web archiving even in the surface Web. Long term preservation is one of the important areas in which the traditional LAM and the Web must depend on each other.

Information Property

One of the most challenging but important areas of complementarity between the traditional LAM and the Web

is information property management. The LAM are expert on copyright laws and conventions that have evolved over the past two centuries. Copyright was designed originally to provide authors with a limited monopoly as an inducement to creativity, but it has expanded in scope and duration and placed constraints on alternatives to purchasing items or leasing access. The digital realm provides many new challenges for copyright.

Laws and licensing agreements usually permit libraries to provide access to authenticated or on-site users, but they strictly prohibit wholesale downloading of entire databases. They also limit the number and future uses of copies of individual articles, and forbid manipulation of digital objects to create extracts or derivative works. Content providers are beginning to use encryption and digital rights management software to prevent duplication of content and access by users who do not purchase an item or pay to view it.

Some scholars such as Lawrence Lessig argue that copyright restrictions on digital content have become so draconian that they are counter-productive to innovation and knowledge generation. The Internet was once seen as a neutral platform that encouraged the free flow of content. Legal constraints on intellectual property are rapidly eroding that nascent tradition, with considerable downside possibilities for knowledge communities. Corynne McSherry contends that the "propertization" of knowledge is transforming key knowledge communities such as universities from "gift" economies to "market" economies.

The effects that such a shift might have on high-quality scholarship, academic freedom, collaboration, and creativity are unknown, but it is clear that these knowledge communities have deeply developed and productive traditions that might be damaged in this process. The information objects that circulate in academic communities are "gifts" where the donor relinquishes knowledge to the larger community as a contribution to that community's larger mission of producing science, knowledge, or truth. In return, the scholar receives recognition and enhanced reputation that enhances the value of the scholar's future work.

The scholar's personal economic welfare is tied only indirectly to this process, through promotion and improved marketability to more prestigious universities that compensate better. Only in rare circumstances does a specific contribution contribute directly to the scholar's economic welfare. This has been the fundamental social contract of university for several hundred years, and has produced universities that are the envy of the world. No for-profit equivalent has ever materialized. In principle, it is possible that propertization of knowledge might produce new knowledge communities that rival universities in content and quality.

But it is more than likely that propertization of knowledge within universities will encourage petty squabbles over attribution and revenue sharing that erode content and quality. Fortunately, the Web does not require the propertization of knowledge to be effective. Alternative strategies for evaluating and distributing intellectual property on the Web are evolving along the lines of the "gift" model. An early project initiated by physicists to submit and deposit "pre-prints" of journal articles electronically has mushroomed into a much larger movement for digital deposit and open archives for scholarly communications.

The open archives movement retains many of the community-oriented value-added functions of a "gift economy," especially peer review and editorial oversight for quality control. It replaces the strict intellectual property rights enforcement regime of publishers with "rules of the road" and community norms for attribution and recirculation of ideas that appeared earlier in published works. Lessig and others advocate the development of "knowledge conservancies" where owners of intellectual property voluntarily place their works in the public domain either to contribute to the larger social good, or in exchange for tax incentives that partially compensate donors for foregone royalty payments.

An important example of an alternative is SPARC, an alliance of more than 200 universities, research libraries, and organizations in North America, Europe, Asia and Australia to innovate in the scholarly communications system. It provides for incubation of competitive alternatives to current high-priced commercial journals and digital aggregations. It also publicly advocates fundamental changes in the system and culture of scholarly communication.

SPARC education campaigns are aimed at improving awareness of scholarly communication issues and supporting expanded institutional and scholarly community roles in and control over the scholarly communication process. It remains to be seen whether open archives, knowledge conservancies, or coalitions such as SPARC will fundamentally change the parameters of information property or create a fundamentally new means for valuing and distributing knowledge. But experiments of this kind are important to developing the complementarity between the LAM and the Web most likely to bring benefits in the future.

7

International Library Associations

INTRODUCTION

International organizations have experienced a recent remarkable increase in numbers. Several possible reasons for the growth of international library associations since World War II are the following: Our shrinking world has caused increasing awareness of other parts of the world with accompanying demands for access to information from those areas.

* Growth of information and publishing throughout the world.
* Awareness through increased automation of resources in other parts of the world.
* Growth of international business interests in the second half of the twentieth century after the war.
* More sophisticated users who demand specialized services and in-creased knowledge of the access to information resources by their librarians.

The World Guide to Library, Archive, and Information Science Associations de-fines international associations as "organizations whose membership includes two or more countries. . . . They may be general in nature . . .or specialized . . ." In its 1990 edition, the World Guide identified seventy-six international associations based on the re-turned questionnaires sent to each association and the compilers' knowledge of additional associations. The World Guide notes that there were 33 international associations in 1973, 41 in 1976, 58 in 1980, and seventy-six in 1990. Dates of establishment are broken down in table.

Table 7.1: Dates of Associations Established by Decade.

Decade	Number of Association Established
1895	1*
1927	1**
1930	1***
1940	3
1950	11
1960	17
1970	23
1980	17
No Date Listed	7

Notes:

*International Federation for Information and Documentation, FID.

**International Federation of Library Associations and Institutions, IFLA.

***Federation International des Archives du Film, FIAF.

Another reason for this growth in numbers is the development of regional and specialized library associations. For several decades, FID (International Federation for Information and Documentation), founded in 1895, IFLA (International Federation of Library Associations and Institutions), founded in 1927 and, to a certain extent, the conferences and congresses of leading library associations, such as the American Library Association and the Library Association (of the United Kingdom), filled the need for librarians from around the w'orld to meet.

The World Encyclopedia of Library and Information Services offers a detailed early history of international library organizations, pointing out that:

"One of IFLA's major roles has been as a centralizing organization precipitating the emergence of specialist groups that become part of its federal structure".

In fact, an analysis of the seventy-six international organizations listed in the *World Guide* reveals that only six of the associations listed there could strictly be called general and fully global. The others fall into either regional groupings or specialized topical or professional groupings, as shown in Table 7.2.

Table 7.2: Regional or Specialized Associations.

Regional Associations (*Examples:* Middle East, Africa, Latin America)	13
Speciallized Topical or Professional Groupings:	
Agriculture	3
Archives	12
Art and Music	6
Bibliographic Control	3
Library Education	4
Medical and Health-related	3
Religion and Theology	3
Other Specialized Subgects	9
Type of Libraries	10

This article will highlight five international library associations which typify the trends. Only two of them are included in the *World Guide* list of international associations. The other three illustrate important trends in international library associations.

The five associations are as follows:

* The International Association of Technological University Libraries (LATUL),which typifies an association of members from a specific type of library.
* The International Association of Agricultural Librarians and Document lists (IAALD), now known as the International Association of Agricultural Information Specialists, which typifies an association of members from a specific subject area or discipline.
* The Special Libraries Association (SLA), which fits the World Guide's definition of international association, but which was listed incorrectly in the national

section, representing the role of the very large library association struggling with an international identity.

* The International Librarianship Round Table of the Arizona Library Association (AzLA ILRT), which illustrates a trend to localize the relationship between librarians in several countries. Associations covering sub-areas of countries, such as state associations, were not in the scope of the World Guide.

* The Trans border Library Forum/Foro Transfronterizo de Bibliotecas (Foro), which represents a unique grass-roots regional development of the 1990s.

Descriptions of each of these five associations will include historical in-formation about their founding; mission, purpose, and goals of the cur-rent organization; profile of the membership components of the association; services to its membership, such as conferences, publications, and other forms of communication; and future plans. No formalized history of the ILRT and little on the Foro have been written; the author has relied on ephemeral material such as minutes, annual reports, and memoranda to construct these sections.

FID AND IFLA

The two international associations with the most influence in the development of other international library associations are FID and IFLA. This stage would not be complete without a summary of the history and influence of these "grandfather" associations.

FID

The FID, the Federation Internationale de Documentation/ International Federation for Documentation, was founded in 1895as the Institute International de Bibliographie (IIB), concerning itself with the classification of materials and particularly the development of a standard classification scheme. Later, with the name change to FID, came a change in purpose, enlarged to include the "organization, storage, retrieval, dissemination and evaluation of information". In 1990,FID had a published membership of 371 library institutions from sixty-six countries and an additional 300 affiliated members.

FID's Web site states its very general goals for the present and future:

* Advance the frontiers of science and technology;
* Improve competitiveness of business, industry, and national economies;
* Strengthen possibilities for development and enhance the quality of life wherever possible;
* Improve the ability of decision-makers to make appropriate decisions;
* Stimulate educational strategies and life-long learning;
* Make expression possible in all sectors of the Information Society including the arts and humanities and will strive and continue to be at the leading edge of the development of the management of information.

IFLA

The International Federation of Library Associations/ Federation Internationale des Associations de Bibliothecaires, renamed the International Federation of Library Associations and Institutions in 1976, was founded in 1926 at the annual meeting of the American Library Association (ALA),where representatives from many countries had convened to celebrate the fiftieth anniversary of ALA. The IFLA's early purpose was to organize regular world conferences between United States and European library associations.

This mission was greatly expanded in the 1970s "to promote international understanding, cooperation, discussion, research, and development in all fields of library activity, including bibliography, information services, and the education of personnel, and to provide a body through which librarianship can be represented in matters of international interest". From its 1997 Web page, IFLA reasserts its global scope: IFLA is a worldwide, independent organization created to provide librarians around the world with a forum for exchanging ideas, promoting international cooperation, research and development in all fields of library activity.

IFLA's objectives are:

* To represent librarianship in matters of international interest,
* *To* promote the continuing education of library personnel, and to develop, maintain and promote guidelines for library ser vices.

IFLA continues to be an association of associations, with 1,200 members in 1990 in two categories-members representing associations and institutions and personal (nonvoting) members. Today, IFLA reaches out to most of the world's regions, encouraging true worldwide participation at conferences and other IFLA-sponsored meetings.

IATUL

The International Association of Technological University Libraries is:

> A voluntary international nongovernmental organi-sation of a group of libraries, represented by their library directors or university managers, who have responsibility for information services and resource management. It is small enough for individual members to be able to develop a close relationship, yet widespread enough to cover the interests of libraries operating in virtually all modern social, economic, and political situations.

The International Association of Technological University Libraries was founded in 1955 with institutional representatives from thirteen countries. Today's membership has grown to 198 member libraries from forty-one countries. IATUL prefers that its members be directors of technological or scientific university libraries. In its founding year, IATUL became a section of IFLA.

There are four categories of membership:

* "Ordinary membership," available to libraries of academic institutions and research libraries where science and technology degrees at the doctoral level are offered;
* "Official observer membership," available to libraries which do not have the doctoral programme, but have research-level collections;

* "Sustaining membership," for individuals and institutions who are sympathetic to the purposes of IATUL; and
* "Non-voting associate membership," which is extended to libraries which confer science and technology degrees at the Masters level when no doctoral degrees are awarded. The last three categories require IATUL Board approval.

IATUL's purpose is to "provide a forum for library directors to meet for exchange of views on matters of current significance in the libraries of universities of science and technology, and to provide an opportunity for them to develop a collaborative approach to problems".

IATUL's goals focus on increasing opportunities for international cooperation in five areas:

* Sharing current information about technical university libraries;
* Recruiting and training library personnel;
* Discussing the development of new library buildings;
* Standardizing and enlarging international lending schemes; and
* Creating exchange opportunities of the publications of the respective institutions.

IATUL takes pride in its ability to communicate with members through conferences, its publication programme, and visibility on the World Wide Web. Conferences are currently held annually throughout the world. The last two were held in Enshede, The Nether-lands, and Irvine, California, in 1996, in Trondheim, Norway, in 1997. The 1998 conference will convene in Pretoria, South Africa, a first for the organization on the African continent. Themes for these and previous conferences have included user education, service to industry, re-source management, networking, and implications for digital libraries.

Conferences are lively opportunities to demonstrate and discuss new ideas for the advancement of library service in the members' constituencies. They are well attended with the

1996 conference attracting approximately 250 attendees. IATUL originally distributed reprints, then began publishing a small bulletin with news of the organization, especially its upcoming conferences. This "grey literature," defined by Dieter Schmidmaier, a former L4TUL board member, as "publications outside of the bookshop, not bibliographically recorded and to a large extent unknown," nevertheless comprised the publication effort of IATUL for the first ten years of its existence. Today, IATUL's publication programme is strong.

The *IATUL NEWS* and the *IATUL Proceedings* are distributed to member libraries, although there is no one library which holds all publications of the organization. In addition, IATUL has a presence on the World Wide Web. Its home page contains information about the organization, upcoming meetings, institutional member linkages, projects, publications, membership information, and links to other relevant Web sites. In October 1996, forty countries had Web sites on the IATUL home page. The future for IATUL encompasses some activities related to its length of time as an organization and its growth in size and global representation.

These activities include developing an archive as a permanent record of IATUL's history, increasing the opportunities for personnel exchanges between the member institutions, essay prizes for papers presented at conferences, and exploring the idea of regional groups. The statutes provide for the establishment of groups to organize member activities on a regional basis, and a North American Regional Group was established in 1985. Similar groups are under consideration for Australasia and South Africa. Cooperation with other international organizations continues. IATUL is an International Member of IFLA, an Official Observer of Unesco, and a member of the Inter-national Federation for Information and Documentation.

IAAAD

Like IATUL, the International Association of Agricultural Librarians and Documentalists was founded in 1955 with sixty founding members in thirteen countries. It clearly met a need, as one year later the member-ship had grown to thirty-five countries and then to fifty-three countries by 1960. Founded by agriculture professors in Germany and Austria, this organization was a direct result of the chaos of World War I1 in Europe and called for renewed cooperation in the identification and exchange of scientific information. IAALD was established "to promote, inter-nationally and nationally, agricultural library science and documentation, as well as professional interests of agricultural librarians and documentalists. . ."

Founders agreed to foster connections to IFLA, Unesco, and the Food and Agricultural Organization (FAO) of the United Nations. Indeed, for the first five years of IAALD's existence, its secretariat was located at the FA0 Library in Rome. Despite this association's strong European roots, the United States was an early active participant, and the first three presidents, serving five years each, were from the United States. IAALD hosts an official World Congress once every five years. Members find that this is not enough, and additional regional meetings, symosia, and workshops reduce the average time between IUD-sponsored events to 1.9 years.

A regional meeting was held in Tucson, Arizona, in April 1996, as a joint conference with the U.S. Agricultural Information Network (USAIN).This is an example of a successful mid-conference meeting that has grown beyond "regional"-twenty Latin American members participated thanks to a grant from the W. K. Kellogg Foundation, and delegates from Asia, South Asia, and Europe were present. In all, the delegates to this conference encompassed 200 attendees from thirty-six countries. IAALD has a robust publications programme.

The *IAALD Quarter4 Bulletin, IAALB Naus,* and *IAALB Lettre d'Infomation* are its official serial publications, but it has supported many other publications, including the several editions of *Agricultural Information Resource Centers: A World Directory,* recently republished, which contains listings for 4,903 libraries and documentation centers from 171 countries. It contains IAALD's mission statement, membership information, upcoming events, and publications information.

IAALD's constitution and chronological history are avail-able in three languages. The latest edition of the IAAIB News is available, full text, at the Web site.

AzLA ILRT

In 1988, the Arizona Library Association (AzLA), then the Arizona State Library Association (ASLA),approved the formation of a new round table concerned with international librarianship. Requested by a large group of Arizona librarians with international experience, its objective, spelled out in its bylaws, was to advance the cause of international librarianship and was called the International Librarianship Round Table.

The goals of ILRT, established at the first bylaws meeting, were to be:

* To develop the interests of librarians and libraries in issues, activities, and opportunities in the field of international librarianship;
* To pro-mote the exchange of materials, information, librarians, and other re-sources throughout the world; and
* To serve as a channel of communi-cation and counsel for members of AzLA in the field of international librarianship.

ILRT's first membership listing in the *Am'zona State Library Association Directory* listed twenty-eight individual members from an association membership of about 1,200. In its first year of activities, ILRT grew to seventy members; membership has fluctuated between seventy and ninety members throughout its existence. The publication programme of ILRT is ephemeral: one renegade newsletter published outside the auspices of the parent organization, then fairly regular columns in the *ASIA Newsletter.* ILRT occasionally receives wider exposure through the publications and presentations of its members. The AzLA Web site enhances its existence. The programs and activities of ILRT establish it as one of the most active groups in AzLA.

Every annual conference and mid-year conference of the association offers several programs of international significance, such as reports of exchanges and other international professional experiences of librarians. The mid-year conference (MIDCON) in 1990 featured a panel of three Arizona librarians speaking of their experiences on three continents.

Speakers from other countries, such as Ana Maria Magalone, director of public libraries in Mexico, draw interest from the larger AzLA membership. Why has ILRT been such a success? One reason is that this group, at the state association level, fills an immediate and accessible need for librarians who are not directors of libraries or the official representatives to larger organizations or for whom travel to expensive international locations for meetings is beyond their budget or the travel budgets of their organizations. Another reason for its success is that it is a trailblazer for state associations.

ILRT established some precedents. It may have marked the first time a state association established a formal international librarianship subdivision, though the California Library Association recently established an International Relations Round Table (IRRT) similar to the IRRT of the American Library Association (ALA). ILRT was the first group to monitor an international travel/exchange endowment programme at the state level. Third, it recommended the establishment of an international conference separate from the association's annual conference.

In addition, Arizona, as a state bordering another country, employs librarians in all types of libraries who see an immediate need to learn about the extensive resources and common interests of Mexico, especially the border states of Mexico. Arizona librarians have extensive experience in international situations all over the world, and this core of leadership sets the tone for the round table. Finally, the projects pro-posed by ILRT becomes reality.

Projects include library exchanges between Arizona and Mexican librarians for education and training; the creation of its own subgroup, the Arizona-Mexico Committee, whose purposes were to report to Arizona members on the work of the Arizona-Mexico Commission, a statewide initiative; to report on Arizona's participation at the Guadalajara Book Fair;

and to begin the organization of the Binational Conference which became the Trans border Library Forum, now organizing its eighth conference.

Finally, ILRT became the administering body for the Horner Japanese Exchange Fellowship Award from an endowment established by Dr. and Mrs. Layton (Jack) Horner, Arizona residents who lived for many post-World War II years in Japan. This fund was initiated with the Arizona State Library Association in 1988 to promote professional cooperation and international understanding through an exchange programme between Arizona and Japanese librarians. The fellowship from the endowment is unique among state library associations in the United States and is still active. Several Arizona librarians have visited Japan, primarily the Osaka area, and on at least three occasions Japanese librarians have officially visited Arizona. ILRT remains strong. Its 1996 annual report, published at the AzLA Web site, indicates a membership of eighty-nine, four programs during the year, and four additional programs at the 1996 Annual Conference

FORO

The Trans border Library Forum developed because of the Arizona Library Association's growing international librarianship interests in the 1980s and because Sonoran librarians were available and interested in engaging in binational networking. The group of meetings is referred to collectively as the foro, which is Spanish for "forum". It was established as a forum, rather than a conference, because of ASLA's reluctance to provide sponsorship for a gathering which could be seen to compete with its annual conference. The Foro was conceived by a group of fifteen librarians from Arizona and Mexico who gathered at the 1989 ASLA Annual Conference in Tucson. That conference was exceptional because the participation of fifty-seven Mexican librarians brought a fresh new perspective on Arizona librarianship, and attendees expressed a need to continue the contact.

The leadership of the International Librarianship Round Table be-came the logical pool for Arizona organizers, but the

Special Libraries Association Arizona Chapter and the members of the ASLA Spanish Speaking Round Table quickly joined in. In Sonora, Jalisco, and Baja, California, librarians expressed interest in helping organize another opportunity to bring together these two countries' librarians. It took eighteen months for the first For to occur, but that early planning set the stage for future successes. For example, programme planning topics were selected by librarians in both countries by means of a questionnaire.

Planning meetings, called "encounters", were held in Mexico and on the Arizona border. Bilingual keynote speakers and dual facilitators in the breakout sessions were essential. The first Foro, held in Rio Rico, Arizona in 1991, was a huge success and, at the closing banquet, the librarians from Sonora invited the group to attend a second Foro the following year in Hermosillo. This invitation set the stage for alternating meetings in Mexico and the United States with the exception of the fourth and fifth Foros which were both held in Mexico. The Trans border Library Forums are unique in the library world. Held every year since 1991, these events are organized without benefit of a secretariat, an association umbrella, dues, or elected officers.

Each forum is administered by a different volunteer group of librarians whose motivation is increased library contact between the two countries. The highlight of all of the Trans border Library Forums has been the networking opportunities between the border librarians of the two countries. Informal exchanges, internship opportunities, and materials exchanges are frequent topics of discussion, and everyone works on language proficiency. Communication about the Foro is enhanced by the existence of a listserv, FORO-L.' Printed proceedings of the first conferences were pre-pared for attendees. Selected proceedings of the sixth Foro, held in Tucson in 1996, are available on the WWW. Plans to make the proceedings of the seventh Foro available in this manner are pending.

The sixth, seventh, and eighth Foros all have Web sites. Consistent with the grassroots and non-centralized nature of the forum, however, each is at a different site with a different U'ebmaster and format. Links are being developed to unite them. The future of the Foro relates to its "growing pains". Attendance at the annual meetings is now consistently 300, three times the size of the first few meetings. This size requires more programming, more logistics, as well as more fund-raising to subsidize expenses because the Foro is operated on a cost-recovery basis.

Further, Trans border Library Forum members are now working to establish a statement of mission and objectives that reflects its continued growth and relevance to long-standing, as well as to new, participants. Programme planning documents, including budget information, the exhibitor and sponsor pool, and tips for success are handed down from one planner to another.

8

Sources of Information

INTRODUCTION

Information is power and an essential ingredient in decision-making. To obtain timely, relevant and quality information for your study or research work, you need to know the various sources of information available. This module is expected to deepen your knowledge of sources of information in print, non-print and electronic formats. It presents the definition, originators/producers, types, formats, and categories of information sources. The module also shows where information sources could be found *e.g.* archives, libraries and the Internet.

PRODUCERS/ORIGINATORS OF INFORMATION

There are four main producers/originators of information, these are:

* Government Agencies
* Academic institutions
* The private Sector
* Individuals

GOVERNMENT AGENCIES

Government departments and agencies publish lots of information in print and electronic formats. In various countries of the world, governments at all levels play an important role in producing information for the society they serve. In many occasions, government officials may need information about the society in order to make decisions relating to economic, social and political issues. Some of the information produced by government is grey literature comprising reports such as National HIV/AIDS reports, gazettes, population statistics, census data, government notices, policy documents etc. Since government documents are generated with public funds, they are made available either free of charge or at low cost. This can be done through the various government agencies including the public libraries or the government Websites.

In Nigerian for instance, some government departments and agencies Websites include:

* National Agency for the Control of AIDS (NACA),
* National Bureau of Statistics (NBS),
* Federal Ministry of Information and Culture (FMIC).

ACADEMIC INSTITUTIONS

Academic institutions such as universities and colleges are major producers of information in a society or country. Academic institutions around the world especially those in the United States, United Kingdom, Africa have conducted extensive researches in various specialties including the health sciences. Numerous publications and knowledge materials are generated from these research studies as technical reports, books and articles in peer reviewed journals. Academic institutions also have other publications such as Newsletters, Magazines, Technical reports, Manuscripts, Maps and lots of other Grey literature.

Web addresses of some academic institutions in Africa are listed below:

* University of Ibadan, Nigeria;
* University of Zambia;
* Kenyatta University, Nairobi, Kenya;
* University of Zimbabwe;
* Makerere University, Uganda; and
* University of Bamako, Mali.

PRIVATE SECTORS

A third major producer of information in a country is the private sector. This consists of print and electronic media organizations, commercial business outfits, publishers/vendors and aggregators, performing/film industry that publish and or make their information products and services accessible on the Web either free or by subscription.

Others are:

* Non-profit professional organizations.
* Profitable organizations and commercial agencies.
* International Agencies.
* Professional Associations or organizations.
* Private institutions.
* Corporate laboratories.

Unlike government departments and agencies, published reports of research carried out by most organizations, agencies and commercial outfits in the private sector are not made available for public consumption. However, non-profit organizations and agencies do make their publications available to those that need them.

Some examples of agencies in the private sector or non profit category are:

* The World Health Organization (WHO).
* Joint United Nations Programme on HIV and AIDS (UNAIDS).
* Elsevier Publishers.
* Cables News Network (CNN).

PRIVATE INDIVIDUALS

Individuals also create information. Many print and web documents available today are created by private individuals, some of whom have their own Websites/pages. Some individuals disseminate information through Facebook, Twitter, Blogs, You-tube etc, while others publish information in print as text books, monographs or articles in journals, magazines or newsletters. On the other hand, some important information is not published rather, it is passed on from generation to generation. For example, some parents pass information to their children by word of mouth on how diseases were treated using traditional unorthodox methods in their communities.

DEFINITION OF INFORMATION/ INFORMATION SOURCES

Information is processed data. An information source is where you got your information from; this can be a book or a Website. Information sources are the various means by which information is recorded for use by an individual or an organization. It is the means by which a person is informed about something or knowledge is availed to someone, a group of people or an organization. Information sources can be observations, people, speeches, documents, pictures, organizations. Information sources can be in print, non-print and electronic media or format.

TYPES OF INFORMATION SOURCES

Information can come from virtually anywhere: personal experiences, books, articles, expert opinions, encyclopedias, the Web. The type of information needed will change depending on its application. Individuals generate information on a daily basis as they go about their work. In academic institutions, staff and students consult various sources of information. The choice of the source to consulted is usually determined by the type of information sought.

The three types of information sources are:

* Primary;
* Secondary; and
* Tertiary.

PRIMARY SOURCES

Primary sources are original materials on which other research studies are based. Primary sources report a discovery or share new information; they present first-hand accounts and information relevant to an event. They present information in its original form, not interpreted or condensed or evaluated by other writers. They are usually evidence or accounts of the events, practices, or conditions being researched and created by a person who directly experienced that event. Primary sources are the first formal appearance of results in print or electronic formats. Examples of primary sources are:

eyewitness accounts, journalistic reports, financial reports, government documents, archeological and biological evidence, court records, ephemerals, literary manuscript and minutes of meetings etc. The definition of a primary source may vary depending upon the discipline or context. A diary would be a primary source because it is written directly by the individual writing in the diary. Interviews are primary sources because the individual talks about the topic directly from what he/she knows about it.

Other examples are:

* Video of the inauguration of the first female president in Brazil.
* A scientific publication reporting the development of a new medication to manage patients with sickle-cell anemia.

A newspaper article reporting the bomb blast in Abuja, Nigeria, during the celebration of the country's 50th Independent Anniversary.

Note: The types of information that can be considered a primary source may vary depending on the subject discipline, and how the material is being used.

For example:

* A research article in a peer-reviewed journal that proved the effectiveness of a newly developed vaccine for the prevention of HIV virus would be a primary source.
* A magazine article that reports the development of a new vaccine for the prevention of HIV infection would be regarded as a primary source.
* Information in a magazine article that reports a study of how compact fluorescent light bulbs are presented in the popular media could be considered a primary source.

SECONDARY SOURCES

A secondary source of information is one that was created by someone who *did not* have firsthand experience or did not participate in the events or conditions being researched. They are generally accounts written after the fact with the benefit of hindsight. Secondary sources describe, analyse, interpret, evaluate, comment on and discuss the evidence provided by primary sources.

Secondary sources are works that are one step removed from the original event or experience that provide criticism, interpretation or evaluation of primary sources. Secondary sources are not evidence, but rather commentary on and discussion of evidence. A secondary data are one that has been collected by individuals or agencies for purposes other than those of a particular research study. However, what some define as a secondary source, others define as a tertiary source. For example, if a magazine writer wrote about the speech Nelson Mandela delivered when he was inaugurated President of South Africa in 1990, it will be a secondary source.

The information is not original, but an analysis of the speech. If a government department has conducted a survey of, say, family food expenditures, then, a food manufacturer might use this data in the organization's evaluations of the total potential market for a new product. Similarly, statistics prepared by a pharmaceutical company on the production of a particular drug will prove useful to a host of people and organizations, including those marketing the drug. For secondary sources, often the best are those that have been published most recently.

If you use a secondary source that was published decades ago, it is important to know what subsequent scholars have written on the topic and what criticism they have made about the earlier work or its approach to the topic. The definition of a secondary source may vary depending upon the discipline or context. Most often how a source is used determines whether it is a primary or secondary source. For the purposes of a historical research project, secondary sources are generally scholarly books and articles. Also included in this category would be reference sources such as encyclopedias.

Other examples of secondary sources are:

* Bibliographies
* Biographical works;

* Commentaries;
* Criticisms;
* Dictionaries;
* Histories;
* Journal articles;
* Magazine and newspaper articles;
* Monographs, other than fiction and autobiography;
* Textbooks; and
* Websites.

TERTIARY SOURCES

Definition

Tertiary sources consist of information which is a distillation and collection of primary and secondary sources. Generally, tertiary sources are not considered to be acceptable material on which to base academic research. Tertiary sources are usually not credited to a particular author. They are intended only to provide an overview of what the topic includes, its basic terminology, and often references for further reading.

Some reference materials and textbooks are considered tertiary sources when their chief purpose is to list, summarize or simply repackage ideas or other information. Examples of tertiary sources include dictionaries and encyclopedias, *Wikipedia* and similar user-contributed online 'encyclopedias' and reference materials, as well as various digests and schoolbooks.

In a nutshell, tertiary sources are:

* Works which list primary and secondary resources in a specific subject area.
* Works which index, organize and compile citations to, and show secondary sources can be used.
* Materials in which the information from secondary sources has been "digested"-reformatted and condensed, to put it into a convenient, easy-to-read form.
* Sources which are once removed in time from secondary sources.

Table 8.1: General Classification of Selected Primary, Secondary and Tertiary Sources of Information

Primary Sources	Secondary Sources	Tertiary Sources
* Autobiographies	* Biographies, Encyclopedias, dictionaries, handbooks	* Chronologies
* Correspondence: e-mail, letters	* Textbooks and monographs on a topic	* Classifications
* Descriptions of travel	* Literary criticism and interpretation	* Dictionaries
* Diaries,	* History and historical criticism	* Encyclopedias
* Eyewitnesses	* Political analyses	* Directories
* Oral histories	* Reviews of law and legislation	* Guidebooks and manuals
* Literary works	* Essays on morals and ethics	* Population registers statistics
* Interviews	* Analyses of social policy	* Abstracts
* Personal narratives	* Study and teaching material	* Indexes
* First-hand newspaper and magazine accounts of events	* Articles, such as	* Bibliographies
* Legal cases, treaties	* Commentaries, research articles in all subject disciplines	* Manuals/Guide books
* Statistics, surveys, opinion polls,	* Criticism of works of literature, art and music	
* Scientific data, transcripts		
* Journal articles		
* Records of organizations literature reviews, and government agencies		
* Original works of literature, art or music		
* Cartoons, postcards, posters		
* Map, paintings, photographs, films		

DIFFERENCE BETWEEN PRIMARY, SECONDARY AND TERTIARY SOURCES OF INFORMATION

Primary sources of information are original manuscripts, documents or records used in preparing a published or unpublished work. For example, an article in a peer reviewed journal that discussed the development of a new vaccine for the prevention of HIV infection will be considered a primary source. Secondary sources are published or unpublished works that rely on primary source.

A commentary by a magazine reporter based on the peer reviewed journal article on the newly invented vaccine for HIV prevention, would be a secondary source. Tertiary sources are published or unpublished works that are based on secondary sources. Tertiary sources are index to primary sources. Science Citation Index would be considered a tertiary source. It is sometimes difficult to differentiate between primary, secondary and tertiary sources.

The following publication details of the information adapted from University of Wisconsin libraries can be helpful in determining whether a material is primary, secondary or tertiary source:

* *Timing of the Event Recorded*: If the article was composed close to the time of the event recorded, chances are it is primary material. For instance, a letter written by a soldier during the Second World War is primary material, as is an article written in the newspaper or a soldier's letter home during the Liberian Civil War. However, an article written analysing the results of the battle during the Liberian Civil War is secondary material.
* *Rhetorical Aim of the Written Item*: Often, an item that is written with a persuasive, or analytical aim is secondary material. These materials have digested and interpreted the event, rather than reported on it.
* *Context of the Researching Scholar*: Primary materials for a critic studying the literature of the Civil War are different from primary materials for a historian studying Civil War prisons. The critic's primary materials are the poems, stories, and films of the era. The research scientist's primary materials would be the diaries and writings of the prisoners.

FORMATS OF INFORMATION SOURCES

Information is available and accessible in two main formats namely, print and non-print and these include published and unpublished sources.

PRINT MATERIALS (PUBLISHED SOURCES)

Information could be in print format and these include: all printed books, periodicals, maps, bibliographies, indexes and abstracts, photographs, government documents, technical reports, etc. Books are the most common type of printed materials. *The Oxford Advanced Learner's Dictionary* defines a book as 'a set of printed pages that are fastened inside a cover so that you can turn them and read them.

A book is described by some people as a written work or composition that has been published, printed on pages bound together while others say it's just the content, separate from its container.

Books are categorized into two, namely: fiction and non-fiction. Fiction contains information that are not true and all the scenes and characters are made up by the author. Non-fiction books deals with information that is true, about real things, people, events and places.

NON-PRINT MATERIALS

In addition to printed materials, information is also produced in other formats (non-print) including audio, audiovisual, multimedia, microform and electronic books, journals, images, texts/records from the Internet.

AUDIO-VISUAL AND MULTIMEDIA

In the past decades, much of the information created by members of a given society is produced in audio, audio-visual and multimedia formats. Example of audio information is music recorded on CDs and books on audio or video tapes. Video information includes VCR tapes of TV shows, movies and documentaries. Other examples are information on CD-ROMs, DVDs, Flash drives and Web documents etc.

MICROFORM

The American Heritage Dictionary defines microform as an arrangement of images reduced in size, as on microfilm or microfiche. Microforms are any form, either films or paper, containing micro reproductions of documents for transmission, storage, reading, and printing. Microform images are commonly reduced about 25 times from the original document size, (miniaturized or compressed images) which cannot be read without special display devices (the reader). Archival materials are frequently placed in microform format because this medium is very stable and economical for storage of information for extended periods of time. There are two major types, namely: Microfilm and Microfiche.

MICROFILM

Microfilm is a roll of transparent film used to store microscopic images of documents. A microfilm reader is required to read the images in the microfilm. Documents are recorded in microfilm because of the risk of damage to a fragile original or to save storage space. Microfilm when properly processed and stored within special envelopes and placed in a climate-controlled room, has a life expectancy of approximately 500 years. Most libraries have a collection of microfilm stored in their archives.

MICROFICHE

Microfiche Is a small sheet of transparent photographic film usually 4 inches by 6 inches containing printed information in a size too small to be seen by the naked eye and needs a special device to read the images. The major advantages of microfiche include storage in a small space, stability of the format, and not needing knowledge to read it. As long as a microfiche machine is available to magnify the print to a readable size, anyone who can read the language can read the information on microfiche. When kept in a temperature-controlled environment, it can last for approximately 500 years; it is a good medium for saving and preserving cultural documents.

UNPUBLISHED SOURCES — INDIGENOUS KNOWLEDGE (IK)

In local communities in Africa, there is a rich body of information or knowledge which has been handed down by word of mouth from generation to generation. This is known as indigenous knowledge. It is neither written nor published but provides people in the community with strategies for survival. Indigenous knowledge is the sum total of knowledge and skills which people in a particular geographical area possess that enables them to get the most out of their natural environment. This information/knowledge is not systematically documented. It is oral in nature, usually transmitted through personal communication; it is culture-specific and often generated within communities for local level decision-making in agriculture, healthcare, food preparation, education, natural resources management and other activities. Examples of areas where indigenous knowledge has been very useful include, among others, African traditional medicine, conflict resolution and culture-dance steps and traditional attire.

WHERE TO FIND INFORMATION SOURCES

Places to begin looking for information are:

* Human sources;
* Archives;
* Libraries; and
* Internet.

HUMAN SOURCES (COLLEAGUES/PEERS)

Communication with peers and colleagues are a good way of obtaining vital information. For example, doctors have been found to rely on their colleagues for information in order to solve a patient's problems. The value of informal sources of information especially colleagues and peers cannot be overstressed. The good side of it is that human sources (colleagues/peers) are readily available to provide needed information at the right time. If the right person is contacted, quality and up-to-date information will be obtained. The downside of using human sources is that there may be some element of bias in the information provided, or some people will say things from their own point of view or exaggerate it.

ARCHIVES

Archives are places where records of all types and formats are kept and made accessible for research and other purposes. They are a good place to find primary sources, both unpublished materials and those that have been published for their parent institution's members or constituencies. Personal and institutional records of all types can be found in archives, as well as media, ephemera, oral histories, and even artifacts. The term *archives*can also refer to the records themselves. The materials housed in the archives are unique, usually one of a kind items. Archives store, preserve and make accessible records of enduring value that have not been produced in great quantities for the general public for research and understanding. Archival materials are rare and irreplaceable and therefore they are not loaned out to users.

LIBRARY

When you think about libraries, the first things that come to mind are probably printed materials such as books, journals and magazines. Libraries also provide access to resources such as fulltext journal and magazine articles, periodical indexes, and online encyclopedias. Libraries collect quality information in a wide variety of formats. Academic libraries purchase these sources for their "community" of students, faculty, and staff. Unlike archives, libraries have mass produced items such as books, government reports, CDs, DVDs, magazines and journals. The exceptions are rare books, manuscripts, map and other special collections. These resources are different from most of the information that is freely available to you over the Web because they have been reviewed and recommended by the library with input from the faculty members.

Like archives, libraries have primary source materials in many forms: historical newspapers, published letters, diaries, and government reports are just a few of the types of primary sources that can be found in libraries. In addition, some libraries are similar to archives in that they specialize in information materials such as rare books and unpublished manuscripts.

WHY GO TO A LIBRARY FOR INFORMATION

The main purpose of libraries, particularly those situated in University campuses, is to collect a large quantity of scholarly materials from different time periods and on diverse topics to make research easier for members of the community they serve (staff and students in the case of a university.) Library resources are free for use by members of the community. Libraries purchase materials that are normally too expensive for library patrons. Library materials, unlike those found on the Internet, go through a review process. Librarians select books, magazines, journals databases and even Websites for use by their patrons. This selection process enables the library to collect resources considered to be reliable, relevant and valuable. In addition, library resources are organized by subjects thus making them easy to find.

For easy access, each item of library material has a call number that indicates where it is located on the stack/shelf. Libraries have collections with in-depth information that has been published over time. Both current and out of print books and magazines are stocked in libraries most of which are in print formats. With the advent of the electronic age, some of these are now accessible through digital libraries collections on the Web. Libraries have trained staff called librarians who serve as a bridge between users and information sources. They assist users in sorting through the maze of information in their library collections. Librarians answer reference questions and also help patrons to learn how to use new information tools. If you need help with accessing information, contact your librarian.

SEARCHING THE LIBRARY CATALOG

For example, you can search the library catalog of a University such as the University of Maryland or University of Zimbabwe to find primary, secondary and tertiary sources of information.

Table 8.2: Sample Catalog Searches.

Primary	Diaries Nigerian Civil War
Secondary	Biography Nigerian Civil War
Tertiary	Encyclopedia Nigerian Civil War

When seeking information for academic purposes, it is advisable to start your search from the library and save yourself time and effort, as well as obtain relevant and quality information. You can then search the Internet if you need more information. Also, if you do not have the skills to search the Internet for relevant information, the librarians are there to assist you.

THE INTERNET

Definition of the Internet and the World Wide Web

The Internet is a global system of networked computers that allow user-to-user communication and transfer of data files from one computer to another on the network. It is a worldwide system of computer networks – a network of networks in which users at any one computer can, if they have permission, get information from any other computer (and sometimes talk directly to users at other computers) on the network. On the other hand, the World Wide Web (WWW) provides the technology needed to navigate the Internet is vast sea of resources. The WWW is a path-way of accessing information over the Internet via Uniform Resource Locator (URL) or web address.

Types of Information on the Internet

In the distant past humans sought to record information for future reference using clay tablets, papyrus, parchment and paper. However; the development of the printing press in the 16th Century forever changed the communication process. Currently the introduction of computers and the Internet has sky rocketed the amount of information now available to students, researchers, scientist, healthcare workers, policy makers, and faculty among others. Unlike the libraries, some of the information available on the Web is not peer-reviewed or referred as no one individual or group dictates what information should be published or how it should be presented. This freedom to post items allows individuals to publish their opinions, ideas and creative works on the Internet. As a result, the Internet has some information that may be interesting but cannot be referenced and used for academic purposes because no authority takes responsibility for it. Unlike libraries where librarians help users in accessing information, the Web is primarily a do-it-yourself endeavor.

The Internet contains all kinds of information sources including, among others:

* Bibliographic information such as library catalogs.
* Multimedia-Audio, video and graphical sources of information.
* Reference sources such as Encyclopedias, Dictionaries, Handbooks, and others.
* Journals, Newspapers, Magazines and Databases.
* Subject related gateways.
* Reports/Grey literature.
* Movies and videos.

INFORMATION SOURCES IN THE LIBRARY/INTERNET

The Internet has become a big library for all kinds of information. Some information sources are available online free of charge while others are fee-based. Examples include online books, databases, journals and reference resources. Some of these are free on the Internet while others are based on subscription or purchase. MEDLINE/PubMed is a good example of a free online database while EMBASE is based on subscription.

The various categories of information sources that could be accessed through the Web:

* Reference;
* Monographs;
* Periodicals;
* Indexes and abstracts;

* Drug information; and
* Databases.

REFERENCE SOURCES

These are authoritative works that provide specific answers or information. As you go through school, you will need to use reference sources to find information about topics, locate facts, and answer questions. There are many types of reference sources, including atlases, dictionaries, encyclopedias, thesauri, directories, almanacs, manuals, biographies, and handbooks, among others. Each type is available either in print, on CD-ROMs and the Internet. Reference information sources can be general or subject specific. For example, The Encyclopedia *Britannica* is general while *The Encyclopedia of Stem-Cell* Research, *The Encyclopedia of Pain,* and *The Gale Encyclopedia of Medicine* are subject encyclopedias. Other reference sources such as dictionaries, atlases, directories also have both general and subject categories.

Fig. 8.1. A Set of Encyclopedia Britannicagale Encyclopedia of Medicine.

MONOGRAPHS

A monograph is a scholarly piece of writing in form of an essay or book on a specific, often limited subject. It is a book that stands on its own rather than being part of a series. National Research Council (NRC), a monograph is a specialized scientific book. Monographs are written by specialists for the benefit of other specialists and demand the highest standards of scholarship. Most monographic manuscripts are critically reviewed and edited resulting in books that are expected to have a reasonably long shelf life. Monographs serve as an important means for conveying basic background information, such as a narrative description of a disease, path-physiology, diagnostic techniques and common therapeutic regimes etc. This trend remains true today, whether the monograph is in the print or electronic format.

Monographs can be located using bibliographies that list references of books with detailed bibliographic information (author, title, year of publication, publisher and date of publication). Bibliographies serve as tools for verification, location and selection of monographs. Today, many print sources for monographs are now in electronic formats. To locate monographs in a library collection requires using the library catalog and most libraries now have Online Public Access Catalog (OPAC). A good example is the National Library of Medicine LOCATOR plus.

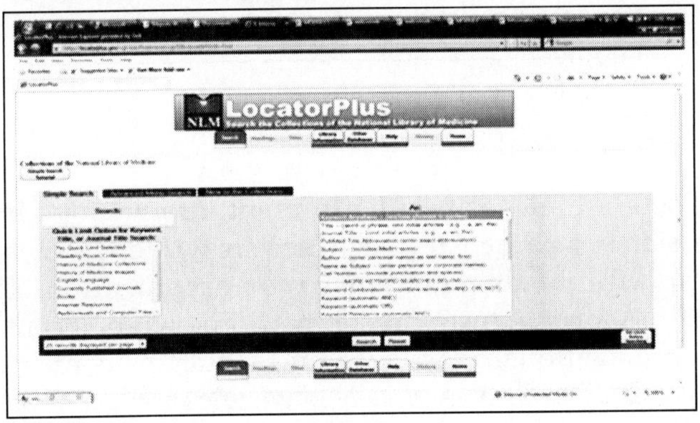

Fig. 8.2

PERIODICALS

Periodicals are publications such as journals, newspapers, or magazines published on a regular basis-daily, weekly, bi-weekly, monthly, bimonthly, quarterly, yearly, etc. The information in periodicals covers a wide variety of topics and is very uptodate. Periodicals are available in both print and electronic formats. Common examples of periodicals include popular magazines (or general interest magazines), professional and trade magazines, scholarly journals, newsletters, and newspapers. The two basic types of periodicals are: popular (or general interest magazines), and scholarly.

POPULAR

Popular magazines are periodicals of non-specialist nature. The published articles are usually written by staff writers, and chosen by the editor of the publication. Magazine articles are usually shorter, written in non-technical language, and designed for the general population. Articles in popular magazines are reviewed by one or two members of staff of the organization where they are published. Popular magazines have a glossy appearance, contains many photographs and advertisements.

Examples of popular magazines are:

* O, The Oprah Magazine.
* Readers Digest.
* People.
* Time Magazine.

TRADE MAGAZINES

These are magazines that present information about a profession or a particular trade. They are written for members of a specific business, industry or organization. Trade magazines cover industry trends, new products or techniques, and organizational news written by staff or contributing authors. Good examples of trade magazines are: *The Economist*, *APA Monitor* and *Computer World.*

SCHOLARLY JOURNALS

Journals are written by experts or specialists in a particular field/discipline and geared towards other scholars. The purpose of scholarly publications is to report research or advance knowledge. The articles are usually longer and may contain charts, graphs, statistics, etc., as well as extensive bibliographies. The articles usually involve extensive research and in-depth studies. The writing style is more complex and the language may be technical. Examples of this type of periodical are academic journals and professional journals. Academic journals are written by members of an academic community and are reviewed by their peers while professional journals are written by member of a professional body including librarians, lawyers, doctors and nurses.

Examples of academic journals are:

* *British Medical Journal.*
* *New England Journal of Medicine.*
* *African Journal of Medicine and Medical Sciences.*
* *East African Medical Journal.*
* *African Health Sciences.*

Examples of professional/academic journals include:

* *Journal of the American Medical Association.*
* *Journal of the Medical Library Association.*
* *African Journal of Library, Archival and Information Science.*

Access to journals either in print or electronic formats is based on subscription, however; fulltext articles of some electronic journals can be accessed free on the Internet. Also, more than 7000 electronic journals are available to students, researchers, scientists, healthcare workers, and policy makers in Africa through the Health Internetwork Access to Research Initiative (HINARI). Using this resource requires institutional registration and login with the User Identification and Password.

NEWSPAPERS

Newspaper articles are short and written in non-technical language. They provide first-hand account of an event and so are primary sources. Newspapers come in different forms and are designed for the general public and are business in nature. Newspaper articles are usually short and written in an easy to understand language by staff reporters and reviewed by staff within the organization. Newspapers are also good sources for secondary information. However, not all information in newspapers is reliable. Newspapers are published daily, weekly or monthly. Example of newspapers include: *The New York Times, The Guardian,* and *Nigerian Tribune* etc.

INDEXES AND ABSTRACTS

Abstracts and indexes provide citations to papers dealing with specific topics in a field of knowledge. Indexes provide the essential bibliographic information needed to identify an article or other publications and usually include information about the author of the work, the source journal or other publication, volume, issue, and pagination. Abstracting tools include the same key elements but also a summary of the work usually written by the author or sometimes generated by the reviewer where an author did not submit one. Most indexing and abstracting services allow access to their content through subject and author indexes. However, each tool differs on how data is presented and the nature by which access is organized.

Examples of abstracts and indexes include:

* *Index Medicus.*
* *International Pharmaceutical Abstracts.*
* *Index to Dental Literature.*
* *Science Citation Index.*
* *Current Contents: Clinical Practice.*
* *Psychological Abstracts.*
* *Cumulative Index to Nursing and Allied Health Literature* (CINAHL).

Most of the popular databases searched by librarians and library users originated from printbased abstracting and indexing services. For example, the Index Medicus resulted in MEDLINE now accessible online through PubMed.

DRUG INFORMATION SOURCES

Butros and McGuinness, drug information sources cover the fields of pharmacology, pharmacy and toxicology. There are as many drug information sources as there are various specialties.

DATABASES

These are systematically organized collections of information covering different subject matters or specializing in one given subject or topic. They may be arranged in a table of contents, alphabetically, in numerical order, in an index or in subject categories. A database is made up of records. Each item in the database has one record. Records consist of smaller units of information called fields.

Common bibliographic database fields are: author, publication title, article title, subject or keywords, publication date, volume, issue and page number. For example, in the MEDLINE/PubMed database, each journal citation has one record. The record consists of the following fields: author, article title, journal title, date of publication, volume, issue, page number, PubMed ID, and abstract. A digital database (8.3) is a computer programme that organizes, describes, and indexes information. It permits the user to search for specific types of information, depending upon the selected search parameters.

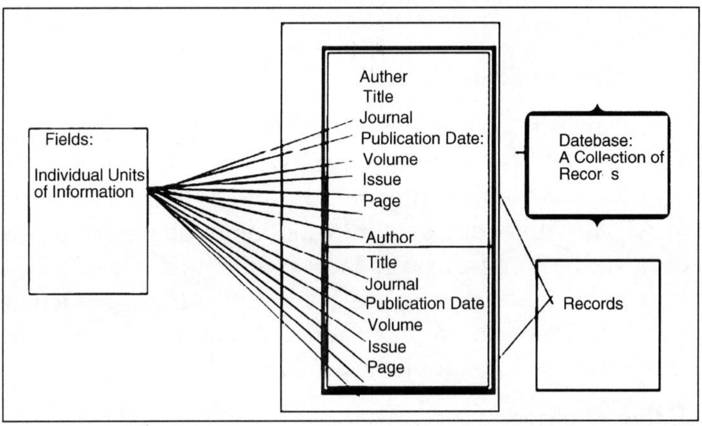

Fig. 8.3: Components of a Biblographic Database

INVISIBLE OR DEEP WEB

The "invisible Web" is what you cannot find using search engines and what you see in almost all subject directories. They are gold mines of information you need to search directly. These includes all of the licensed article, magazine, reference, news archives, and other research resources that libraries and some industries buy for those authorized to use them. There is lots of helpful information locked away in databases that can never be indexed by search engines. The services that let you search this "invisible Web" or "deep Web include: Invisibleweb.com, Lycos Invisible Catalog, Direct search and WebData.

Examples of searchable databases containing invisible web pages valuable in academic research are:

* ipl2.
* Infomine.
* Online Bibliographic Databases:
    - African Index Medicus (AIM);
    - MEDLINE/PubMed;
    - Cumulative Index to Nursing and Allied Health Literature (CINAHL);
    - Web of Knowledge;
    - Scopus; and
    - EMBASE.

African Index Medicus (AIM)

African Index Medicus (AIM) is a collaborative effort between the World Health Organization (WHO) and the Association for Health Information and Libraries in Africa (AHILA). AIM gives access to information published or related to Africa and also encourages local publishing. A total of 140 journals published in Africa are indexed in AIM as of October 1, 2010. This database provides access to mainly abstracts and a few full-text articles published in African journals.

MEDLINE/PubMed

MEDLINE is the premier bibliographic database of the National Library of Medicine, Bethesda, Maryland, USA. It covers the field of medicine, nursing dentistry, veterinary medicine, the healthcare systems, the preclinical sciences and other areas related to the life sciences and is updated daily. MEDLINE records contain bibliographic citations from over 5,000 print and electronic biomedical journals published across the globe. It has over 12 million citations of which approximately 76% include abstracts.

Cumulative Index to Nursing and Allied Health Literature (CINAHL)

Cumulative Index to Nursing and Allied Health Literature (CINAHL) CINAHL gives access to citations and abstracts for nursing and allied health information. It includes citations from over 2000 journals and abstracts are available for over 1200 titles with full text of over 7,000 records available in the database. This database also provides some coverage of biomedicine, alternative/complementary medicine and consumer health information. CINAHL is based on subscription. However, it could be accessed free of charge through HINARI by institutions in Africa.

Web of Science

Web or science Provides access to the Science Citation Index Expanded and Social Science Citation Index. It covers science and provides technical journals in biochemistry, biology, genetics, biomedicine, genetics, microbiology, nuclear science with abstracts. It covers more than 8,000 journals. It offers current and retrospective bibliographic information, author abstracts and cited references and allows users to conduct broad-based comprehensive searches that uncover all the relevant information they need. It provides cited reference searching, the unique ISI search and retrieval feature that lets users track the literature forward, backward and through the database. It is updated weekly. Web of Knowledge (PubMed) is accessible free of charge via HINARI.

Scopus

Scopus is an interdisciplinary bibliographic database that indexes the content of more than 15,000 peer-reviewed journals from more than 4000 international publishers. It covers subjects such as the physical sciences, engineering, earth and environmental sciences, life and health sciences, social sciences, psychology, business, and management. Scopus content includes MEDLINE and EMBASE citations. Also, Scopus covers 1,000 Open Access Journals, 500 Conference Proceedings, Over 600 Trade Publications and over 125 Book titles. In addition, Scopus covers 386 million quality Web sources including 21 million patents.

Embase

Provides content to biomedical (clinical and experimental) information with extensive coverage of drug research, pharmacology, pharmacy, and toxicology, public health and mental health topics with abstracts back to 1974 and it is updated daily with pharmacological information. The database indexes more than 7000 journals, has over 18 million records. It has more than the 11 million EMBASE records from 1974 to date and seven million for unique MEDLINE records from 1966 to the present.

EVIDENCE-BASED MEDICINE (EBM) RESOURCES/ DATABASES

Evidence-Based Medicine is about using information from the medical literature in making informed decision about patient care.

Many EBM databases are now accessible online including, among others:

* Clinical Queries.
* Cochrane Library.
* Clinical Evidence.
* DynaMed.
* Best Evidence.

In this module, Clinical Queries and the Cochrane Library will be discussed

Clinical Queries

This is accessible through PubMed and covers three main areas namely:

* *Clinical Study Category Query*: This filters citations to a specific clinical study category and scope.
* *Systematic Reviews:* These filter citations for systematic reviews, meta-analyses, reviews of clinical trials, evidence-based medicine, consensus development conferences, and guidelines..

* *Medical Genetics:* Filter citations to topics in medical genetics.

The Cochrane Library

The Cochrane Library is a collection of databases, published on CD-ROM and the Internet and updated quarterly, containing the Cochrane Database of Systematic Reviews, the Cochrane Central Register of Controlled Trials, the Database of Abstracts of Reviews of Effects, the Cochrane Methodology Register, the HTA Database, NHSEED, and information about The Cochrane Collaboration. The Cochrane Library has about 4,000 reviews meant for use by health care workers to enable them to make informed decisions with respect to patient care. Reviews are unique because they are both produced by, and are relevant to everyone interested in the effects of health care. Based on the best available evidence, healthcare providers can decide if they should fund production of a particular drug. Practitioners can find out if an intervention is effective in a specific clinical context.

Patients and other healthcare consumers can assess the potential risks and benefits of their treatment:

* Systematic reviews seek to collate all evidence that fits pre-specified eligibility criteria in order to address a specific research question.
* They aim to minimize bias by using explicit, systematic methods.
* The Cochrane Collaboration prepares, maintains and promotes systematic reviews to inform healthcare decisions (Cochrane reviews).
* Cochrane reviews are published in the *Cochrane Database of Systematic Reviews* in *The Cochrane Library.*

CONSUMER HEALTH INFORMATION RESOURCES/ DATABASES

* MEDLINEPlus.
* National Institute of Health (NIH) Senior Health.
* New York Online Access to Health (NOAH).
* HealthyRoadsMedia.

* Toxtown.
* Toxnet.
* Household products database.

Medline Plus

Medline Plus is a product of the National Library of Medicine (NLM). Medline Plus offers information on selected, organized links to online consumer health information on hundreds of topics about diseases, conditions, and wellness issues in language you can understand. Medline Plus offers reliable, up-to-date health information, anytime, anywhere for free. You can use Medline Plus to learn about the latest treatments, look up information on a drug or supplement, find out the meanings of words, or view medical videos or illustrations. You can also get links to the latest medical research on your topic or learn about clinical trials on a disease or condition. It also includes tutorials.

Also featured are an online encyclopedia, medical dictionary, audio-visual resources, and extensive links to Spanish-language health information. Medline Plus is the premier consumer health site. It should be any consumer health information seeker's first stop, and can fill the vast majority of information needs. The homepage is very well-organized; everything is accessible from there. When searching, multiple search terms automatically combined with "And". Search engine will detect misspelled words and suggest alternatives.

NIH Senior Health

This is a website for the elderly, developed by the National Institute on Aging and the National Library of Medicine. Senior-friendly features include the ability to adjust font size and contrast, an audio option that reads text on the page aloud, and videos. Seniors with low vision, and anyone with low literacy needs, although most topics are senior-specific (*i.e.* Exercise for Older Adults). A short list of topics is easy to browse. No search option is included. Audio text reading function is very literal and function is spotty: may repeat phrases several times and/or skip words or sentences.

NOAH: New York Online Access to Health

A collaborative effort of New York librarians, NOAH provides access to selected, organized links to online consumer health information. It has a wide range of topics and extensive Spanish-language content. Non-Spanish-speaking users can navigate organized topic pages in English, and then click on "en espanol" link at bottom of page to access available Spanish language links for that topic. It is well-organized and easy to browse; browsing is often more efficient than using the search engine.

Healthy Roads Media

A collaborative effort of many different public health agencies, social services organizations, and librarians, HealthyRoadsMedia collects, creates and provides free online access to multilingual health information overviews on various topics in a variety of formats: audio, audiovisual, and written. Health topics provided in English and eight other languages: Arabic, Bosnian, Hmong, Khmer, Russian, Somali, Spanish, and Vietnamese. It is best for patients with lower literacy English and/or need for information in a language other than English. Focus is on prevention and wellness, and safety. Not all topics are available in all languages.

Household Products Database

This database links over 10,000 consumer brands to health effects from Material Safety Data Sheets (MSDS) provided by manufacturers and allows scientists and consumers to research products based on chemical ingredients. Household product database was developed by the Specialized Information Services Division at the National Library of Medicine, National Institutes of Health, Bethesda, Maryland, USA.

The database is designed to help answer the following typical questions:

* What are the chemical ingredients and their percentage in specific brands?
* Which products contain specific chemical ingredients?

* Who manufactures a specific brand? How do I contact this manufacturer?
* What are the acute and chronic effects of chemical ingredients in a specific brand?
* What other information is available about chemicals in the toxicology-related databases of the National Library of Medicine?

Tox Town

Tox Town: is designed to give you information on:

* Everyday locations where you might find toxic chemicals.
* Non-technical descriptions of chemicals.
* Links to selected, authoritative chemical information on the Internet.
* How the environment can impact human health.
* Internet resources on environmental health topics.

Tox Town uses colour, graphics, sounds and animation to add interest to learning about connections between chemicals, the environment, and the public's health. Tox Town's target audience is students above elementary-school level, educators, and the general public. It is a companion to the extensive information in the TOXNET collection of databases that are typically used by toxicologists and health professionals.

Toxnet

Toxnet is a database on toxicology, hazardous chemicals, environmental health, toxic releases and other information resources from the Toxicology and Environmental Health Information Programme. Developed by the U.S National Library of Medicine.

INTERNET PORTALS, DIGITAL ARCHIVES AND INSTITUTIONAL REPOSITORIES

* Health Internetwork Access to Research Initiative (HINARI) African Journals Online (AJOL).
* PubMed Central (PMC).

* *Bioline International (BI):* Through this site you can search through free and open access medical journals.
* *Biomed Central*: Open Access (OA) journal publisher that allow readers free access to published full text journal articles while authors pay fees to get published.
* *Scientific Online Library (SciELO):* An AO publisher that gives access to full text articles.
* *Directory of Open Access Journals (DOAJ):* Gives you free access to online journals related to your subject area.
* Loughborough University's Institutional Repository.
* *Google Scholar:* While regular Google can be a helpful tool, sometimes you just need scholarly results, and that's just what this tool does, paring down results to the most reliable and academic sources.

INFORMATION SOURCES ON SOCIAL NETWORKING APPLICATIONS

In recent years social networking applications popularly known as Web 2.0 are now being used as a means of communication, especially in sharing and dissemination of information. Libraries are also using this media to reach out to their clients.

Common Web 2.0 applications that have become sources of information include:

* Facebook;
* Blogs;
* Twitter;
* MySpace;
* YouTube; and
* RSS.

9

Reference and Information Services

In this first decade of the twenty-first century reference and information services are a vital yet changing part of the function and mission of the library institution. While the continually expanding availability of electronic resources and digitized materials has changed the nature of reference, the essential service remains central. Indeed, far from minimizing the need for reference services, the rise of the Internet, and with it the availability of a tremendous number of subscription and free online resources, makes this aspect of library service all the more crucial.

Librarians and their users are constantly bombarded with a wide range of information choices that must be evaluated for authenticity and accuracy. Whether at home on their computers or wandering through the stacks, many people feel as though they are drowning in a sea of information. New media and technologies are like tributaries leading to this great new body of knowledge, and each stream makes the waters deeper and more perilous. Reference services are at once a life raft, map, and compass to those who feel adrift.

In providing them with a combination of personalized service in a timely manner, libraries reaffirm their centrality as twenty-first century public institutions par excellence:

* For all its contemporary relevance, the concept of reference service is more than a century old. In 1876, Samuel Green, librarian of the Worcester Free Public

Library in Massachusetts, developed the idea of having librarians assist the user in the selection of books to suit their needs. This served a dual function, increasing the use of his library's collection and thereby demonstrating the need for the library. Green saw the role of the public library as one of welcoming users by having a pleasant and cultivated female staff. Some forty years later, in 1915 at the thirty-seventh meeting of the American Library Association, a paper on reference work was delivered by W.W. Bishop, the superintendent of the Reading Room of the Library of Congress. Bishop defined reference work as "the service rendered by a librarian in aid of some sort of study" holding that it was "an organized effort on the part of libraries in aid of the most expeditious and fruitful use of their books."

The idea of reference service was further developed by Charles Williamson in his 1923 report, "Training for Library Service: A Report Prepared for the Carnegie Corporation of New York," which included a course description for reference work:

* A study of the standard works of reference, general and special encyclopedias, dictionaries, annuals, indexes to periodicals, ready reference manuals of every kind, special bibliographies, and the more important newspapers and periodicals. Works of similar scope are compared, and the limitations of each pointed out. Lists of questions made up from practical experience are given, and the method of finding the answers discussed in the class.

Several authors, including James I. Wyer, Margaret Hutchins, William A. Katz, Richard E. Bopp, and Linda C. Smith wrote reference texts in which they continued to refine the role of the reference librarian over the subsequent decades. Perhaps the most important point to remember is that reference service seeks to fulfill the greater mission of the library by helping individual users. Despite the many transformations that have been wrought on reference work by both developments of our information society and paradigm shifts in the selfunderstandings of the library, much has remained the same.

First and foremost, it is still a service in which the librarian interacts with a patron on a one-to-one basis. This level of personal service has become even more important in the twenty-first century in light of the alienating and depersonalizing effects of many information technologies. On the other hand, the way such service is provided has changed considerably—it now extends beyond face-to-face assistance thanks to the availability of the telephone, e-mail, and the technology for chat and IM reference.

ETHICAL AWARENESS AND ENGAGEMENT

Ethical awareness and engagement is a crucial aspect of all library services, and the ideals that have been established for the profession generally apply fully to those working in reference services. Just as therapists would do their patients little good if they did not keep their information confidential, reference librarians must follow certain standards of behaviour if the service they provide is to be effective. The American Library Association's Current Code of Ethics, adopted in 1995, provides a useful guide. This code, composed of eight broad statements, upholds a variety of the principles essential to the modern library.

The first statement of the Code insists that librarians should provide the "highest level of service to all library users" and service that is equitable for all with information provided that is "accurate, unbiased and courteous." This statement is at the heart of good reference service, which strives to provide good quality information and information that can be documented.

Reference staff must understand what constitutes a good reference interaction and must strive to meet that standard with each user query. The second statement of the Code calls for the protection of the "principles of intellectual freedom" and resistance to "all efforts to censor library resources." Library selection is reflected in this statement, as librarians attempt to provide information on a subject from many points of view.

The third statement protects the user's right to privacy and confidentiality in requesting and using library resources. Reference librarians must be particularly cognizant of this professional obligation. They must respect the privacy of a user by keeping their reference interview and the resources used confidential. The fourth statement, intellectual property rights should be recognized and respected. It is important that librarians keep current with changes in intellectual property laws, especially copyright, and keep their users aware of these laws.

Librarians must know when copying is covered under the "fair use" provision of the law and when copying violates the copyright law. This is more than a good in itself; it also helps protect the institution, its employees, and its users from claims of copyright infringement and intellectual dishonesty. The fifth through the eighth statements of the Code all treat the relationship between personal interests and professional responsibilities. The fifth encourages the respectful treatment of coworkers and colleagues and the safeguarding of the rights of all employees. This is a statement that encompasses the whole library and its staff.

Every staff member should ensure that others are treated fairly. In the sixth statement, library employees are cautioned not to put private interests ahead of library interests. This means that employees should be circumspect in their dealings with library vendors and others outside the library so their decisions are made on professional merit and are not influenced by personal interest. The seventh statement cautions library employees not to put personal convictions or beliefs ahead of library interests. This is also of special significance to reference librarians.

Sometimes a librarian must help a user research an area that is personally against the librarian's beliefs or philosophy. But by putting professional duties first, the librarian can successfully assist the user and provide the information needed. The eighth statement encourages all library staff to continue to grow in their knowledge and skills and to assist those entering the profession. We live in a time when change is constant, so all library staff must continue to learn and change. Other professional library organizations have their own codes of ethics. These include the *American Society for Information Science* (ASIS), the Society of American Archivists, the Medical Library Association, and the American Association of Law Libraries.

KINDS OF INFORMATION SERVICE

Information service, in the most general sense, is the process of assisting library users to identify sources of information in response to a particular question, interest, assignment, or problem. Sometimes referred to as reference service, the *Reference and User Services Association* (RUSA) of the American Library Association defines reference transactions as "information consultations in which library staff recommend, interpret, evaluate, and/or use information resources to help others to meet particular information needs". These reference transactions can take place in person or via the telephone, e-mail, or virtual reference technologies.

Librarians are also creating Web sites, answer archives, and links to answers to "frequently asked questions" all designed to anticipate user questions and help people find information independently. Traditional reference desk service continues to be highly valued by library users in many settings, but the newer forms continue to grow in popularity. Consequently, it is all the more important that librarians understand the range of enquiries that can be expected, allowing them to provide a full and ready answer, regardless of the form in which the query arises.

ANSWERING REFERENCE QUESTIONS

In light of the immense diversity and range of possible questions, being approached by a patron with a reference need can seem like a daunting prospect. Indeed, much of the difficulty of information services arises from uncertainty about the kind of service or breadth of information called for by a given question. Categorizing reference questions by type is a useful way to make sense of such concerns. Three common types of information service are ready reference questions, research questions, and bibliographic verification. *Ready reference questions* such as "Where was Abraham Lincoln born?" "Who won the 1992 World Series?" "What is the capital of Nicaragua?" or "Where can I find a copy of the United States' Declaration of Independence?" can be readily answered using one or two general reference sources.

The librarian may be tempted to tell the user the answer to simple ready reference questions. Yet here the old saying that "giving a man a fish feeds him for a day while teaching him to fish feeds him for a lifetime" is proven true. No matter how simple they seem initially, ready reference questions provide the possibility of teachable moments. Whenever possible, librarians should lead users through the process of looking up the information rather than simply providing the solution.

Librarians who assist users with ready reference enquiries on a regular basis sometimes choose to create a "ready reference" section of the most commonly used resources either in print or on the library's Web site to answer quick questions. Typically, such sections include a general all-purpose encyclopedia, dictionaries, almanacs, and handbooks. Care must be taken to keep the sources uptodate and to avoid depending so heavily on this subset of the collection that other sources are overlooked by library users and librarians.

Librarians may find that ready reference questions have diminished due to the ease of answering basic questions through online information portals such as Google. Nevertheless, ready reference remains a cornerstone of information services, and librarians should be primed to provide it at any time. *Research questions* are more complex, may take much longer to answer, and typically require multiple sources of information. These questions often require the user to consider a variety of sources and viewpoints and to subsequently draw conclusions.

Sometimes questions that initially seem like ready reference questions are far more complex as previously hidden facets of the user's enquiry are revealed. Here, the variety of possible sources increases with the complexity of users' questions. Librarians should, for example, guide the user in the use of bibliographic sources, citations, and the back-of-the-book bibliographies. Likewise, users with complex questions may need to be taught how to find or request the full text of articles for which only citations are given in a search of electronic databases, allowing them to move beyond cursory surveys of the literature.

Research questions, especially if the user is unable to fully articulate the nature of his or her query, require librarians to ask questions of their own, trying to get at the nature of the request before setting out to help the patron answer it. The librarian may, for example, have to determine how much information is needed, what level of information is needed, and what other sources have already been consulted. Information services call for mutual engagement, especially with more complex questions.

Reference librarians should never be passive participants, pointing the way to an answer. Instead, they should play the part of dynamic guides, joining users on their journeys to knowledge. Naturally, the extent of such engagement may vary from one circumstance to another. Different types of libraries tend to have their own standards for how long librarians should spend with users on research questions. Many public libraries recommend that users be given five or ten minutes of personal assistance and then asked to return if more help is needed.

A university library may have a similar standard, or depending on the institution, may be able to invite the user to make an appointment for more in-depth research assistance. Some libraries may suggest that users call or e-mail ahead of their visit so the librarian can be prepared to offer the best possible assistance. Other libraries, including special libraries, may only be able to provide a basic level of help during the first visit. Libraries may refer users to other libraries with more specialized materials in the area of the user's research or may offer to call back if additional information is found.

Finally a library user may seek *bibliographic verification* when he or she has already obtained the information needed but must verify the sources. Sometimes this service is a matter of fact checking, whereas on other occasions users may have completed their research but lack full citation information. As users increasingly depend on electronic databases for information, compiling and formatting bibliographic citations becomes easier. Verifying and citing material found on Web pages is more difficult since the information needed for the citation is not always easy to find.

READER'S ADVISORY SERVICE

Reader's advisory service, sometimes considered a type of information service, is the quest to put the right book in the hands of the right reader. Librarians are increasingly expected to provide an answer to the dreaded question, "Can you help me find a good book?" Fortunately, as demand has increased, so too has the ease of providing this service. Although there is no substitute for one's own knowledge or experience, many new technologies serve to make the reader's advisory far easier than it was in the past. Many online databases, for example, have functions that automatically recommend other books for those who like a given title. Others have searchable lists of works by genre, helping readers match their favourite books to others like them.

As always, however, remember that reader's advisory, like other reference work, is predicated on the interaction between librarian and library user. Asking directed questions, listening carefully to the users' responses, and tailoring assistance accordingly is the basis of excellent, truly helpful service. The reader's advisory service is generally associated with public libraries and tends to be employed primarily by those looking for fiction. In academic libraries, it is far less common as users rarely come in searching for a mystery to read. Even so, reader's advisory may be needed to help lay researchers looking to deepen their knowledge of a particular field.

A patron who has read and enjoyed Stephen Ambrose's *Undaunted Courage,* but is troubled by allegations about

Ambrose's questionable accuracy and academic honesty, may want to know the titles of books about the Lewis and Clark expedition that are both reputable and engaging. Successful reader's advisory librarians are skilled at asking users questions that enable them to assess users' reading level, language, or educational background. They must know a great deal about various genres of fiction and nonfiction and be intimately familiar with their library's collection. Significantly, it is important that they be able to convey their expertise in a friendly and conversational manner.

INFORMATION LITERACY

User instruction, which is now usually referred to as *information literacy*, may range from showing an individual how to use the library's online catalog and basic print reference sources to formal classroom sessions about conducting research in the library. The basic component of information literacy includes demonstrating how, when, and why to use various reference sources in an integrated way that will capture the user's attention at the teachable moment. In today's educational settings, the ease of using electronic resources often results in a failure to teach more traditional research strategies. While finding superficial information has grown easier, in-depth information has become increasingly obscure for many students.

In the library too, approaches to instruction may vary and librarians often question whether to simply answer questions posed by users or to teach users how to employ the available resources. This may be contingent on the mission or purpose of the library. Academic institutions may call on their librarians to help students understand how to engage effectively and independently in the research and information evaluation process. Public librarians, by contrast, may try to teach users about reference sources in a more informal manner as they lead users to the answers they seek.

Thus, while instruction is always an important part of reference work, the degree to which they go about providing it is highly contingent on the circumstances. In any case, all reference librarians must be skilled at helping users find information and answers quickly and be ready to teach users how to use the reference sources that are available. The best reference librarians develop an intuition for when to be information providers and when to be bibliographic instructors.

In some libraries, only specific, designated librarians are charged with conducting library instruction courses. Nevertheless, an increasing number of librarians are required to participate in their libraries' bibliographic instruction programme, and library school graduates are expected to be capable of teaching basic classes on the use of library resources. As should be clear, even those librarians not charged with providing formal instruction have the opportunity to teach those they serve.

SELECTING AND EVALUATING PRINT AND ELECTRONIC INFORMATION

Selecting and evaluating print and electronic information for the library's collection can be as professionally rewarding as providing expert information service. Reference librarians' involvement in evaluating and selecting titles for the collection helps them develop rich knowledge of the sources at their disposal, increasing their effectiveness. The responsibility for selecting reference materials depends largely on the size and scope of the library. In large academic libraries, selecting reference materials may be assigned to subject bibliographers whose work may be limited to collection development responsibilities.

On the other side of the continuum, the evaluation and purchase of resources in very small libraries may be the work of a single reference librarian or coordinator of reference. A range of shared evaluation and selection possibilities between these points include reference materials selection committees or group assignments. The question, "What makes a book a reference book?" has long been debated in our profession. For the purpose of this discussion, reference books are those texts set aside to be consulted for specific information rather than to be read as a whole. In other words, reference books contain content meant to be "looked up".

Typically, one turns to a reference source in search of something in particular rather than to the text as a whole. Another common characteristic of reference books is that they do not leave the library premises. This ensures that all works in the reference collection are always on hand, making for a consistently available body of knowledge. Note that labeling narrative or non-reference books as "reference" to deter theft or ensure that a popular volume is always available may lead to bloated reference collections, and it is not generally recommended.

Finally, with the addition of electronic reference sources, which are increasingly available to remote library users from their homes, dorm rooms, offices, and elsewhere, reference collections encompass much more than print books and serials and may be available twenty-four hours a day.

As the present trend towards shrinking budgets for reference collections, lean reference collections, and the elimination of duplication among print and electronic collections continues, the careful evaluation and selection of reference materials is essential. Libraries should determine the criteria that will be used in selecting sources for its reference collection. The following criteria may help determine whether an item is a worthy addition to a library's collection: scope, quality of content, appropriateness for audience, format, arrangement, authority, currency, accuracy, ease of use, unique coverage and cost.

Criteria for selecting electronic resources may vary, though all of the criteria used to evaluate print resources should be considered, especially in libraries that aim to avoid redundancy in their print and electronic reference collections. Some libraries select reference materials by reading reviews in the library professional literature such as *Library Journal* and *Choice* and *Booklist*'s "Reference Books Bulletin." Other institutions insist on physically reviewing reference sources at trade shows or through special arrangements with publishers of reference materials. Most libraries employ a combination of these two.

CREATING FINDING TOOLS AND WEB SITES

Another strategy employed by many reference departments is the creation of finding tools and pathfinders for library users. Here, librarians act as cartographers, mapping out the best routes through familiar territory and pointing out interesting sites along the way. Pathfinders are often prepared for commonly requested subjects such as high school and college assignments about capital punishment, drug abuse, and the history of Native American tribes. Similarly, public libraries may prepare pathfinders that address frequently asked questions of a quotidian nature such as: finding job information, checking the credentials of a health care provider, or researching a family tree.

Depending on the topic, audience, and needs, the pathfinder may guide the user to a selection of appropriate reference books, relevant databases and search terms, a selection of current and authoritative Web sites, and tips for searching the library's *Online Public Access Catalog* (OPAC) for additional materials. Librarians also create Web sites of carefully evaluated links organized by topic, sometimes known as "webliographies" that serve as finding tools. Who better than librarians to organize the World Wide Web of information, pointing the users to "the best" sources and helping them steer clear of the dubious? Web-based finding tools offer several advantages to print pathfinders.

They are available to users 24/7, they can be updated as often as needed, and they can include direct links to Web sites and electronic reference tools. Depending on the circumstance and the nature of a library's Web presence such webliographies can be either general, providing direction to broadly targeted reference resources, or subject specific.

General all-purpose lists of librarian-selected Web resources include the *Internet Public Library* and the *Librarians' Internet Index*. Examples of library subject-specific webliographies include The New York Public Library's *Best of the Web* and the University of Washington's *Information Gateway*. Larger libraries, whether academic or public, often produce indexes of both types. Smaller libraries may be better served by developing webliographies for specific areas in which they have subject specialists and linking to a general reference site like the *Internet Public Library* or the *Librarians' Internet Index*.

PROMOTING AND MARKETING LIBRARIES AND REFERENCE SERVICE

Paying attention to promotion and marketing of libraries and reference service is becoming more important than ever. Without support from the community, the library will not stay viable. Promoting reference services among individual library users can go a long way towards achieving this goal, especially insofar as it demonstrates how the library can serve them. In large communities—urban public libraries, for example-promoting the library through individual users is not enough to attract new users and major marketing or publicity campaigns become important. In academic libraries, school libraries, and special libraries, promotion and marketing are equally essential. Use of print and online newsletters, Web sites, and opportunities to meet with faculty and staff can provide opportunities to promote the library's resources.

EVALUATING STAFF AND SERVICES

Libraries may seek to routinely evaluate their reference collections or reference service. In her book *Evaluating Reference Services: A Practical Guide*, Jo Bell Whitlatch wisely emphasizes the importance of defining the purpose of the evaluation before setting a strategy. "The most important questions you must ask," according to Whitlatch, are these: "Why am I evaluating reference services" and "What do I plan to do with the study results?" The quality of the reference interaction, from either the user's or the librarian's perspective, may be assessed to help determine how effective the reference service is. Evaluating reference staff is one way to help determine how effective the reference service is, and is one way to help assure quality reference service.

The American Library Association's Reference and User Services Association has developed "Guidelines for

Behavioural Performance of Reference and Information Service Professionals," which are intended to be used in the training, development, or evaluation of library professionals and staff. The performance of reference librarians is typically evaluated on both the information conveyed to users and the satisfaction of the interaction on the library user.

The following factors are covered by the ALA Guidelines:

* *Approachability:* Are users able to identify that a reference librarian is available to help?
* *Interest:* Does the librarian demonstrate a high degree of interest in the reference transaction?
* *Listening/Enquiring:* Does the librarian identify the user's information need in a manner that puts the user at ease? Are good communication skills used throughout the transaction?
* *Searching:* Is the librarian skilled at creating search strategies that yield accurate and relevant results?
* *Follow-up:* Does the librarian determine if the user is satisfied with the results of the search/interaction?

These performance guidelines may form the backbone of a library's staff evaluation instruments, whether the instrument is a simple self-evaluation checklist, a peer-evaluation tool, or a formal evaluation system influencing earning potential. In addition to evaluating staff, the library may measure its productivity or efficiency with quantitative measures that include the number of questions answered and the frequency with which print and/or electronic sources are consulted. Smaller libraries may continuously count the number and type of in-person questions answered by the reference staff.

In larger libraries, quarterly one-week periods are frequently used to estimate the number of questions answered over the course of a year. Depending on the available resources, data may be recorded using hand-held computers, by making hash marks on a form, or by any means in between. Avariety of other evaluation strategies are also available to libraries: Assessing the quality of the resources available may, for example, be another useful measurement. Issues of resource allocation may also be incorporated into departmental evaluations, if one includes how the library's budget allocates for library staff, print and electronic resources, computers and networks, and buildings.

Evaluation methods frequently used to gauge users' satisfaction with reference services and sources include questionnaires, surveys, focus groups, observation and interviews. It is crucial that library administrators determine what is to be measured and against what standards before choosing the preferred method of evaluation. Many sources are available for detailed information on designing evaluation instruments for libraries. Selecting the best method, developing and field testing the instrument, administering the survey, questionnaire, or interview, planning the observation, avoiding interviewer bias and scores of ethical issues should be carefully considered. Analysing data and developing conclusions and recommendations may require advanced training and in some cases evaluation experts are hired.

THE CHANGING NATURE OF REFERENCE

As the form of the library has evolved in the years since Samuel Green's seminal pronouncements in 1876, so too has the nature of reference services. Today it stretches far beyond the walls of the library and strives to far loftier ends than welcoming users to the library with a "cultivated female staff." Academic libraries in particular have already seen a slowing of traffic to the physical library and the increasing use of the library's online resources. Users can ask questions 24/7 through virtual reference and expect an immediate response. Likewise, they can access electronic resources that the library provides through its Web site.

Virtual reference is growing quickly; the appeal of instant messaging and like services point to a generational paradigm shift ahead. These online reference services have the advantage of being convenient and necessary in our fast-paced world. In numerous forms and fashions, technology continues to change reference services. Libraries must be ready to learn new technology and adapt to the needs of users unable to imagine a world without technology. Like few other professionals, librarians must be willing to ride the waves of such change, adapting to meet the needs of their users. Whether it is the cell phone, the Palm Pilot, the MP3 player, or the iPod, users will want to receive and read their information on this new technology.

New models of reference are also developing to meet different user needs. Libraries are adding more points of service. For example, an information desk near the front of the library, a reference service point combined with other library services or an in-depth reference center where a user can sit down with a librarian and work out a plan for researching a paper have all been instituted to positive effect at libraries around the world.

In other situations, librarians rove the reference area to help users who do not approach the reference desk. These and other new strategies are changing the way information services are offered. As we look ahead, we must be aware that reference work will no doubt be based increasingly on electronic means of communication. It will at the same time continue to be a personal service although not necessarily face to face. There will be more emphasis on electronic materials while some older materials will still need to be consulted in print format. Even so, the way we find information and convey it is as fundamental today as it ever was.

INDEXING AND ABSTRACTING SERVICE

An abstracting service is a service that provides abstracts of publications, often on a subject or group of related subjects, usually on a subscription basis. An indexing service is a service that assign descriptors and other kinds of access points to documents. The word indexing service is today mostly used about computer programs, but may also cover services providing back-of-the-book indexes, journal indexes and related kinds of indexes. An indexing and abstracting service is a service, that provides shortening or summarizing of documents and assigning of descriptors for referencing documents.

The product is often an abstract journal or a bibliographic index, which may be a subject bibliography or a bibliographic database. Guidelines for indexing and abstracting, including the evaluation of such services, are given in the literature of Library and information science.

CENTRAL AUTHENTICATION SERVICE

The *Central Authentication Service* (CAS) is a single sign-on protocol for the web. Its purpose is to permit a user to access multiple applications while providing their credentials only once. It also allows web applications to authenticate users without gaining access to a user's security credentials, such as a password. The name *CAS* also refers to a software package that implements this protocol. The CAS protocol involves at least three parties: a *client* web browser, the web *application* requesting authentication, and the *CAS server*. It may also involve a *back-end service,* such as a database server, that does not have its own HTTP interface but communicates with a web application. When the client visits an application desiring to authenticate to it, the application redirects it to CAS.

CAS validates the client's authenticity, usually by checking a username and password against a database. If the authentication succeeds, CAS returns the client to the application, passing along a security ticket. The application then validates the ticket by contacting CAS over a secure connection and providing its own service identifier and the ticket. CAS then gives the application trusted information about whether a particular user has successfully authenticated. CAS allows multi-tier authentication via proxy address. A cooperating *back-end* service, like a database or mail server, can participate in CAS, validating the authenticity of users via information it receives from web applications. Thus, a webmail client and a webmail server can all implement CAS.

SERIAL DIGITAL INTERFACE

Serial digital interface (SDI) is a family of video interfaces standardized by SMPTE. For example, ITU-R BT.656 and SMPTE 259M define digital video interfaces used for broadcast-grade video. A related standard, known as *high-definition serial digital interface* (HD-SDI), is standardized in SMPTE 292M; this provides a nominal data rate of 1.485 Gbit/s. An emerging interface, commonly known in the industry as dual link HD-SDI and consisting essentially of a pair of SMPTE 292M links, is standardized in SMPTE 372M; this provides a nominal 2.970 Gbit/s interface used in applications that require greater fidelity and resolution than standard HDTV can provide.

A more recent interface, 3G-SDI, consisting of a single 2.970 Gbit/s serial link, is standardized in SMPTE 424M that will replace the dual link HD-SDI. These standards are used for transmission of uncompressed, unencrypted digital video signals within television facilities; they can also be used for packetized data. Coaxial variants of the specification range in length but are typically less than 300 meters. Fibre optic variants of the specification such as 297M allow for long-distance transmission limited only by maximum fibre length and/or repeaters. SDI and HD-SDI are currently only available in professional video equipment; various licensing agreements, restricting the use of unencrypted digital interfaces to professional equipment, prohibit their use in consumer equipment. There are various mod kits for existing DVD players and other devices, which allow a user to add a serial digital interface to these devices.

DIGITAL SERVICES

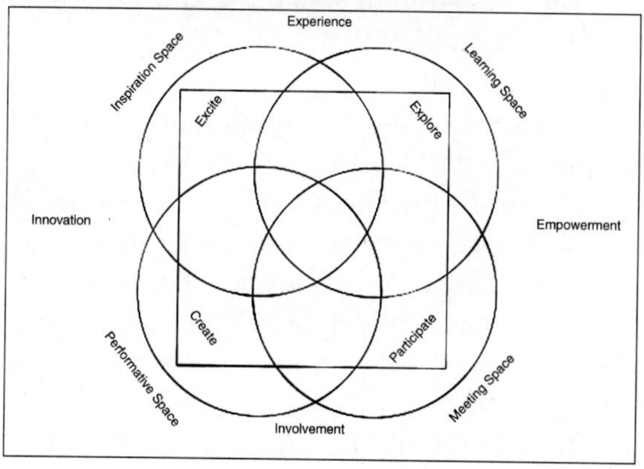

Fig. 9.1 A New Library Concept.

Do we agree on the vision:

* To establish a coherent digital library covering all fields of media and library services from baby-to researcher level.
* Corresponding with the library space.
* Aiming at all citizens with segmented services and building on partnerships of all kind.

How do we get there:

* Establish a convincing strategy.
* Demonstrating capability by good working examples on new services.
* Lobbying and marketing for a new political understanding of a library concept meeting the needs in the knowledge-and innovation society.

Digital means 'change' and 'divide':

* The gap between analogue and digital media is growing.
* The 'traditional' library still works well but we loose more and more users if we do not move faster building digital libraries.

The digital media landscape is part of a bigger agenda:

* The knowledge and innovation society.
* The changed economic balance between Europe and the new economies.
* The fragmentation of social life and growing tension
* Needs for better skills.

A European agenda:

* Knowledge societies imply globalization and a new competition pattern–jobs are moving east.
* The answer to the challenge is 'innovation' based.
* On more research, better education, lifelong learning, a strong identity and cohesion in society.
* We are in badly need of all these elements facing illiteracy, social tension in a more and more multicultural society.
* The fragmentation and cultural changes in the 'late modern society' are roaring for counter strategies.

E-book service is also part of a bigger agenda:

* An e-book platform is not enough.
* Developing a new library concept.
  – Public service concept: services for all citizens, segmentation.
  – Competing with other information services: the library niche.
* Creating new organizational frames
  – No library is an island: (inter)national development
  – Partnerships.
  – Break up of traditional library collection oriented organization.

Analogue and digital services should be integrated:

* The library space is for public libraries still the hub.
* The activities in the four spaces of the new library concept are virtual and real.
* The programs support the agenda of society, from innovation to democratic inclusion and participation.
* Partnerships basic for organization.

10

Organization of Knowledge

KNOWLEDGE ORGANIZATION SYSTEMS: AN OVERVIEW

The term *knowledge organization systems* are intended to encompass all types of schemes for organizing information and promoting knowledge management. Knowledge organization systems include classification schemes that organize materials at a general level, subject headings that provide more detailed access and authority files that control variant versions of key information. They also include less-traditional schemes, such as semantic networks and ontologies. Because knowledge organization systems are mechanisms for organizing information, they are at the heart of every library, museum, and archive.

Knowledge organization systems are used to organize materials for the purpose of retrieval and to manage a collection. A KOS serves as a bridge between the user's information need and the material in the collection. With it, the user should be able to identify an object of interest without prior knowledge of its existence. Whether through browsing or direct searching, whether through themes on a Web page or a site search engine, the KOS guides the user through a discovery process. In addition, KOSs allow the organizers to answer questions regarding the scope of a collection and what is needed to round it out.

All digital libraries use one or more KOS. Just as in a physical library, the KOS in a digital library provides an overview of the content of the collection and supports retrieval. The scheme may be a traditional KOS relevant to the scope of the material and the expected audience for the digital library, a commercially developed scheme such as the Yahoo or Excite categories, or a locally developed scheme for a corporate intranet.

The decision of what knowledge organization system to use is central to the development of any digital library. The KOS must be applicable, either automatically or by human catalogers, to the resources included in the digital library. Once the material is included in the collection, the KOS must be meaningful to its users. This section outlines the characteristics of KOSs, describes the common types, and discusses their origins and traditional uses.

COMMON CHARACTERISTICS OF KNOWLEDGE ORGANIZATION SYSTEMS

It is often said that humans are inherent organizers. From an early age, children play sorting and matching games. We cope with our ever-changing world by comparing new objects or experiences with those with which we are familiar, identifying patterns and categorizing what is new into our existing frame of reference. The emphasis on developing comprehensive KOS's can be seen in the writings of our earliest philosophers, many of whom continue to influence our view of the world. For example, Aristotle's effort to categorize knowledge into groups is reflected in our language, our education, and our science.

The original classification scheme of the Library of Congress, used between 1800 and 1814, was based on the philosophical works of Sir Francis Bacon and inherited from the English tradition. Beginning in 1814, the influence of Thomas Jefferson can be seen on the Library of Congress collection. Jefferson, who reclassified the library, reflected a more humanist philosophy. There is no single knowledge classification scheme on which everyone agrees.

Michael Lesk speculates that while a single KOS would be advantageous, it is unlikely that such a system will ever be developed. Culture may constrain the knowledge classification scheme so that what is meaningful to one culture is not necessarily meaningful to another. Therefore, we live in a world of multiple, variant ways to organize knowledge.

Despite their diversity, KOSs have the following common characteristics that are critical to their use in organizing digital libraries:

* The KOS imposes a particular view of the world on a collection and the items in it.
* The same entity can be characterized in different ways, depending on the KOS that is used.
* There must be sufficient commonality between the concept expressed in a KOS and the real-world object to which that concept refers that a knowledgeable person could apply the system with reasonable reliability. Likewise, a person seeking relevant material by using a KOS must be able to connect his or her concept with its representation in the system.

TYPES OF KNOWLEDGE ORGANIZATION SYSTEMS

A review of some typical knowledge organization systems shows their scope and applicability to a variety of digital library settings. While there are specific definitions for many of these KOSs in the computer science and information science literature, and even in standards documents, there is debate over these definitions. Terms are often used, particularly in the popular press and in the book trade, in nonstandard ways. Reflecting the scope of this practice, a recent *National Information Standards Organization* (NISO) work shop on electronic thesauri emphasized the need to improve the definitions of "terminology relating to terminology".

The descriptions given here provide an overview of possible systems for organizing digital libraries. The descriptions are based on characteristics such as structure and complexity, relationships among terms, and historical function. The list is not comprehensive; nor are the definitions of these terms contained in specific standards documents. They are grouped into three general categories: term lists, which emphasize lists of terms often with definitions; classifications and categories, which emphasize the creation of subject sets; and relationship lists, which emphasize the connections between terms and concepts.

Term Lists

Authority Files

Authority files are lists of terms that are used to control the variant names for an entity or the domain value for a particular field. Examples include names for countries, individuals, and organizations. Nonpreferred terms may be linked to the preferred versions. This type of KOS generally does not include a deep organization or complex structure. The presentation may be alphabetical or organized by a shallow classification scheme. A limited hierarchy may be applied to allow for simple navigation, particularly when the authority file is being accessed manually or is extremely large. Examples of authority files include the Library of Congress Name Authority File and the Getty Geographic Authority File.

Glossaries

A glossary is a list of terms, usually with definitions. The terms may be from a specific subject field or from a particular work. The terms are defined within a specific environment and rarely include variant meanings. Examples include the *Environmental Protection Agency* (EPA) Terms of the Environment.

Dictionaries

Dictionaries are alphabetical lists of words and their definitions. Variant senses are provided where applicable. Dictionaries are more general in scope than are glossaries. They may also provide information about the origin of a word, variants and multiple meanings across disciplines. While a dictionary may also provide synonyms and through the definitions, related words, there is no explicit hierarchical structure or attempt to group them by concept.

Gazetteers

A gazetteer is a list of place names. Traditional gazetteers have been published as books or have appeared as indexes to atlases. Each entry may also be identified by feature type, such as river, city, or school. An example is the U.S. Code of Geographic Names. Geospatially referenced gazetteers provide coordinates for locating the place on the earth's surface. The term *gazetteer* has several other meanings, including an announcement publication such as a patent or legal gazetteer. These gazetteers are often organized using classification schemes or subject categories.

Classifications and Categories

Subject Headings

This scheme type provides a set of controlled terms to represent the subjects of items in a collection. Subject heading lists can be extensive and cover a broad range of subjects; however, the subject heading list's structure is generally very shallow, with a limited hierarchical structure. In use, subject headings tend to be coordinated, with rules for how they can be joined to provide concepts that are more specific.

Examples include:

* The Medical Subject Headings (MeSH); and
* The Library of Congress Subject Headings (LCSH).

Classification Schemes, Taxonomies, and Categorization Schemes

These terms are often used interchangeably. Although there may be subtle differences from example to example, these types of KOSs all provide ways to separate entities into "buckets" or broad topic levels. Some examples provide a hierarchical arrangement of numeric or alphabetic notation to represent broad topics. These types of KOSs may not follow the rules for hierarchy required in the ANSI NISO Thesaurus Standard and they lack the explicit relationships presented in a thesaurus.

Examples of classification schemes include:

* The Library of Congress Classification Schedules,
* The Dewey Decimal Classification, and
* The Universal Decimal Classification.

Subject categories are often used to group thesaurus terms in broad topic sets that lie outside the hierarchical scheme of the thesaurus. Taxonomies are increasingly being used in object-oriented design and knowledge management systems to indicate any grouping of objects based on a particular characteristic.

Relationship Lists

Thesauri

Thesauri are based on concepts and they show relationships among terms. Relationships commonly expressed in a thesaurus include hierarchy, equivalence and association or relatedness.

These relationships are generally represented by the notation:

* BT (broader term),
* NT (narrower term),
* SY (synonym), and
* RT (associative or related term).

Associative relationships may be more detailed in some schemes. For example, the *Unified Medical Language System* (UMLS) from the National Library of Medicine has defined more than 40 relationships, many of which are associative. Preferred terms for indexing and retrieval are identified. Entry terms point to the preferred terms to be used for each concept. There are standards for the development of monolingual thesauri and multilingual thesauri. In these standards, the definition of a thesaurus is fairly narrow.

Standard relationships are assumed, as is the identification of preferred terms, and there are rules for creating relationships among terms. The definition of a thesaurus in these standards is often at variance with schemes that are traditionally called thesauri. Many thesauri do not follow all the rules of the standard but are still generally thought of as thesauri. Another type of thesaurus, such as the *Roget's Thesaurus*, represents only equivalence. Many thesauri are large; they may include more than 50,000 terms. Most were developed for a specific discipline or a specific product or family of products. Examples include the Food and Agricultural Organization's *Aquatic Sciences and Fisheries Thesaurus* and the *National Aeronautic and Space Administration (NASA) Thesaurus* for aeronautics and aerospace-related topics.

Semantic Networks

With the advent of natural language processing, there have been significant developments in semantic networks. These KOSs structure concepts and terms not as hierarchies but as a network or a web. Concepts are thought of as nodes, and relationships branch out from them. The relationships generally go beyond the standard BT, NT, and RT. They may include specific whole-part, cause-effect, or parent-child relationships. The most noted semantic network is Princeton University's WordNet, which is now used in a variety of search engines.

Ontologies

Ontology is the newest label to be attached to some knowledge organization systems. The knowledge-management community is developing ontologies as specific concept models. They can represent complex relationships among objects, and include the rules and axioms missing from semantic networks. Ontologies that describe knowledge in a specific area are often connected with systems for data mining and knowledge management. All of these examples of knowledge organization systems, which vary in complexity, structure, and function, can provide organization and increased access to digital libraries.

THE ORIGIN AND USE OF KNOWLEDGE ORGANIZATION SYSTEMS

In the physical library, classification schemes such as *Library of Congress* (LC), Dewey Decimal System, and the

Universal Decimal Classification reflect, among other things, the need to store a single item at a single location on a shelf. To provide multiple access points beyond the limits of a single physical location, subject headings are applied. Libraries use subject heading schemes such as LCSH, Sears, or other specialized schemes developed for specific content or specific collections. At the level of specific content, libraries have used authority files to control variant forms of personal, organizational, and geographic names. However, KOSs can be found in settings other than libraries. An awareness of the KOSs available from alternative sources is valuable when considering the development of digital libraries for a specific audience.

Abstracting and Indexing Services

Abstracting and indexing (A&I) services developed as an outgrowth of traditional bibliographies and the explosion of journal literature. In the sciences, the development of A&I services was spurred by the post-World War I concerns about inadequate access to scientific information. In the 1950s, investment in A&I services was fueled by the Cold War and Sputnik. Abstracting and indexing services in the humanities, such as the Bibliography of the History of Art or the *Modern Languages Association* (MLA) Bibliography, generally took a different growth path than did their scientific and technical counterparts, but they also quickly became important resources for scholarship in the online environment.

The scope of A&I services varies from broad discipline-oriented services to narrowly defined aspects of the literature and subdisciplines. Special KOSs, such as thesauri and subject categories, were developed to support A&I services and their specific products and audiences. These organizations applied increasingly complex schemes to provide subject access to the literature in a variety of subjects.

By the 1960s, A&I services were moving from the provision of printonly products to print and online services through large online vendors such as Dialog. Later, the products were distributed on CDROM and now, increasingly, on the Web. In many cases, the KOSs migrated from print to electronic media following the products they supported. While increased computing power, more sophisticated search engines, and more independent end-user searching have led to changes in some KOSs, most have retained their importance, even in the Web environment.

For many years, the KOSs related to A&I services were applied only by catalogers and indexers trained in using the KOS indexing for a particular product or products. The primary users of KOSs were librarians and other professional searchers. However, the proliferation of electronic data, the explosion of electronic publishing, and increasing concerns about the difficulty of locating information have led to a renewed interest in these KOSs for use not only by professionals but also by end users.

Publishers

As publishers have migrated to electronic composition systems, they have become increasingly involved in the production of A&I products. Large journal publishers such as Academic Press and Elsevier have developed their own systems to provide bibliographic records linked to the full text of documents. As the content of online journals has grown, it has become necessary to move from systems that provide browsing by table of contents and journal issue to systems that support searching by both free text and by KOS. Electronic journals have resulted in additional KOSs, particularly classification and categorization schemes. For example, Elsevier's Web site has a subject categorization scheme to provide access to individual Web sites of its more than 2000 titles.

Trade, Professional, and Governmental Organizations

A variety of authority files and classification schemes are used to support business and commerce. They range from the *Standard Industrial Classification* (SIC) code and the *North American Industrial Classification System* (NAICS), used in procurement and government statistics, to disease codes used to communicate patient illnesses and treatments among physicians, hospitals, and insurance companies. As more organizations develop Web sites, additional KOSs are being developed to support them.

Internal Projects

Organizations are among the most prolific creators and users of KOSs. Developers of corporate intranets and knowledge management systems have discovered hundreds of specific classification schemes, glossaries, categorization schemes, and other vocabularies in use within organizations. Many of these are geared towards specific tasks and are, therefore, very narrow both in subject scope and target audience. However, for these audiences, they can also be rich sources of information. For example, the *Department of Energy* (DOE), *Environmental Management Science Programme* (EMSP) and the Office of Scientific and Technical Information are developing a digital library to support EMSP programme managers.

Programme managers and researchers have developed "needs categories" and "science categories" to organize the *Environmental Science Network* (ESN). The categories are used primarily to support the process of grant submission and award; however, the ESN also uses them to provide access to related material from within DOE and from other distributed databases from the EPA, the Department of Defence, and NASA. Vocabulary is currently being organized around these categories for use with a Web mining tool that will provide highly relevant Web resources for project managers in specific areas.

LINKING DIGITAL LIBRARY RESOURCES TO RELATED RESOURCES

This section emphasizes the ability of knowledge organization systems to link digital library resources to other related resources. The basis for this linking is the identification of information within a digital resource that can be extracted and used to search and locate information within a KOS. The KOS may then be used to expand codes to more explanatory full text, to provide more descriptive records, or to link entity names to resources of physical specimens.

EXPANDING CODES TO FULL TEXT

Practitioners of a discipline use coding schemes to facilitate communication within that discipline. It is often helpful to connect these coding schemes to the full names for which the code stands. The examples provided here include links between databank registration codes and the biological sequence data, and between industrial codes and the full name that the code represents.

Linking Sequence Numbers to Biosequence Databanks

The lengthy biochemical and genetic sequences that molecular biologists, biotechnologists, and geneticists identify each day are kept in databanks. Several databanks have been developed, for example, to cover protein sequences, nucleotides, and cell lines. One of the largest databanks contains information on the mapping of the human genome. As molecular biologists began to discover these sequences, they reported them in scientific journals. Difficulties in composing, proofreading, and printing the text soon arose.

Through an ad hoc standards process, major biomedical publishers agreed to require the inclusion of codes or databank numbers for these sequences in articles when they are published. In addition, the sequence itself must be registered in a databank before the paper can be published. Some of the most frequently referenced databanks are listed on the Web site of the National Center for Biotechnology Information. They include GenBank and the Research Collaboratory for Structural Bioinformatics Protein Data Bank.

Each sequence number is different, but all begin with a persistent code identifying the databank. How can the link be made between the literature and the databank? Through a search profile, a text analysis programme, or keyword indexing, the text can be analysed and the sequence databank numbers identified. An active link can be embedded. The active link consists of a search strategy to locate that sequence number in the databank where the actual sequence is stored. When the user clicks on the active link, the script is generated and launched from the user's browser.

The Web-enabled database is searched, and the sequence record is returned to the user. Depending on the services provided by the databank site, the user can analyse the sequence using a number of tools provided by the databank or download the sequence for local manipulation. This type of connection exists between the *National Library of Medicine's* (NLM) search service, PubMed, and GenBank at the National Center for Biotechnology Information. If a search in PubMed yields records that have GenBank numbers, the user can automatically search and display the sequence records from GenBank.

Linking Individual Industrial Codes to the Full Scheme

In business, classification schemes serve to communicate important facts about a company or product. These codes are generally controlled by a government, professional, trade, or international standards organization. They often serve as shorthand for users interested in material in a particular area of industry or a specific business sector. Perhaps the most familiar scheme is the SIC code, which was last updated in 1987. The SIC codes have been used by the U.S. government, economists, financial markets, regulators, and procurement offices to identify manufacturing, agriculture, and service sectors of the economy.

In 1997, a new scheme was approved for use within the United States. The North American Industrial Classification System was developed with Canada and Mexico as a means of providing an agreed-upon scheme for the collection, reporting, and analysis of information about the economy by sector, both within and across borders. Information about NAICS is available from the Web site of the U.S. Census Bureau. The digital library can provide related information by using the authority files for the coding schemes as a linked authority file.

If a company or economic sector mentioned in the digital library's collection can be linked to an SIC or NAICS code, the code can be searched against the official tables of definitions maintained by the U.S. Census Bureau. These files provide definitions of the codes and place each code in the classification scheme with other economic sectors. The digital library's content can be further enhanced by making a link between the

SIC and NAICS codes. If the digital library resource has the SIC code, it can be extracted and searched against the Census Bureau's *1997 NAICS and 1987 SIC Correspondence Tables.* The table returns the corresponding code from the alternate scheme.

LINKING TO DESCRIPTIVE RECORDS

Linking the name of an entity, such as a personal name, organization, or location, to additional information about that entity was one of the first uses of hyperlinking. Knowledge organization systems such as dictionaries, glossaries, and classification schemes can be used to link the entities in one resource to richer descriptions of that entity in another resource. This is particularly helpful for users who are new to a topic and in cases where the additional information can make the user's task more efficient. The examples that follow are from three disciplines. The first example links organism names to records that not only describe the species more fully but also put it in the context of the overall classification scheme for living organisms. The second example links chemical names to descriptive records and molecular structures. In the third example, proper names are linked to the biographies for the person.

Linking Organism Names to Taxonomic Records

Genus-species names are the Latin names for organisms—*e.g.*, plants, animals, and microorganisms. Taxonomists, who study and classify living organisms, create records for each of these organisms. Generally, these records are linked relationally to the other organisms in a hierarchy. Beyond the organism name and the information that it and its placement in the hierarchy convey, taxonomic records use other elements to describe the organism. These may include distribution patterns, the authority for naming and classification, and the date the organism was identified.

Scientists base the information on specimens that are retained because they serve as the physical evidence of the description. Natural history museums, private collections, and individual scientists number, or code, the specimens in their collections. Sometimes specimens are supported by photographs or line drawings, which may be digitized. By using a taxonomic authority file as an intermediate authority file, one can link a text or an image file containing a name or picture of an organism to additional related information.

By automatically processing the text or embedding a link from the organism name in the text or from the image to the taxonomic authority record, one can extend the knowledge conveyed by the text. The text can include the descriptive and historical information in the taxonomic record and, ultimately, link to a photograph, a drawing, or appropriate video or audio segments. Because of the ambiguity in organism names, many examples of this type are now created manually. However, depending on the extent of the files involved, the ambiguity of the Latin and common names for organisms can be overcome.

An example of a taxonomic intermediate file is the *Integrated Taxonomic Information System* (ITIS). ITIS is a partnership of U.S., Canadian, and Mexican government agencies, private organizations, and taxonomic specialists cooperating to develop an online, scientifically credible list of biological names of North American plants and animals. It is used by many U.S. government agencies for consistent naming of plants and animals for regulatory and monitoring purposes. To link textual material in a digital library to the ITIS record, the organism name can be identified manually or automatically in the text and submitted as a query to the ITIS database. When a match is found, ITIS presents the ITIS record, which provides essential information about the organism. The information includes synonymous names, including some common names, and an indication of the placement of the organism in the larger taxonomic classification scheme.

Linking Chemical Names to Molecular Structures

The unique identification for a chemical substance is not its name but its molecular structure. However, chemical names are commonly used in research documents, project plans, catalogs, and directories, all of which may be resources in a digital library. There are competing systems of nomenclature as well as common and commercial synonyms. The ambiguity is resolved by providing links between the chemical names in the text and the molecular structure. This is done through a chemical registry number or code that is connected to a particular chemical name and an authority record that provides additional information about the chemical. This information includes the chemical's synonyms and some of its chemical and physical properties.

Most important in today's research environment is the link from this authority file to a chemical structure file. Structure files, used with the appropriate software, graphically depict the molecular structure. This sophisticated software allows for three-dimensional visualization, rotation, and substitution of the chemical bonds. An example of the use of the chemical registry number to link chemical names with molecular structures can be seen in the work of BIOSIS, the world's largest not-for-profit producer of biological and biomedical databases.

In 1993, BIOSIS began processing its bibliographic citations to automatically identify chemical names. BIOSIS assigns CAS *Registry Numbers* (RNs) to the chemical names identified in this process. In the STN International online system, hosted in the United States by CAS, a user of BIOSIS can select one or more of the records resulting from a search and extract the RN. The extracted RN can be applied against the CAS Registry File, which contains more than 21 million substances, including organics, inorganics, biosequences, metals, and alloys.

The registry file record for the chemical name, including the link to the synonyms for the chemical name and the structure file itself, can then be accessed. With special tools developed by CAS, the structure can be viewed and manipulated. It can be imported into modeling tools that allow the chemist to manipulate the structure and thereby envision new chemicals. Alternatively, the user can start with any database that contains CAS RNs and extract the resulting RNs to perform a search for complementary bibliographic records in the BIOSIS database. Linking chemical names to structures using RNs on a large scale is neither inexpensive nor easy. There are two approaches to identifying chemical names in text.

Some journal articles include the CAS RN for the major chemicals discussed. In this case, an analysis of the text for the terms "RN", "CAS RN", and variations preceding numerics can identify RNs that can be used as a link. Alternatively, a programme to identify chemical names in text, similar to that developed by BIOSIS, could be devised.

Developing the identification programme, as well as searching chemical databases, is costly; however, if the digital library has license agreements for chemistry databases, this type of linkage may be possible. In addition, many organizations have small chemical files of their own that may include RNs and other information of particular relevance to the organization's research. It may be possible to link to these local databases using methods that are more direct.

Linking Personal Names to Biographical Information

A common type of authority file is the personal name authority, which controls variants of personal names. For example, the *Library of Congress Name Authority File* (LCNAF) is used to control variant personal names for authors, editors, artists, and others. The *Union List of Artist Names* (ULAN), developed by the Getty Vocabulary Programme, is another example. Name authorities serve as tools for catalogers and indexers. They ensure that the proper form of the name, rather than an unapproved variant, is used and bring together all works by or about the person.

A name authority file can also be used to link a bibliographic record or document containing the person's name to a variety of other related materials. If the digital library's resource has a standardized form of the name, it can be identified and searched against the authority file to locate variants. The standardized and variant forms can be joined in a search against a variety of other resources that can provide related information. For example, in the case of a digital library of images of artists' works or biographical or critical text, a name authority file such as the ULAN or the LCNAF can act as an intermediate file to provide additional information.

The file, which contains integrated variant names, can be searched by the name appearing in the digital library collection. When the record is found, the information about the artist can be displayed, providing a wide range of contextual material for the user. Citations to significant biographical or critical works about the artist, some of which may also be available on the Web, may also be provided in the name authority file. The variant names from a name authority can also be used to locate and provide automatic links from the personal name in the text to a biography, without requiring that the name be presented in the same fashion in the two resources.

One such resource that could be linked to for biographical information is Gale's Biography Resource, which contains more than 142,000 biographies and related citations from more than 1,000 periodicals. However, to produce this kind of link, there must be a mechanism for locating personal names in text. Several programs can do this type of text analysis; among those that have been developed commercially are NameFinder from the Carnegie Group and the Intelligent Agent from IBM. In addition, variant names can be extracted from the name authority itself, grouped, and run as a search against the text to locate name occurrences.

LINKING ENTITY NAMES TO PHYSICAL SPECIMENS

In some cases, it is possible to go another step and connect entity names in the digital library resources to physical specimens. The curation of physical specimens or artifacts is critical to the advancement of many disciplines. Exhibition catalogs describe the art objects in a particular exhibition. Museum catalogs provide inventories of the art, natural history, or cultural objects held by a particular museum.

These catalogs, increasingly available as computerized databases, are knowledge organization systems that not only provide descriptive records but also point to the location of the object in a museum, an archive, or another collection. For example, in biology, a physical specimen is particularly important when it is the result of the discovery and description of a new organism or of the reclassification of a known organism.

A type specimen is the example collected from the field by a taxonomist to serve as the prime example for the description of the organism and the validation of its taxonomic classification and naming. These specimens are held by natural history collections, and their deposit is required by the rules of various taxonomic societies. As part of the curatorial activity, the collections assign identification codes. While the primary use of identification codes has been to organize the physical collections, numerous projects are under way in the natural history community to digitize photographs of specimens and create database records for the specimens, including their identifiers, and thereby make them more rea dily accessible.

The degree of digitization varies from specialty to specialty. For example, in botany, virtually all significant research herbaria are digitally cataloging their type collections instead of maintaining paper records. Many are also making digital photographs of the type specimens available over the Web. The publication of identification codes in the journal literature is also changing. Historically, identification codes have been presented in the "Materials Used" sections of journal articles. The level of specificity of the identification code has varied, depending on the biological discipline. For example, botanical journals tend to list only the institution and the catalog, while vertebrate journals provide the code to the specimen level.

The current trend is to require lists of specimens that are more detailed. As the lists become longer and the printing costs increase, journal publishers are beginning to request links to independent Web sites maintained by the researchers or their organizations that carry all the specimens used in the study and provide some level of identification.

If the digital library collection contains resources that include the identification codes, these codes can be extracted and matched against the Web-based catalogs or databases. This link can provide users with location and contact information to allow them to access the physical object mentioned in the digital library resource. Curators or registrars of artistic, archaeological, and cultural history collections also assign inventory or accession numbers to items in their collections.

Identification numbers may also be found in scholarly catalogues raisonnés. Links similar to those described for natural history can be made between text related to works of art and the physical work in a particular collection. An article about a work of art can be linked to additional information about the physical specimen by linking the identification number in the text with an online catalog containing the number and additional information about the work.

As museums digitize their collections to establish a presence on the Web or to reduce the handling of the physical objects, KOSs that can link the digital library resources to the physical object are being developed. If there is a museum with a collection that complements that of the digital library, it is worthwhile to discuss ways in which the digital library and digital museum collections may "co-evolve."

MAKING RESOURCES ACCESSIBLE TO OTHER COMMUNITIES

Someone recently compared the Web with a large room filled with books that were scattered all over the floor. The Web is the world's largest mass of bits and bytes. It is a meeting place that brings together disparate communities. The "Internet Commons," as this meeting place has been called, requires connections between and among disparate communities in order for an "economy" to develop. This economy will provide the framework within which both commercial and noncommercial transactions can occur. KOSs are one means of connecting these disparate communities.

Knowledge organization systems can be used to:

* Provide alternate subject access,
* Add modes of understanding to digital library resources,
* Support multilingual access, and
* Supply terms for expansion of free-text searches in domains that are relatively unknown to the user.

PROVIDING ALTERNATE SUBJECT ACCESS

Alternate subject access refers to the provision of one or more additional subject orientations that make the resources of the digital library accessible to different audiences. This approach is particularly valuable when the digital library resources appeal to groups that do not share a common terminology. It can be a system of subject headings, a classification scheme, or any other subject-oriented system.

Alternate subject access can be provided by:

* Indexing or classifying the resources using multiple schemes,
* Retaining original schemes from organizations that contribute to the digital library, or
* Mapping between the primary scheme and an alternate scheme.

Indexing the Material with Multiple Schemes

The most direct method for providing alternate subject access to a collection is by classifying or indexing the resources with multiple schemes, but it may also be the most costly. This approach requires redundant cataloging or catalogers who are knowledgeable in both schemes. It may also require modifications to the cataloging tools and procedures. However, if the cataloging is at a high level or if the schemes are not difficult or detailed, it may be a reasonable approach.

Retaining Alternate Indexing from Contributors

If the digital library is being built through contributions from a variety of sources, the originating organization may have applied an alternate scheme that could be used. For example, the NASA database on aeronautics and astronautics receives relevant bibliographic records from other U.S. agencies, such as the Department of Defence and the Department of Energy.

The controlled vocabulary terms assigned by the contributing organization are processed through a machine-aided indexing process to create candidate indexing terms from the *NASA Thesaurus* for review by NASA's indexers. However, the final records contain both the *NASA Thesaurus* terms and the controlled vocabulary terms from the contributing organization, with the alternate indexing terms retained in a separate data element in the bibliographic record. The terms collected from other organizations can be viewed as an alternate access point, so that at least part of the collection is accessible through another discipline's terminology.

Mapping Multiple Schemes

The third method for providing alternate subject access is the most indirect, that of mapping one or more schemes. Several examples of this approach can be found among A&I services. Both BIOSIS, the world's largest private sector A&I service in the life sciences, and the NLM apply MeSH to BIOSIS documents. The records that BIOSIS contributes to NLM's TOXLINE database are processed automatically to have appropriate MeSH terms added. This is based on a mapping of the natural language terms that occur in the toxicology literature and BIOSIS' normalized natural language keyword indexing with the MeSH terminology.

In the new BIOSIS relational indexing structure, BIOSIS builds and maintains authority files that connect natural language disease names to the MeSH-controlled disease terms. When the BIOSIS indexer assigns the free text keyword for the disease name, the appropriate MeSH term is also added to the record as an alternate access point. The assignment is based on the development over time of a mapping between the terminology used by BIOSIS and the MeSH-controlled terms. In addition to providing alternate access points to BIOSIS products, the inclusion of the MeSH terms makes it possible to perform cross database searching on the indexing field with MEDLINE and other databases that include MeSH terms. From 1999 forward, users can search BIOSIS databases using MeSH disease terms.

The disease terms can be extracted from the MeSH authority file or from a MEDLINE record and then used in a search against the BIOSIS files, or *vice versa*. This helps users find relevant records that are unique to either BIOSIS or

MEDLINE. The inclusion of terms from an alternate KOS, such as MeSH, therefore supports the use of BIOSIS by medical librarians and practitioners who are familiar with MeSH terminology. A more extensive example of mapping variant schemes is the metathesaurus developed by the NLM's *Unified Medical Language System* (UMLS). This system has linked more than 40 separate KOSs from various medical specialties. They range from MeSH to coding and classification schemes used by insurance companies and physicians to describe treatments and diseases on patient records.

The UMLS is licensed by many other organizations for inclusion in applications that can bridge various health care communities. How can digital libraries use alternate indexing? While many digital libraries do not have the A&I resources of large database producers such as NLM and BIOSIS, the concept of applying alternate indexing can be scaled to fit. While the systems described deal with item-level bibliographic records, alternate indexing can be applied at several levels.

Alternate subject access can be applied only at the resource level, for the database, electronic book, electronic journal, or image collection, so that other communities can identify resources of interest that must then by searched or browsed individually. This concept is conducive to use with portals that provide access to the same resources with different views for different audiences. Alternatively, if the digital library has bibliographic records or metadata records at a very detailed level, it may be possible to develop switching programs that will translate concepts from the original organization of the digital library or resource to that of the alternate scheme.

ADDING NEW MODES OF UNDERSTANDING TO THE DIGITAL LIBRARY

People perceive the world through many modes, including textual and graphical. Some people comprehend information more easily in one mode than another. Most people benefit from a variety of modes that reinforce one another or that can be used when appropriate to the context. Many digital library projects remain text-based; however, this text-only dimension is changing as digital libraries become oriented more to multimedia and as other modes of information presentation become viable on the Internet. KOSs can be used to bring new dimensions to an information resource or a collection in a digital library.

In the digital library environment, these dimensions can be viewed as layers that can be added on top of one or more objects. Various tools and services can be developed that are geared to a particular mode. For example, the results of a text search can be presented in graphical or visual form, based on the number of occurrences of a term or concept or on the occurrences of documents from a particular country, journal title, or author. A more complex dimension that can be added is the geospatial dimension, which emphasizes access by place.

A "geolibrary" is defined as a digital library consisting of "geoinformation", or material that can be accessed by place. This so-called geo-referencing can be either direct or indirect. Georeferencing of textual objects is facilitated by a gazetteer, which brings together the place name and the spatial footprint for its location. Many gazetteers also include feature types for each footprint. The vocabulary used for the feature types varies among gazetteers, but may include terms such as "airport", "harbor", and "railroad station".

Although many organizations, including federal and state agencies, are currently required to provide geospatial referencing as part of the National Spatial Data Infrastructure Programme, the geospatial referencing is not readily available for older works. How can the data sets of today be integrated with the textual information of yesterday? The answer is by adding geospatial referencing to the text resource. Geospatial referencing requires that the text name for a place have an associated spatial footprint. This can be achieved by using a georeferenced, digital gazetteer that provides geospatial footprints for place names.

Through this type of knowledge organization system, place names in a library catalog or bibliographic database can have footprints assigned. If one or more of the library's resources have latitude or longitude coordinates in the catalog record or in the full text but no place name, the coordinates can be extracted and submitted to the gazetteer service. The service will return the place name for the footprint.

Alternatively, the resource may have a textual place name. This place name can be extracted and searched against the gazetteer, and the footprint can be provided to a mapping application. The latter search may result in more than one footprint, since place names may be ambiguous. Therefore, it is important that the user interface be designed to allow the user to distinguish the locations. Once the footprint has been determined, a user can access the text resource through a geographic mapping tool. Alternatively, a user of the text resource can find a set of results and have the place names displayed as footprints on a map.

In disciplines such as ecology, environmental science, and even public health and epidemiology, it would be beneficial to build a digital library with access to such a digital gazetteer service. Users could then access the system through the text mode or the geographic mode, depending on their comfort level and the type of information needed. Presenting the results on a map allows users to make new associations and analyse the results more easily. Through a geospatial KOS, they can see connections between disparate data, because the data are presented in an alternate mode.

PROVIDING MULTILINGUAL ACCESS

A third way that KOSs can support the use of digital libraries by disparate communities is to provide multilingual access. A variety of sources, including multilingual dictionaries and multilingual thesauri, can support this type of access. One of the most extensive multilingual thesaurus efforts is the *Generalized Multilingual Environmental Thesaurus* (GEMET) from the *European Environment Agency* (EEA), produced by Italy's research council, the *Consiglio Nazionale delle Ricerche* (CNR).

The GEMET is available in 12 languages, and plans for a global environmental thesaurus in many more languages were recently announced. GEMET is available by agreement with the EEA. The European Topic Centre on Catalogue of Data Sources in Germany is developing a system that will link data sources and metadata information in a virtual library. GEMET will be used to convert a search in one language into searches for the same concepts in other languages. Users will retrieve documents not only in their native language but also in other languages. This will allow data systems from throughout the EEA and beyond to be accessed as a virtual library collection with both controlled vocabulary and free-text term searching in multiple languages.

EXPANDING FREE-TEXT SEARCH TERMS

Free-text searching is the main method of searching on the Web. Only a small percentage of Web resources have metadata, and an even smaller percentage have controlled vocabulary assigned. However, variations in natural language make free-text searching problematic. Even a knowledgeable user may not know all the terminology that can be used in the literature to express a concept. The problem is exacerbated when the user is unfamiliar with the topic or is interested in an interdisciplinary area. How can the user expand his or her search to overcome these terminology differences? One possibility is to use KOSs as aids to the selection of free-text keywords. The Getty Vocabulary Project emphasizes support for searching as a significant application of its vocabularies. Harpring reports that the vocabularies are increasingly being used in search engines to look for different terms that refer to the same concept.

The Getty vocabularies are particularly rich in equivalence relationships. "When these equivalence relationships are exploited in search engines, there are typically two possible scenarios: the user may be allowed to first query the vocabulary database, locating appropriate terms, and then applying those chosen terms in a query across target databases; or there may be little or no user interaction with the vocabulary, when the vocabularies are used behind the scenes..."

Getty developed a prototype called *a.k.a.* to experiment with the use of equivalence terms to broaden or narrow searches across databases on the Web. In addition to expanding routine search queries, KOSs can be used in Web mining tools. Northern Light has developed a Web mining tool that reportedly returns a high degree of relevant hits. The KOS that supports the Northern Light site was built by ingesting large existing vocabularies and thesauri.

The result was then organized under an extensive classification scheme developed by Northern Light. The terms can be used to extend a user's search or to distinguish between multiple meanings of the terms supplied by the user. The results of a search are organized into "folders" based on the classification scheme. These high-level categories, represented by the folders, help distinguish multiple meanings of the same term. For example, an ambiguous word such as "pitcher" might result in two folders being presented to the user. One folder would be titled "Sports", the second "Decorative Arts". The user who chooses only the Sports folder will be presented with only those Web resources that use "pitcher" in the baseball sense.

The user who selects the folder called "Decorative Arts" will be presented only with those resources that are related to water pitchers. KOSs can be very powerful in supporting free-text searching within digital libraries and in integrating Web resources into existing digital libraries. However, these systems must be used with caution. KOSs have generally been developed for a specific discipline, task, or function, or for the indexing of a specific collection or database. Therefore, depending on the domain in which the KOS is being used and the complexity of the system, it may or may not suggest relevant free-text terms. Expanding a search with related terms, rather than pure synonyms, may return hits that are only peripherally relevant to the user.

PLANNING AND IMPLEMENTING KNOWLEDGE ORGANIZATION SYSTEMS IN DIGITAL LIBRARIES

This section provides general guidelines that may be useful for an organization that wants to use knowledge organization systems to organize a digital library. The framework described is applicable for KOSs of any type or subject.

PLANNING KNOWLEDGE ORGANIZATION SYSTEMS

Analysing User Needs

Of primary importance to any digital library project is an analysis of its users' needs, in terms of content and functionality. Many volumes have already been written about needs assessment, and providing detailed guidance on this subject is beyond the scope of this paper. However, when analysing how a KOS might be used with a particular digital library, it is essential to thoroughly understand the environment of the user.

One must look not only at the needs for organizing the digital library materials but also at possible links between content within and outside the digital library walls. This is particularly important for KOSs that are acting as intermediate authority files, because in such cases the links may not be readily apparent. It is important to consider other views that might be valuable for users and peripheral communities that might benefit from the digital library's content were it accessible to them through a KOS.

Locating Knowledge Organization Systems

Once the user's needs have been analysed, it is necessary to locate KOSs to meet the need. While an alternate system can be built locally, it is preferable to find an existing KOS for several reasons. First, it is costly and time-consuming to build a KOS. Second, KOSs often benefit by having been built over time. Many of the systems described in this report have been built over decades; some existed in paper before digitization. The value of a KOS comes from its acceptance by the user community; sources built by noted authorities such as learned societies, trade associations, or standards groups will be viewed as more trustworthy than those built internally.

Finally, the networked environment has resulted in both an explosion of primary materials, including documents, electronic journals, and Web-based databases, and in an equivalent explosion of KOSs on the Web. There are several ways to identify KOSs that may be of interest. Many users are already aware of KOSs on the Web within their discipline. Developers may also turn to directories, librarians in the field, and reference sources, or they may perform a general search of the Internet.

Planning the Infrastructure

It is necessary to make decisions about the architecture of the KOS in the context of the digital library setting. The physical location of the KOS is important. Will the system be held externally or internally? There are pros and cons to either approach. If the system is available on the Web, it is possible to consider linking to the KOS as an external system. This architecture requires a script or some search query to locate the resource. One must then launch a query against the resource to obtain the piece of information that will serve as the key between the two files. This key could be a *universal resource locator* (URL) or input to another search query.

A query may be necessary if the KOS is stored in a database. The script may transfer log-on information from the digital library system to the external KOS, in order to provide access to the Web-enabled database. In the case of a more direct link, the access may be by URL. However, the use of a URL as the link has the same problem with persistence as does direct access via a URL from a browser. The organization may move the KOS, thereby changing the URL that is being used as the key. It is important to determine how often the URLs in the KOS change, whether there is a means of notification of these changes, and whether it is possible to consider an alternative that would be more persistent.

Schemes such as the Digital Object Identifier and the Persistent URL have been devised to enable resources to be physically moved among servers without having their names changed. Another alternative is the use of other Uniform Resource Identification (URI) schemes and the *Uniform Resource Name* (URN), which can be sent from the newer Web browsers. The benefit of linking to a remote resource is that the resource will always be upto-date. The maintenance of the

KOS is in the hands of the owner, not the digital librarian. It may also be more apparent to users that the KOS is not owned by the digital library.

Linking to a remote KOS also has disadvantages. Persistence and unexpected changes in the organization and content of the system may cause problems. The software or telecommunications route between the digital library server and the KOS may be unreliable. In systems requiring fast response time or large amounts of data transfer, and, therefore, high bandwidth, the fact that a connection must be made between the digital library and the external KOS may make the system unacceptable to the user. Alternatively, the KOS may be obtained from the owner and loaded locally.

In many cases, this requires licensing that may not be required when the KOS is accessed remotely, because a copy of the whole resource is being provided to the digital library. Loading a KOS locally also requires that one consider issues such as maintenance, local system administration, and disk storage. If the KOS uses special software, such as a database management system, loading the KOS locally will require a copy of that software, which may require additional purchase or licensing. Other considerations are the need for firewalls and interface design.

On the positive side, the KOS is under more local control. Therefore, it may be possible to improve the response time by not accessing the KOS over the Internet. If the KOS is to be used behind the scenes, concerns of speed and integration become more important. If additional modifications need to be made to the KOS to integrate it with the digital library, it will also be necessary to load the KOS locally. If the digital library intends to incorporate numerous secondary KOSs, it is important to consider the degree to which the architecture is scaleable.

The National Library of Medicine's UMLS incorporates more than 40 different sources. While its main purpose has been to develop a metathesaurus for moving among these vocabularies, the management of the systems, regardless of the mapping issues, has been a major consideration. Ingest has been a major concern, with the need to develop a system that can handle a variety of input formats-from ASCII text files to highly structured database output.

The architecture must also accommodate the character sets of the incoming sources. This is particularly important if a mark-up language has been used to represent special characters and diacritical marks. Systems that have been developed in Unicode, which extends ASCII to accommodate diacritical marks and non-Roman character sets, cannot be handled by systems that deal only with ASCII or extended ASCII sets. Since many digital library systems are being built as extensions or applications of existing *integrated library systems* (ILS), it is important to consider how the KOSs will integrate with the library system.

Unfortunately, many ILS vendors have not considered links to external files or databases in their system designs. In some cases, the vendor may require that the information be stored in the proprietary format of the ILS. The system may require that the files be on the same directory or server as the accessing ILS. The fields that can be linked to the Web or searched may be limited. Outside communications may require Z39.50 client-server connections. With relatively closed systems, ILSs may be a difficult environment in which to implement alternative and nontraditional KOSs.

Digital libraries that are interested in using KOSs should consider this integration when developing requirements for the procurement of a system to support them. Vendors should be encouraged to support relatively open architectures and to consider the extension of traditional library systems to support broader digital library functionality.

In addition to these immediate concerns, it is important to consider the incorporation of future KOSs. Initial success may spur the desire for integration of additional KOSs or enhanced functionality for the existing KOS. Success may breed additional requirements and increase the strain on hardware, software, and network architectures.

Maintaining the Knowledge Organization System

For a digital library, an outdated KOS can be more of a hindrance than a benefit. Maintenance, both of content and of the system, should be considered when planning a KOS. This is particularly important if the digital library is to be self-supporting or revenue generating. Version control of the KOS is extremely important.

Reloading a new version from the system provider is one way to accommodate changes; however, this may not be acceptable if the locally held version differs substantially from that held by the system's provider. If there has been significant transformation or processing of the original KOS, it may be difficult, or impossible, to reload the original and recreate the changes that have been made.

A transaction-based approach, whereby only changes are transferred between the KOS provider and the library, is also possible; however, this requires that the system provider have the infrastructure, both machine and human, to produce these transactions. It also requires that the changes to the original KOS be identifiable in order to create change transactions. For example, Stuart Nelson of the NLM's UMLS Project recently reported that many systems can create annual transaction records to inform the UMLS about the changes that have occurred to the original system.

However, the changes are often not indicated with enough detail to support automatic change transactions in the UMLS. If a change date, for example, is recorded only at the level of the concept record, it is impossible to tell whether the term has changed or if the relationship between this concept and another concept has changed. Since the UMLS splits the incoming terminology and its relationships into a variety of files, it is often difficult to tell how the UMLS files must be change based on the changes made during the maintenance of the original KOS.

Presenting the Knowledge Organization System to the User

In addition to deciding which KOS should be used and what functions it should serve, the digital library will need to determine how to present the KOS to its users. A KOS may be exposed to the user or made relatively transparent. The KOS can be exposed to the user in different ways. Material can be grouped into KOS-related themes or categories on the digital library's Web site.

The KOS may be used at a higher level to identify specific portals for different uses or users. If the content of the digital library includes metadata records, the KOS may be displayed as index terms on the records or in its entirety as a navigation aid to searching. In other cases, the KOS may be transparent. For example, a thesaurus can be used behind the scenes to extend the user's search to include synonyms, to connect the digital library's resources to other information and resources, or to filter or rank the information obtained.

IMPLEMENTING KNOWLEDGE ORGANIZATION SYSTEMS

Acquisition and Intellectual Property Issues

It is critical to properly handle the acquisition of knowledge organization systems. The first question is whether the KOS is under copyright. If so, the copyright holder should be contacted concerning the KOS. It is important to ensure that the apparent contact is the official one. Many references have been reprinted or put on the Web without proper acknowledgment of the real owner.

Once the contact has been made, there are several points for discussion:

* If the provider maintains the KOS, how will the digital library find out about any changes that may be made in it? Is there a notification mechanism in place? How frequently must the information be updated to be of benefit to the digital library's users? Will the maintenance be self-evident, or must the agreement include notification requirements? What will the owner do if the maintenance can no longer be performed?
* What will happen if the provider discontinues the product or sells or transfers it to someone else?

* What uses can the digital library make of the KOS under the proposed agreement? As with other licensing, it is advisable to aim for the broadest permissions and the longest term possible. At a minimum, the library should be able to renegotiate the terms of the agreement relatively easily.
* In a networked environment, it is beneficial to develop mechanisms for linking to online versions rather than to maintain a local copy of the resource. This ensures that what is presented is up-todate, and acknowledges more clearly the ownership of the KOS. However, there are numerous factors to consider. Will the KOS be used on an intranet or behind a firewall, where access to the outside or information coming into the organization might be prohibited? Does the KOS service use "cookies" or require knowledge of the user's Internet provider address? Does it require a user ID and password?
* If the KOS is to be accessed remotely, are there service issues? Is it likely to be accessed with bandwidth, model, and computer speeds that are adequate for outside connections of this type? Is the use of such a critical nature that unreliable service on the part of the KOS or the Internet connection will cause the digital library itself to be viewed as less useful? Does the KOS require a specialized search engine or search query formulation? Can the digital library system properly display the results, or would the results be better displayed through the KOS system? Will the resulting information be used in its native form or must it be extracted or transformed? If the KOS is to be loaded locally, in what formats can the content be received?
* If the KOS is not available electronically, can it be digitized? Is the owner interested in a cooperative venture, and are the human and financial resources for such an effort available?

Making the Link

There are two parts to establishing the link between the digital library and the KOS. The first is locating the key anchor information in the digital library's resource. The second involves the look up against the target file. The creation of this link may be more or less automatic, depending on the particular situation. The characterization of this activity is meant to be general and to allow both "on-thefly" links and embedded links.

Regardless of what function the KOS is going to serve in the digital library, the essential information contained in the digital library resource from which the link is to be made must be identified. The mechanism for doing this depends on the type of object from which the link is being made and on the information that is expected to be identified in the digital library's resource. The first step is to review any metadata related to the digital library resource. Do the metadata carry the term that is needed to make the link? If this information is included, the level at which the metadata are assigned should be reviewed.

If the metadata indicate the subject matter of the specific resource in which the user will be interested, the metadata can be used to make the links. However, in some cases, the terms that appear in the title or description at the resource level may not be indicative of the subject at the individual item level. Automatically making a link on the basis of the content description for an entire book may misrepresent the content of a chapter. Whether or not the metadata can be used will depend on the amount and type of information given in the metadata and the level at which the metadata are assigned.

If a text resource in the digital library provides no appropriate metadata, the procedure for identifying the key information may involve text analysis. A programme to perform simple string searching or a search engine that can preserve hit locations can be used if the text string has distinguishing characteristics, such as a database acronym, or a specific structure, such as a latitude and longitude coordinate. If the text string has no such cues, text mining or more complex textanalysis tools may be necessary. These tools use a variety of semantic and syntactic algorithms to locate key information.

There have been significant advances in commercially available text-mining tools, such as IBM's Intelligent Agent, which includes specific algorithms for identification of names of places and persons. The second step of the linking activity is to make the connection to the KOS. The methods for doing this vary, depending on whether the system is being loaded locally or is referenced remotely. If the system is loaded locally, it is possible to perform a significant amount of processing to match the two files, assuming that computer resources of this type are available to the digital library organization. If the system is only available remotely over the Web, the interaction will require knowledge of scripting and various Web-based access techniques.

Scripting should be considered in both local and remote approaches, since the more integrated the linking is with the resource, the more maintenance may be required if there are changes in either the resource or the KOS. Regardless of the approach that is taken, making the link requires an analysis of both the information in the original digital library material and the corresponding information in the KOS. If the KOS is being used as an intermediate file to bridge between the digital library's resource and another resource, it is also important to understand the data and the process whereby the search is performed and information returned from the target resource. If the KOS must return a value to the original digital library resource, the data and process must be evaluated in a bidirectional sense.

Choosing the linking mechanism is equally important. The link may be fixed or "on-the-fly." In the case of a fixed link, a specific URL is embedded at the link point in the digital library material. However, as stated before, problems of persistence are inherent in this approach. Alternatively, a URN can be used. The URN requires the creation of a namespace on the point of the target file, and the search is to this namespace rather than to a specific URL. Persistent locators and *digital object identifiers* (DOIs) can also solve this problem. These schemes are sufficient if the material is an HTML document. Content in databases is more difficult to retrieve.

The National Library of Medicine now supports the searching of a variety of its databases through its *Internet Grateful Med* (IGM) URL function. IGM users can create URLs that will actually perform searches against the databases. Information on the syntax for creating such a URL is provided on the NLM Web site. While the intent is that the search URL will be bookmarked by an individual user, the same concept can be used for creating an active link at the anchor point for the link. With additional scripting, the creation of the term *pneumonia* can be automatically replaced with an active link that picks up the term where the link has been made.

THE FUTURE OF KNOWLEDGE ORGANIZATION SYSTEMS ON THE WEB

As online databases moved to the Web, they began to provide their products, including vocabulary aids, in this environment. *Portable document format* (PDF) versions of printed vocabulary aids are common, since PDF can be easily produced from a Postscript file and it retains the look of the printed product. With Adobe's tools for indexing and searching, the PDF file can provide some level of support for linking. Many of these aids, however, remain in the form of HTML files only—there is no database structure to easily support the linking and searching.

In some cases, the full structure of the KOS is not made available on the Web; the only format for a Web-based thesaurus may be an alphabetical list of terms that does not enable the user to navigate easily the hierarchical structure. As unique ways of using these resources are developed, it is hoped that more KOS providers will be encouraged to provide their systems in formats that are conducive to such networked uses. Some of the requirements for such electronic KOSs were identified at a workshop entitled "Electronic Thesauri: Planning for a Standard" and sponsored by NISO. While the focus of this meeting was digital thesauri, consideration was also given to other KOSs in digital form.

The identified requirements include persistent identification at the concept level, the need for a simple protocol for the distributed querying and response from a KOS, and the development of a standard set of metadata attributes for describing a remote KOS. To facilitate the search and display of information from a previously unknown KOS, the system must have unique and persistent identifiers for each of the concepts in the system. For example, the California Environmental Resources Evaluation System and the U.S. Geological Survey have developed a system for remote querying and response. It requires that each concept in the thesaurus have a unique identifier.

In the case of the previously described ITIS, which is accessed remotely by the CERES system, the ITIS record number is used as the identifier. Other unique identifiers could include the DOI, or a classification notation that has been made unique by appending the scheme name or the URL to the notation. The second requirement is a protocol for the distributed querying and response of KOSs. This is particularly critical for highly structured systems such as thesauri, semantic networks, and ontologies. Work has been done in this area within the Z39.50 community.

A profile has been proposed by the Zthes Working Group to tailor the Z39.50 protocol to operate on thesauri that follow the Z39.19 standard. A similar effort is under way at the CERES Project. Instead of a Z39.50-based protocol, CERES has developed a structure that is based on the *Resource Description Framework* (RDF) and the HTTP protocol of standard browsers.

The RDF's concept of containers is a natural for managing the hierarchical structure of complex systems such as thesauri. The structure proposed by CERES is likely to be encoded using XML, a mark-up format that lends itself to structured information. This protocol for linking distributed vocabularies will support both searching and cataloging.

The user will be presented with remote vocabularies that can be displayed and navigated by a local client. The third major finding from the NISO workshop was the need for a metadata content standard for the description of KOSs. Such a standard is key to provision of knowledge organization services over the Internet. The metadata identify the Web resource as a KOS and provide important information to allow an application to use it remotely without prior knowledge of its content or structure.

A draft set of attributes for describing KOSs available in a networked environment has been developed by a task group of the *Network Knowledge Organization Systems* (NKOS) Working Group, an ad hoc group of terminology experts from organizations that are interested in issues related to the use and interoperability of KOSs over the Internet. The draft attributes are based on work originally done by Linda Hill and Michael Raugh.

The attributes describe the KOS so that content from the system can be transferred over the Internet and handled by a remote browser or client application. The attributes include the depth of hierarchy, the types of relationships included, the subject, storage format, copyright and rights management, and contact information.

To facilitate the transfer of information, the attribute set also includes information on character set and file size. To facilitate the acquisition and licensing of the KOSs, the draft content description includes point of contact information. During discussions about the metadata content standard, workshop attendees identified three methods for storing the metadata for a KOS. First, the metadata could be stored with the KOS, as metadata elements for that resource. Second, the metadata could be stored in a physically separate knowledge organization registry.

The third possibility is a hybrid approach, where a minimal set of metadata elements is contained in a central registry. The more detailed information would be stored with the KOS itself. There is significant interest in the use of KOSs to organize and search material on the Internet. It is hoped that this interest will result in knowledge organization services that will make these sources more readily accessible to a variety of software applications and to a variety of users. As services and enabled software proliferate, it will be easier to integrate these KOSs into digital libraries.

CONCLUSION

Given that the digital library field is still quite new, it seems strange to be talking already about enhancing digital libraries. However, in this fast-moving environment, the initial digital libraries resulting from digitization projects, or even virtual collections, are being enhanced as user expectations and technology capabilities allow. In the midst of this furious activity, it is valuable to analyse users' needs and interests and then to identify KOSs that can be used to enhance the digital library. Knowledge organization systems refer to a range of traditional and nontraditional systems for the organization of knowledge.

The systems have been developed in numerous environments outside the traditional library environment, including those of A&I services, publishers and professional organizations, and corporations. Examples exist in many disciplines and for many target audiences. Knowledge organization systems can enhance the digital library in a number of ways. They can be used to connect a digital library resource to a related resource. The related information may reside within the KOS itself or the KOS may be used as an intermediary file to retrieve the key needed to access it in another resource. A KOS can make digital library materials accessible to disparate communities.

This may be done by providing alternate subject access, by adding access by different modes, by providing multilingual access, and by using the KOS to support free text searching. A well-planned infrastructure for KOSs is required. This includes the resources, processes, and policies for analysing user needs; locating KOSs to answer these needs; and acquiring, implementing, and maintaining the KOS. Traditional and nontraditional KOSs provide an opportunity to extend the boundaries of the digital library. By going beyond the initial organization of the digital library, digital librarians can use the network environment to provide additional value to its users.

Bibliography

Ahuja, M. L.: *Financial Assistance for Library and Information Studies*, Bangalore: Geological Society of India, 2002.

Allan, B.: *Encyclopaedic Dictionary of Library and Information Science*, New Jersey: Facet Publishing, 2007.

Allan, M.: *e-Learning and Teaching in Library and Information Services*, New Jersey: Facet Publishing, 2002.

Anderson, T.: *Restructuring of Library and Information Science*, India: Cambridge University Press, 2008.

Bates, M. J. and Maack, M.N.: *Encyclopedia of Library and Information Sciences*, USA: CRC Press, 2010.

Chaube, S. K.: *Foundations of Library and Information Science*, New Delhi: Oxford University Press, 2000.

Datta, P. S.: *International Library and Information Science Research*, Madras: University of Madras, 1999.

Depuis, E. A.: *LCSH and PRECIS in Library and Information Science*, India: Neal Schuman Publishers, 2003.

Dewey Decimal: *Library and Information Sciences*, USA: CRC Press, 2003.

Galvin, T. J.: *Encyclopedia of Library and Information Science*, New York: Pittsburgh University, 1977.

Ghosh, S. K.: *Library and Information Science: Parameters and Perspectives*, Agartala: Benign Hills, 2004.

Hodges, C. B.: *Indian Library and Information Science Literature*, Scotland: University of Glasgow 2004.

Horam, M.: *Career Opportunities in Library and Information Science,* Bangalore: Geological Society of India, 1996.

Johnston, P.: *Dimensions of Library and Information Science,* UK: Clarkson University, 2001.

Jolliffe, A: *Investigative Methods in Library and Information Science,* UK: Taylor and Francis, 2005.

Kumar, Amrit: *Critical Theory for Library and Information Science,* Manson: Manson Publishing, 2004.

Kumar, M.: *Library and Information Science: Current Trends in India,* Madras: University of Madras, 1997.

Mishra, U.: *Case Studies in Library and Information Science Ethics,* Mumbai: Manaktalas, 2003.

Pertti Vakkari and Blaise Cronin: *Conceptions of Library and Information Science. Historical, Empirical and Theoretical Perspectives,* London: Taylor Graham, 1992.

Sarin, V. I. K.: *Leadership in the Library and Information Science,* Mumbai: Manaktalas, 2003.

Sen, A.: *Encyclopedia of Library and Information Science,* Delhi: Oxford University Press, 2002.

Sinha, A. C.: *The Management of Library and Information Studies Education,* Mumbai: Manaktalas, 1999.

Sreen, S. K.: *Opportunities in Library and Information Science,* New Delhi: Oxford, University Press, 1999.

Index

L

M

N

O

P

R

S

T

U

V

W